Cromwell and the Interregnum

Blackwell Essential Readings in History

This series comprises concise collections of key articles on important historical topics. Designed as a complement to standard survey histories, the volumes are intended to help introduce students to the range of scholarly debate in a subject area. Each collection includes a general introduction and brief contextual headnotes to each article, offering a coherent, critical framework for study.

Published

The German Reformation: The Essential Readings
C. Scott Dixon

The English Civil War: The Essential Readings
Peter Gaunt

The Italian Renaissance: The Essential Readings
Paula Findlen

The Scientific Revolution: The Essential Readings
Marcus Hellyer

Stalinism: The Essential Readings
David L. Hoffmann

The Cold War: The Essential Readings
Klaus Larres and Ann Lane

The Third Reich: The Essential Readings
Christian Leitz

The Counter-Reformation: The Essential Readings
David M. Luebke

The Crusades: The Essential Readings
Thomas F. Madden

The Russian Revolution: The Essential Readings
Martin Miller

The French Revolution: The Essential Readings
Ronald Schechter

Cromwell and the Interregnum: The Essential Readings
David L. Smith

Cromwell and the Interregnum

The Essential Readings

Edited by David L. Smith

Blackwell
Publishing

Editorial material and organization © 2003 by Blackwell Publishing Ltd

350 Main Street, Malden, MA 02148-5018, USA
9600 Garsington Road, Oxford OX4 2DQ, UK
550 Swanston Street, Carlton South, Melbourne, Victoria 3053, Australia
Kurfürstendamm 57, 10707 Berlin, Germany

First published 2003 by Blackwell Publishing Ltd

Library of Congress Cataloging-in-Publication Data

Cromwell and the interregnum : the essential readings / edited by David L. Smith.
    p.   cm. – (Blackwell essential readings in history)
    Includes bibliographical references and index.
    ISBN 0-631-22724-5 (alk. paper) – ISBN 0-631-22725-3 (pbk. : alk. paper)
    1. Great Britain – History – Commonwealth and Protectorate, 1649–1660.   2.
Cromwell, Oliver, 1599–1658.   I. Smith, David L. (David Lawrence), 1963–   II. Series.

DA425 .C76 2003
941.06 – dc21
                                                                    2002038284

A catalogue record for this title is available from the British Library.

Set in 10 on 12 pt Photina
by SNP Best-set Typesetter Ltd., Hong Kong
Printed and bound in the United Kingdom
by MPG Books Ltd, Bodmin, Cornwall

For further information on
Blackwell Publishing, visit our website:
http://www.blackwellpublishing.com

Contents

Acknowledgements

Davis, Colin, 'Cromwell's religion', from *Oliver Cromwell and the English Revolution*, ed. John Morrill (Longman, 1990). Reproduced by permission of Pearson Education.

Fletcher, Anthony, 'Oliver Cromwell and the Localities', from *Politics and People in Revolutionary England*, ed. Colin Jones et al. (Blackwell, 1986). Reproduced by permission of Blackwell Publishing.

Gaunt, Peter, '"The single person's confidants and dependents"? Oliver Cromwell and his Protectoral councillors', from *Historical Journal*, 32 (Cambridge University Press, 1989). Reproduced by permission of Cambridge University Press and the author.

Morrill, John and Baker, Philip, 'Oliver Cromwell, the Regicide and the Sons of Zeruiah', from *The Regicides and the Execution of Charles I*, ed. Jason Peacey (Palgrave, 2001). Reproduced by permission of Palgrave Macmillan and the authors.

Smith, David L., 'Oliver Cromwell, the first Protectorate Parliament and Religious Reform', from *Parliamentary History*, 19 (2000). Reproduced by permission of Edinburgh University Press.

Stevenson, David, 'Cromwell, Scotland and Ireland', from *Oliver Cromwell and the English Revolution*, ed. John Morrill (Longman, 1990). Reproduced by permission of Pearson Education.

Woolrych, Austin, 'The Cromwellian Protectorate: a Military Dictatorship?', from *History*, 75 (Blackwell, 1990). Reproduced by permission of Blackwell Publishing.

Worden, Blair, 'Oliver Cromwell and the Sin of Achan', from *History, Society and the Churches: essays in honour of Owen Chadwick*, ed. D. Beales and G. Best (Cambridge University Press, 1985). Reproduced by permission of Cambridge University Press and the author.

Editor's Introduction[1]

Ever since his own lifetime, Oliver Cromwell has inspired fascination and controversy in equal measure. Some of the finest historians in the English language have worked on his life and times, and interest shows no sign of drying up. Love him or hate him, historians, students and the wider public continue to find his story compelling. This book brings together eight of the most influential recent articles on Cromwell and the Interregnum and deliberately concentrates on the period from Charles I's execution in 1649 to Cromwell's own death in 1658. Any such collection is bound to be personal, and others will no doubt have their own ideas about what constitute the 'essential readings' on this subject. The particular focus of this selection is on the relationship between Cromwell's personality and politics, religion and society during the Interregnum. The nature of his aims, and the reasons why he failed to generate lasting stability, form recurrent themes. Other areas, such as foreign policy or the settlement of Ireland and Scotland, are also covered but much less extensively.

The essays are wide-ranging and indicate the diversity of approaches and perspectives that historians have brought to these issues. This introduction sets the scene by surveying some of the recent writings on the subject, and is divided into three sections. The first examines Cromwell's personality, beliefs and motives; the second considers the nature of his role and influence during the Interregnum, especially through his relationships

1 I am most grateful to John Morrill for his helpful comments on an earlier draft of this introduction.

with Parliaments, the Army and the Council; and the third explores the impact and legacy of the Interregnum.

I   Cromwell's Personality and Motives

In 1980, John Morrill wrote that there were 'innumerable biographies of Oliver Cromwell', and that he 'would be very surprised' if Cromwell were 'not the most biographied Englishman'.[2] Since then, at least three more major biographies have appeared, together with an important collection of essays and a string of other articles, all of which explore Cromwell's personality and beliefs.[3] Although these writings have their different perspectives and emphases, their common denominator is an attempt to understand Cromwell as a man of his times and to examine his complex character on its own terms. They try, in particular, to reconstruct his mental world using the ideas and categories of the seventeenth century and consciously to avoid imposing anachronistic values and ideas. This has had the effect of moving discussion beyond terms such as liberty or tyranny and instead placing his religion at the centre of the stage. That religion needs to be seen not as a rationalization for some other secular or material motive, but as part of a web of beliefs that locates Cromwell within the world of mid-seventeenth-century England.

One of the beliefs that Cromwell shared with many of his contemporaries was his conviction that God's will manifested itself regularly in the events of this world in 'providences'. The idea of a providentialist God, whose interventions offered guidance and signified divine approval or anger, lies at the heart of Cromwell's surviving letters and speeches. Blair Worden has shown how this providentialism was typical of the Puritan background from which Cromwell emerged.[4] Cromwell may have differed in the intensity with which he held this belief, and in the way in which his military and political careers enabled him to apply it directly to national events, but the

2   J. S. Morrill, *Seventeenth-Century Britain, 1603–1714* (Folkestone, 1980), p. 43.
3   The three major biographies are: Barry Coward, *Oliver Cromwell* (Harlow, 1991); Peter Gaunt, *Oliver Cromwell* (Oxford, 1996); and J. C. Davis, *Oliver Cromwell* (London, 2001). The important collection of essays is John Morrill (ed.), *Oliver Cromwell and the English Revolution* (Harlow, 1990), two of which appear as chapters 6 and 8 in this volume. Of the many other recent articles that focus directly on Cromwell, some of the most significant, in addition to those collected here, are Blair Worden, 'Toleration and the Cromwellian Protectorate', in W. J. Sheils (ed.), *Persecution and Toleration: Studies in Church History*, 21 (Oxford, 1984), pp. 199–233; Blair Worden, 'Providence and Politics in Cromwellian England', *Past and Present*, 109 (1985), pp. 55–99; Peter Gaunt, 'Oliver Cromwell and his Protectorate Parliaments: Co-operation, Conflict and Control', in Ivan Roots (ed.), *Into another Mould* (Exeter, 1998), pp. 70–100; and the Cromwell Day addresses collected in Peter Gaunt (ed.), *Cromwell 400* (Brentwood, 1999).
4   See especially Worden, 'Providence and Politics'.

basic premise was one that he shared with many of his contemporaries. In his letters and speeches, Cromwell referred constantly to the role of 'providences' in pointing towards God's will and the 'necessity' of conforming to it. To give just two examples from many, in November 1648, amidst the events leading up to the trial and execution of Charles I, Cromwell wrote to his cousin Robert Hammond:

> As to outward dispensations, if we may so call them, we have not been without our share of beholding some remarkable providences, and appearances of the Lord . . . If thou wilt seek, seek to know the mind of God in all that chain of Providence . . . Let us look into providences; surely they mean somewhat. They hang so together; have been so constant, so clear and unclouded.[5]

Later, in April 1657, as he wrestled with the dilemma of whether or not to accept the offer of the kingship, Cromwell declared:

> Truly, the Providence of God hath laid aside this title of King providentially de facto; . . . God hath seemed providentially, seemed to appear as a Providence, not only to strike at the family but at the name . . . I will not seek to set up that, that Providence hath destroyed, and laid in the dust; and I would not build Jericho again.[6]

Such rhetoric pervades most of Cromwell's recorded utterances, and the thrust of recent scholarship has been to take these statements very seriously as a genuine indication of his inner frame of mind. Most recent writers have inclined towards seeing Cromwell as basically sincere even if there was an element of self-deception that allowed him to put the most favourable possible gloss on his own motives.[7]

One good reason for believing in the sincerity of Cromwell's providentialism is that he followed the logic of it even when it was deeply troubling for him to do so. The clearest case of this was in 1655–6, when the failure of his campaign against Spain in the West Indies forced him to wonder why God had ceased to favour English troops in battle. In chapter 2 of this book, Blair Worden charts Cromwell's prolonged period of self-examination in which he wondered if it was some sin in himself that had provoked God's anger. Old Testament parallels, especially the story of the 'sin of Achan',

5   S. C. Lomas (ed.), *The Letters and Speeches of Oliver Cromwell with Elucidations by Thomas Carlyle* (3 vols., London, 1904), 1, pp. 393–6 (Cromwell to Colonel Robert Hammond, 25 November 1648).

6   Lomas (ed.), *Letters and Speeches*, 3, pp. 70–1 (Cromwell to the representatives of the second Protectorate Parliament, 13 April 1657).

7   See, for example, Davis, *Cromwell*, pp. 128–30; Morrill (ed.), *Cromwell and the English Revolution*, pp. 13–14; Gaunt, *Cromwell*, pp. 233–8.

haunted Cromwell during these introspective reflections and may well have contributed to his decision to decline the kingship in 1657 lest he be thought self-seeking and greedy.

This in turn leads to another aspect of Cromwell's religious beliefs that looms large in recent biographies, namely his constant drawing of parallels between England's experiences during the late 1640s and 1650s and those of the Israelites in the Old Testament. Just as the Israelites had broken free of bondage in Egypt by crossing the Red Sea, so England had overthrown Stuart tyranny by executing Charles I. Now the English were journeying across the desert towards the promised land, guided by 'providences' (the equivalent of a pillar of fire). This metaphor cast Cromwell – in both his own eyes and those of his supporters – in the role of Moses. Intriguingly, in all his surviving letters and speeches, Cromwell never defined what the promised land would look like; indeed, he probably believed that this could not be known until it was actually reached.

Nevertheless, one very important step along the way was to ensure that 'liberty of conscience' was extended as widely as possible among the godly. Much recent work has drawn out the significance of this goal, and again discussion has focused on Cromwell's own phrase, 'liberty of conscience', rather than the vaguer and possibly anachronistic term 'toleration'. Indeed, Blair Worden has argued that there were significant limits to how far Cromwell was willing to accept religious diversity outside the godly Protestant mainstream.[8] Against this, Colin Davis has suggested that Cromwell's sympathies may have been rather broader than Worden allows, and that Cromwell perceived 'liberty of conscience' as only the first step towards reuniting the godly.[9]

Davis in turn links this to another idea that he believes is central to our understanding of Cromwell's religion, namely his antiformalism. Davis argues that Cromwell deeply mistrusted human institutions and outward forms of religious practice, and believed that the godly should rise above differences of form in order to rediscover what united them. It is for this reason, Davis suggests, that Cromwell so resolutely resists being identified with any one church or religious group. Just as he was not 'wedded and glued to forms of government', so he was never 'wedded and glued' to any particular religious form.[10] This also helps to explain why so many different groups or sects initially regarded him as an ally yet later came to see him as an apos-

8   See especially Worden, 'Toleration and the Cromwellian Protectorate'.
9   On this, see chapter 6 of this book, and Davis, *Cromwell*, chapter 6.
10   See chapter 6, below; Davis, *Cromwell*, chapters 6–8; Lomas (ed.), *Letters and Speeches*, 3, p. 362 (Cromwell at the Putney Debates, 28 October 1647). Davis explores the issue of antiformalism more generally during this period in J. C. Davis, 'Against Formality: One Aspect of the English Revolution', *Transactions of the Royal Historical Society*, 6th series, 3 (1993), pp. 265–88.

tate or a hypocrite. That charge forms a recurrent theme in many contemporary accounts of Cromwell, and the importance of antiformalism in his thought is vital in understanding why.[11]

Cromwell's mistrust of forms went along with a consistent commitment to the ends of government. In Morrill's view, he 'cared about ends not means', and 'was loyal to no one but God'.[12] Similarly, Davis feels that Cromwell's 'religion was almost invariably the ultimate determinant of his action'.[13] Cromwell seems to have believed that God had a purpose for England, and that it was his duty to drive that forward. He had a consistent, albeit very vague, vision of the 'necessity' of creating a godly nation. But he was pragmatic about the means that might be used to achieve that end. His own preference was probably for government by a 'single person and a Parliament',[14] but equally, if a Parliament failed to 'do the work of the Lord, in fulfilling the end of [its] magistracy', then he was willing to resort to more authoritarian solutions, such as the Major-Generals experiment of 1655–7.[15] This was the outlook that lay behind Cromwell's chilling intention to rule 'for [the people's] good, not what pleases them',[16] and that enabled him to justify breaking the rule of law on the grounds that 'if nothing should ever be done but what is according to law, the throat of the nation may be cut while we send for some to make a law.'[17] His contempt for human forms, be they religious or governmental, as 'dross and dung in comparison of Christ' helps to explain his periodic disregard for legal and constitutional propriety.[18]

Cromwell's overarching hope was that the godly would become more and more numerous until they ultimately comprised the whole nation. He insisted that there should be no incompatibility between their interests and those of England as a whole. As he put it on 3 April 1657:

If anyone whatsoever think the interest of Christians and the interest of the nation inconsistent, or two different things, I wish my soul may never

11   Morrill (ed.), *Cromwell and the English Revolution*, chapter 8.
12   Morrill (ed.), *Cromwell and the English Revolution*, p. 14.
13   Davis, *Cromwell*, p. 128.
14   Lomas (ed.), *Letters and Speeches*, 2, p. 381 (Cromwell to the first Protectorate Parliament, 12 September 1654).
15   Lomas (ed.), *Letters and Speeches*, 1, p. 343 (Cromwell to William Lenthall, 20 August 1648). On the Major-Generals, see chapter 5 below, and the recent excellent study by Christopher Durston, *Cromwell's Major-Generals: Godly Government during the English Revolution* (Manchester, 2001).
16   Lomas (ed.), *Letters and Speeches*, 3, p. 345 (Cromwell to the 'Council of War' at Reading, 16 July 1647).
17   Lomas (ed.), *Letters and Speeches*, 2, p. 543 (Cromwell to the second Protectorate Parliament, 17 September 1656).
18   Lomas (ed.), *Letters and Speeches*, 3, p. 373 (Cromwell at the Putney Debates, 1 November 1647).

> enter into their secrets . . . And upon these two interests, if God shall
> account me worthy, I shall live and die.[19]

Or again, on 21 April 1657:

> I think you have provided for the liberty of the people of God, and for the
> liberty of the nation. And I say he sings sweetly that sings a song of rec-
> onciliation betwixt these two interests! And it is a pitiful fancy, and wild
> and ignorant to think they are inconsistent.[20]

Yet in a nation where, as Derek Hirst has shown, evangelical Puritanism
advanced only patchily at best and attachment to the old Church of England
was still widespread by the time of Cromwell's death,[21] these interests
clearly were inconsistent. Furthermore, Cromwell's relations with successive Parliaments were bedevilled by the tension between his own commitment to 'liberty of conscience' and the strong desire of many members to
suppress religious 'errors' and 'horrid blasphemies'.[22]

There was thus a basic conflict between two principles both of which
Cromwell regarded as 'fundamentals': government 'by a single person and
a Parliament' and 'liberty of conscience'. Many of the recent writings on
Cromwell have suggested that these tensions lay so deep within his own
character that he was never able to reconcile them. Instead of trying to
resolve these contradictions, it seems wiser for historians to live with them
and not to invest Cromwell's beliefs with greater coherence and consistency
than he did himself. Nearly thirty years ago, Worden advanced an influential argument that the collision between Cromwell's religious radicalism
and his social and political conservatism produced in him 'a kind of ideological schizophrenia, setting him on an almost predictable course of political self-destruction'.[23] More recently Morrill has suggested that the very
religious zeal that enabled him to rise from fenland obscurity to become
Lord Protector also prevented him from generating lasting stability once in
power.[24] The biographies by Davis, Coward and Gaunt all draw out these
tensions and contradictions within Cromwell's personality and show how
they lay at the heart of his flawed achievement. They in turn lead naturally
into consideration of the role that Cromwell played during the Interregnum,
and its broader significance.

19 Lomas (ed.), *Letters and Speeches*, 3, p. 31 (Cromwell to the representatives of the second
Protectorate Parliament, 3 April 1657).
20 Lomas (ed.), *Letters and Speeches*, 3, p. 101 (Cromwell to the representatives of the second
Protectorate Parliament, 21 April 1657).
21 Derek Hirst, 'The Failure of Godly Rule in the English Republic', *Past and Present*, 132
(1991), pp. 33–66.
22 See chapter 7, below.
23 Blair Worden, *The Rump Parliament, 1648–1653* (Cambridge, 1974), p. 69.
24 Morrill (ed.), *Cromwell and the English Revolution*, p. 281.

II   Cromwell's Role and Significance

Here again, we are faced with a series of paradoxes. Cromwell was a dominant personality who also respected the advice of others; a figure with a
deeply authoritarian streak who yet wanted to rule with Parliaments; a
remarkably successful soldier whose own relationship with the Army was
frequently troubled; a republican Head of State who was increasingly
surrounded by monarchical trappings; and a leading proponent of the
Regicide who was himself offered, and very nearly accepted, the Crown. All
these tensions have been particularly prominent themes within the recent
historiography on this subject.

Many of Cromwell's contemporaries believed that his role during the
Interregnum gave him sweeping powers. Yet, as Peter Gaunt argues in
chapter 4 of this book, such a view overlooks not only the limitations placed
on protectoral powers in the two written constitutions of the 1650s, the
Instrument of Government (1653) and the *Humble Petition and Advice* (1657),
but also Cromwell's own reluctance to assume unchecked powers. That
reluctance apparently stemmed partly from his feeling that such powers
might have a corrupting influence on him, and partly from a belief that he
had a duty to seek advice and share power with others. Gaunt argues that
Cromwell was far from overbearing or manipulative in his handling of the
Council, and was willing to defer to the majority view even when it conflicted with his own preferred course of action. The Council was certainly
not a mere cipher, and Cromwell seems genuinely to have valued its advice.

However, as Gaunt, Worden, Woolrych and others have shown,
Cromwell's relationship with Parliaments was far less stable and effective
than his dealings with the Council. Time and again, Cromwell opened a new
Parliament with great optimism that it would embrace its responsibility to
further God's purpose. But every time he was disappointed and, despite his
own pledges to intrude as little as possible in parliamentary business, he felt
himself obliged to intervene and ultimately to dissolve Parliament. Gaunt
shows that the problem lay not so much in a failure of management as in
the basic divergence of outlook, especially on religious matters, between
Cromwell and his army allies on the one hand and the majority of members
of Parliaments on the other. Chapter 7, below, offers a case study of how
this divergence undermined the first Protectorate Parliament. Throughout
the Interregnum, Cromwell and his Parliaments found themselves locked
into a relationship in which they needed each other yet were unable to work
harmoniously together.[25] He believed in the importance of a Parliament

25   Worden, *Rump Parliament*; Austin Woolrych, *Commonwealth to Protectorate* (Oxford,
1982); Gaunt, 'Cromwell and his Protectorate Parliaments'; Peter Gaunt, 'Law-Making in the
first Protectorate Parliament', in C. Jones, M. Newitt and S. Roberts (eds.), *Politics and People in*

within England's constitutional arrangements, yet it had to be a Parliament on his terms. Equally, although he felt compelled to disband any Parliament that he thought had betrayed its trust, Gaunt and Egloff have shown that Cromwell carefully distanced himself from the purges of members of both the first and second Protectorate Parliaments, and was content that the *Instrument of Government* empowered the Council to make such exclusions.[26]

Much of Cromwell's dominant role during the Interregnum rested on his capacity to straddle the worlds of the army and the civilian politicians. Yet, just as his relations with Parliaments remained volatile, so his dealings with his army colleagues were far from untroubled. Cromwell's status in the army stemmed from his unbroken run of victories from 1642 to 1651, and there is no evidence that a military coup against him was likely at any stage during the Interregnum. There was, however, considerable unhappiness at his brutal suppression of a Leveller-inspired mutiny at Burford in May 1649, and strong opposition to him becoming King in 1657.[27] In the end, it seems that the army's attitude was important in Cromwell's decision to decline the kingship: he perceived the army as God's instrument and apparently interpreted its hostility as a direct sign of divine disapproval. But although he did not go against the army's wishes over the kingship, Cromwell's deteriorating relationship with his fellow-officers, his annoyance at their interference in politics and his suspicion that they had been an obstacle to a lasting settlement, showed through plainly in two speeches he made to them in 1657 and 1658.[28]

One reason for these tense relations was the army's concern that even though he had declined the title of king, Cromwell had in effect assumed the role of monarch in all but name. There has recently been considerable

Revolutionary England: Essays in honour of Ivan Roots (Oxford, 1986), pp. 163–86. See also chapter 7, below; David L. Smith, 'Oliver Cromwell: a great Parliamentarian?', in Gaunt (ed.), *Cromwell 400*, pp. 73–8; David L. Smith, *The Stuart Parliaments, 1603–1689* (Oxford, 1999), pp. 136–44; and Ivan Roots, 'Lawmaking in the second Protectorate Parliament', in H. Hearder and H. R. Loyn (eds.), *British Government and Administration: Essays presented to S. B. Chrimes* (Cardiff, 1974), pp. 132–43.

26   Peter Gaunt, 'Cromwell's Purge? Exclusions and the first Protectorate Parliament', *Parliamentary History*, 6 (1987), pp. 1–22; Carol S. Egloff, 'The Search for a Cromwellian Settlement: Exclusions from the second Protectorate Parliament', *Parliamentary History*, 17 (1998), pp. 178–97, 301–21.

27   Ian Gentles, *The New Model Army in England, Ireland and Scotland, 1645–1653* (Oxford, 1992), chapter 10. On the offer of the kingship, the older accounts by C. H. Firth have not been superseded: C. H. Firth, 'Cromwell and the Crown', *English Historical Review*, 17 (1902), pp. 429–42, and 18 (1903), pp. 52–80; C. H. Firth, *The Last Years of the Protectorate, 1656–1658* (2 vols., London, 1909), 1, pp. 128–200.

28   Lomas (ed.), *Letters and Speeches*, 3, pp. 487–8, 509–10 (Cromwell to the Army Officers, 27 February 1657, 6 February 1658); David Underdown, 'Cromwell and the Officers', *English Historical Review*, 83 (1968), pp. 101–7; John Morrill, 'King Oliver?', in Gaunt (ed.), *Cromwell 400*, pp. 79–84.

interest in the trappings and iconography that surrounded Cromwell, especially as Lord Protector. Roy Sherwood has stressed how much the protectoral court and the symbolism associated with the office of Lord Protector owed to monarchical models. These echoes continued to surround Cromwell in death, when his funeral effigy depicted him robed in ermine, wearing a crown, and carrying an orb and sceptre.[29] By contrast, Laura Knoppers has argued that depictions of Cromwell during the Interregnum did not slavishly adopt Stuart forms of portraiture, ceremony or panegyric, but adapted them in the process.[30] Equally, what seems profoundly ironic is that Cromwell who, as John Morrill and Philip Baker show in chapter 1, had played a crucial if reluctant role in the events leading to the execution of Charles I and the abolition of monarchy, subsequently made as much use of royal symbols and imagery as he did. This debate forms part of a wider controversy – examined more fully below – over how far the Interregnum saw the emergence of distinctively republican strains of political thought and culture.

Interestingly, Cromwell emerges in Knoppers' account as quite passive and not at all proactive in the development of his public image during the Interregnum. This would tie in with Gaunt's view that he shied away from unrestrained powers, and with Woolrych's argument in chapter 3 that the Protectorate was never a military dictatorship. It also fits with Cromwell's modest perception of his own role as 'a good constable set to keep the peace of the parish'.[31] Yet, even if Cromwell's role was not that of a monarch or a military dictator, historians seem agreed that it was immensely influential and significant. That is a common denominator of all the essays in this volume. Even the most critical assessments still acknowledge Cromwell's influence, for example the following by J. P. Kenyon:

> It is clear that much of the praise lavished on [Cromwell] then and since is misplaced. In the early 1650s he alone stood between the English people and a peaceful and permanent settlement; without his leadership and his military genius, the republic would have foundered in its first two years; single-handed he postponed the inevitable restoration of the monarchy for another ten.[32]

Many recent historians would take a rather more positive view, including Davis, who argues that Cromwell confronted

---

29   Roy Sherwood, *The Court of Oliver Cromwell* (London, 1977); Roy Sherwood, *Oliver Cromwell: King in all but name, 1653–1658* (Stroud, 1997).

30   Laura Lunger Knoppers, *Constructing Cromwell: ceremony, portrait, and print, 1645–1661* (Cambridge, 2000). See also John Cooper, *Oliver the first: contemporary images of Oliver Cromwell* (London, 1999).

31   Lomas (ed.), *Letters and Speeches*, 3, p. 63 (Cromwell to the representatives of the second Protectorate Parliament, 13 April 1657).

32   J. P. Kenyon, *Stuart England* (2nd edition, Harmondsworth, 1985), p. 184.

a revolutionary situation in which moderate men could only struggle to make an ordered and stable society out of the wreckage. This was Cromwell's tragedy. His greatness is that he did so much more than cling to the debris . . . It was a settlement far less radical than those who have aspired to an English Revolution, then and since, would have wished . . . But it was admirable none the less.[33]

It was a similar story among Cromwell's own contemporaries. Regardless of whether they loved or loathed him, few doubted the importance of the role that he played during the Interregnum.[34] Such assessments in turn raise the broader questions of the impact of Cromwellian government during the Interregnum, the extent to which it produced any lasting achievements, and the legacy that it left behind. These issues will form the subject of the final section of this introduction.

III   The Impact and Legacy of the Interregnum

Most recent work on the Interregnum regimes has taken a pessimistic view of their impact on the English localities. Cromwell's hopes for a godly reformation were clearly disappointed. Derek Hirst, Anthony Fletcher and others have argued that godliness advanced patchily at best and the overriding impression in the provinces is of islands of godliness in a sea of apathy, ignorance and conservatism.[35] The majority of the population acquiesced grudgingly to godly rule, but what eluded Cromwell was the active and zealous support of more than a minority. A key reason for this lay in the reluctance of most of the traditional governors of local society to embrace Cromwell's radical religious agenda. Christopher Durston's recent study of the Major-Generals has concluded that although they had some success in improving the regime's security, their campaign for moral reform was 'a clear failure'.[36] Their remit was too ambitious, and they were given too little

33   Davis, *Cromwell*, p. 201. Cf. Morrill (ed.), *Cromwell and the English Revolution*, pp. 1–3, 281; Derek Hirst, *England in Conflict, 1603–1660* (London, 1999), p. 315.
34   For some examples of contrasting contemporary perceptions of Cromwell, see Morrill (ed.), *Cromwell and the English Revolution*, chapter 10; Blair Worden, 'Andrew Marvell, Oliver Cromwell, and the Horatian Ode', in Kevin Sharpe and Steven N. Zwicker (eds.), *Politics of Discourse: The Literature and History of Seventeenth-Century England* (Berkeley and Los Angeles, 1987), pp. 147–80; and Blair Worden, 'John Milton and Oliver Cromwell', in Ian Gentles, John Morrill and Blair Worden (eds.), *Soldiers, Writers and Statesmen of the English Revolution* (Cambridge, 1998), pp. 243–64.
35   Hirst, 'Failure of Godly Rule'; Anthony Fletcher, 'Oliver Cromwell and the godly nation', in Morrill (ed.), *Cromwell and the English Revolution*, pp. 209–33; Coward, *Cromwell*, pp. 98–114, 160–8; Ann Hughes, 'The Frustrations of the Godly', in John Morrill (ed.), *Revolution and Restoration: England in the 1650s* (London, 1992), pp. 70–90.
36   Durston, *Cromwell's Major-Generals*, p. 179.

time and insufficient support, for them to achieve more than fairly minimal progress towards godly reformation. Where they had the assistance of sympathetic local commissioners, as in Staffordshire,[37] a degree of success was possible, but in general there was a striking lack of popular enthusiasm for Cromwell's vision. Furthermore, Cromwell's pursuit of godly reformation, by seeking to advance what remained a minority agenda, also undermined his efforts to achieve what he called the 'great end' of 'healing and settling'.[38]

Perhaps the most positive and lasting legacy of the Interregnum in England lay not in building a godly nation but in liberating the godly minority and allowing them to establish the deep roots that enabled dissent to survive after the Restoration. Barry Coward writes that the 'one positive lasting effect' of Cromwell's career was 'the establishment of Protestant nonconformity as a permanent feature of life in Britain from that day to this', and he concludes that Cromwell 'left as his major legacy an indelible religious imprint on the development of his country'.[39] Cromwell's commitment to 'liberty of conscience', and his refusal to create ecclesiastical structures with coercive or didactic powers, helped him to give genuine freedom to the minority of godly Protestants. But, by another of the many ironies that surround his career, his unwillingness to impose punitive authority also impeded his own attempts to create a godly nation.

That vision of a godly nation was focused on England and, as David Stevenson argues in chapter 8, Cromwell was concerned with Ireland and Scotland mainly to safeguard English security and to turn them into 'little Englands'. In both kingdoms, he accomplished the first goal much more successfully than the second. Conquest and subjugation were carried out with ruthless effectiveness, but popular acceptance and support proved elusive. In Ireland the traditional Catholic elite was expropriated and the foundations laid for the Protestant ascendancy that endured until the early twentieth century.[40] A recent provocative study has argued that Cromwell's conduct in 1649–50 was within the codes of early-modern European warfare.[41] This is probably correct, but equally the Irish campaign involved

37   John Sutton, 'Cromwell's commissioners for preserving the peace of the Commonwealth: a Staffordshire case study', in Gentles, Morrill and Worden (eds.), *Soldiers, Writers and Statesmen*, pp. 151–82.

38   Lomas (ed.), *Letters and Speeches*, 2, p. 341 (Cromwell to the first Protectorate Parliament, 4 September 1654).

39   Coward, *Cromwell*, pp. 176–7.

40   See, in particular, Toby Barnard, 'Planters and Policies in Cromwellian Ireland', *Past and Present*, 61 (1973), pp. 31–69; Toby Barnard, *Cromwellian Ireland: English Government and Reform in Ireland, 1649–1660* (Oxford, 1975).

41   Tom Reilly, *Cromwell: An Honourable Enemy* (Dingle, 1999). Cf. James Scott Wheeler, *Cromwell in Ireland* (Dublin, 1999); James Scott Wheeler, *The Irish and British Wars, 1637–1654: Triumph, Tragedy, and Failure* (London, 2002), chapter 8.

a level of brutality (which Cromwell justified on the grounds of religious vengeance and a mission to bring the benefits of Protestantism and liberty to Ireland) that was not seen in England or Scotland. The same military efficiency was evident in Scotland, but the settlement was less savage and rather more akin to that in England, mainly because Cromwell regarded the Scots as fellow Protestants, albeit misled politically.[42] The three kingdoms were forcibly integrated into a single republic, yet what was lacking – and what Cromwell probably never intended to create – was a *British* republican identity during this period.[43]

How far there was an *English* republican identity has been strongly debated in recent years. A number of scholars have reconstructed the remarkable ferment of republican ideas during the 1650s.[44] This was associated, especially in the period of the Commonwealth, with the emergence of a republican political culture and a distinctively republican literature.[45] Yet Cromwell himself was a highly ambivalent figure in this context. A reluctant regicide, and a republican by default rather than conviction, he offended many committed republicans by dissolving the Rump Parliament in April 1653 and assuming the mantle of Lord Protector the following December. For staunch republicans, such as Henry Marten or Sir Henry Vane, or poets like John Milton and Andrew Marvell, this seemed a flagrant betrayal of all that they believed Cromwell had previously stood for.[46] Although explicable in terms of Cromwell's pragmatic approach to 'forms of government', discussed above, his actions dealt a blow to the republican cause from which it arguably never recovered.

That failure to recover also reflected the lack of any agreed republican ideology or framework from 1649 onwards. Kevin Sharpe has argued that monarchical symbols and forms continued to pervade English political

---

42   James Scott Wheeler, 'The Logistics of the Cromwellian Conquest of Scotland, 1650–1651', *War and Society*, 10 (1992), pp. 1–18; Wheeler, *Irish and British Wars*, chapter 9; John D. Grainger, *Cromwell against the Scots: The Last Anglo-Scottish War, 1650–1652* (East Lothian, 1997); F. D. Dow, *Cromwellian Scotland, 1651–1660* (Edinburgh, 1979).

43   Derek Hirst, 'The English Republic and the Meaning of Britain', in Brendan Bradshaw and John Morrill (eds.), *The British Problem, c. 1534–1707* (London, 1996), pp. 192–219.

44   Sarah Barber, *Regicide and Republicanism: politics and ethics in the English Revolution, 1646–1659* (Edinburgh, 1998), chapters 6–8; David Wootton (ed.), *Republicanism, Liberty, and Commercial Society, 1649–1776* (Stanford, 1994), chapters 1–3; Jonathan Scott, *England's Troubles: Seventeenth-Century English Political Stability in European Context* (Cambridge, 2000), especially chapters 13 and 14.

45   David Norbrook, *Writing the English Republic: Poetry, Rhetoric and Politics, 1627–1660* (Cambridge, 1999), chapters 5–8; Sean Kelsey, *Inventing a Republic: the Political Culture of the English Commonwealth, 1649–1653* (Manchester, 1997).

46   Norbrook, *Writing the English Republic*, chapters 6–8; Worden, 'Milton and Cromwell'; Derek Hirst, ' "That Sober Liberty": Marvell's Cromwell in 1654', in John M. Wallace (ed.), *The Golden and the Brazen World: Papers in Literature and History, 1650–1800* (Berkeley, 1985), pp. 17–53; Barber, *Regicide and Republicanism*, chapter 8.

culture, and that visual, non-textual sources demonstrate their remarkable resilience. He suggests that, by concentrating too much on written evidence, historians may have overestimated the impact and importance of republican ideas and languages.[47] The most powerful symbols associated with Cromwell during the Protectorate, despite efforts to 'republicanize' him, were not those of a republic, or even of empire, but those of a monarchy.[48] Cromwell may eventually have declined the kingship, but to convinced republicans the really amazing thing was that he agonized for three months before reaching what to them seemed the only acceptable decision. The monarchical overtones undoubtedly grew stronger the longer the republic lasted. Equally, as Sharpe argues, even if republican discourse was never dominant, the republic created a situation where the case for monarchy could no longer simply be assumed; it had henceforth to be argued. In political and constitutional terms, the Interregnum's legacy lay more in what it had shown to be possible – the execution of the king, the abolition of the monarchy and the House of Lords, the creation of a republic – than in any permanent changes.

The Interregnum also demonstrated that an English republic could conduct a successful foreign policy and earn the respect of its continental neighbours. This theme, although touched on relatively briefly in this volume, has been the subject of two recent monographs, both of which indicate the impossibility of separating material and ideological motives.[49] They show that in his aggressive settlement of Ireland and his obsessive hostility towards Spain, Cromwell developed his foreign policy within an English Protestant tradition dating back to the later sixteenth century. His search for alliances with northern European Protestant powers and his wish to end the Anglo-Dutch war of 1652–4 as quickly as possible were further expressions of this confessional diplomacy. His hatred of continental absolute (Catholic) monarchy, and especially of Spanish claims to universal monarchy, shows his religious beliefs and strategic aims merging together into a single vision. As with other aspects of his career, the role of religious ideology has played a central part in recent discussions of Cromwellian foreign policy.

If the legacy of the Interregnum thus fell far short of what Cromwell had desired, it should nevertheless not be regarded as a complete failure. It

47 Kevin Sharpe, '"An Image Doting Rabble": The Failure of Republican Culture in Seventeenth-Century England', in Kevin Sharpe and Steven N. Zwicker (eds.), *Refiguring Revolutions: Aesthetics and Politics from the English Revolution to the Romantic Revolution* (Berkeley and Los Angeles, 1998), pp. 25–56.
48 Norbrook, *Writing the English Republic*, chapter 8; David Armitage, 'The Cromwellian Protectorate and the Languages of Empire', *Historical Journal*, 35 (1992), pp. 531–55.
49 Timothy Venning, *Cromwellian Foreign Policy* (London, 1995); Steven C. A. Pincus, *Protestantism and Patriotism: Ideologies and the Making of English Foreign Policy, 1650–1668* (Cambridge, 1996), chapters 2–10.

helped nonconformity to become a permanent feature of English life, it reasserted England as a significant player on the continental scene, and it proved that an English republic could survive, and indeed prosper economically, for over a decade.[50] Above all, however we assess the impact and legacy of Cromwell and the Interregnum, they left behind an indelible memory that has preoccupied historians and many others ever since. Several studies have lately appeared that examine the many contrasting images and interpretations of Cromwell since his own lifetime, be they in print, portrait, statue or music.[51] Of one thing we can be sure: in future decades the writings surveyed in this discussion will themselves appear as but another stage in an on-going debate, and the period will lose neither its power to fascinate, excite and disturb, nor its compelling claim to be studied.

50   William Lamont, 'The Left and its Past: Revisiting the 1650s', *History Workshop*, 23 (1987), pp. 141–53; Derek Hirst, 'Locating the 1650s in England's Seventeenth Century', *History*, 81 (1996), pp. 359–83.
51   Blair Worden, *Roundhead Reputations: The English Civil Wars and the Passions of Posterity* (London, 2001), chapters 8–11; Timothy Lang, *The Victorians and the Stuart Heritage: Interpretations of a Discordant Past* (Cambridge, 1995); R. C. Richardson (ed.), *Images of Cromwell: Essays by and for Roger Howell* (Manchester, 1993).

1

Oliver Cromwell, the Regicide and the Sons of Zeruiah

John Morrill and Philip Baker

Originally appeared as John Morrill and Philip Baker, 'Oliver Cromwell, the Regicide and the Sons of Zeruiah', in Jason Peacey (ed.), *The Regicides and the Execution of Charles I*. Copyright 2001 John Morrill and Philip Baker. Published by Palgrave, Basingstoke.

Editor's Introduction

Historians have long debated Cromwell's attitudes towards the execution of Charles I and his role in bringing it about. Some have argued that he was a late and reluctant convert to the cause of regicide, while others have suggested that he accepted the need to bring Charles to trial rather earlier and was then trying to secure as much support for this course as possible. Morrill and Baker engage with this debate by arguing that it is essential to distinguish between Cromwell's attitudes towards Charles I and his attitudes towards monarchy. They suggest that the evidence of Cromwell's contributions to the Putney Debates reveals that by 1 November 1647 at the latest he had come to acknowledge the severe problems posed by Charles I personally, but that he believed God's views on the future of monarchy were not yet apparent. Furthermore, his reference to the 'sons of Zeruiah' (11 November 1647) indicates that he felt that the army could not get away with killing the king at that stage. Morrill and Baker argue that the key to Cromwell's behaviour from November 1647 to January 1649 lay in the combination of a growing conviction that Charles should be brought to trial – and possibly even executed – with a continuing uncertainty over when, how and by whom this was to be accomplished.

The essay draws out the ways in which Biblical language and allusions saturated Cromwell's 43 letters and 28 speeches that survive from this period. These drew on 21 Old Testament books and 13 New Testament books, but they contain no evidence at all that he had read anything other than the Bible.

The letters during the course of 1648 indicate a particular preoccupation with Isaiah, chapters 8 and 9, and show Cromwell searching for guidance from God as to how to proceed. He was clear from the beginning of 1648 that Charles should be brought to trial; by the autumn of that year he apparently believed that the King deserved to die; but he remained uncertain as to when and how this would be achieved, and he almost certainly did not want to see the monarchy itself abolished. His initial preference was probably for Charles to abdicate in favour of one of his sons, and for a new paper constitution to be brought in prior to the King's trial. Pride's Purge threw him off balance, and in an attempt to restore his preferred sequence of events, Cromwell was forced to accept the 'cruel necessity' of bringing the King to trial and execution sooner than he had envisaged.

The importance of this essay lies in its very close reading of Cromwell's letters and speeches during the 15 months prior to the Regicide, its judicious sifting of other contemporary evidence, and its very precise analysis of Cromwell's motives and attitudes. The authors demonstrate that Cromwell was simultaneously 'a bitter opponent of Charles. a reluctant regicide, and a firm monarchist'. This provides a far subtler and more nuanced account than earlier treatments of the subject as well as a penetrating reconstruction of Cromwell's mind during the late 1640s.

Oliver Cromwell, the Regicide and the Sons of Zeruiah[1]

John Morrill and Philip Baker

I

In the middle of the night following Charles I's execution, Oliver Cromwell stood over the coffin, peering down at the body to which the severed head had been surgically reattached, and is reported to have muttered the words 'cruel necessity'.[2] Whether or not this report – from a very distraught and highly partial observer, with an uncertain oral history before it was written down – is true, these words are, we shall suggest, precisely the words that would have been passing through his mind. Cromwell was, we shall argue, at once a bitter opponent of Charles, a reluctant regicide, and a firm monarchist. To understand how this can be so, and how he attempted to square circles in his own mind and in the making of public policy, we need to look with renewed care at his recorded words and actions over a period of some 15 months from the time of the Putney Debates to the final show trial.

This paper argues that Oliver Cromwell 'fell out of love' with Charles I no later than 1 November 1647 but that it took him a lot longer to decide quite how and when he was to be removed from power and to decide what the implications of Charles' deposition and/or execution were for the future of the monarchy. In doing so, it takes sides in perhaps the greatest single contention in modern scholarship about Cromwell. It does not question, but rather embraces, the near consensus that has acquitted him of the charges of hypocrisy, double-dealing and a craving for power levelled against him by almost all his contemporaries. His sincerity and his deep religious faith are now widely accepted. There may have been a strong capacity for self-deception in his make-up, but not a calculating policy of deceiving others. However, this paper does come up against a more sharply divided modern historiography about his actions and motives from the autumn of 1647 to 1 January 1649 than for any other period in his career.

---

1   This essay is based on extensive discussion between the two authors. It was fully written by John Morrill on the basis of these discussions and then subjected to revision and redraft after further debate between the authors.
2   The words were later recalled by the Earl of Southampton and are printed in Joseph Spence, *Anecdotes* (London, 1820), p. 275. See the full text and context in R. S. Paul, *The Lord Protector: Religion and Politics in the Life of Oliver Cromwell* (London, Lutterworth Press, 1955), p. 195.

The interpretative difficulties are concentrated into that 15-month period. All students of these events agree that Cromwell was at the least *a* and probably *the* driving force sustaining the trial and execution of Charles I throughout January 1649.[3] The evidence for this is plentiful but all of it unreliable. Cromwell himself falls silent as far as the historical record is concerned.[4] In the weeks following Pride's Purge, only one letter of his has survived, a request on 18 December 1648 written to the master and fellows of Trinity Hall that they allocate a room in Doctors' Commons to Isaac Dorislaus.[5] Indeed, between the act of regicide and Cromwell's departure for Ireland in August 1649, in essence we only have letters relating to the marriage of his son Richard to Dorothy Maijor or routine military memoranda. We have to rely on what others report about him, or what they later recalled. So nothing is certain. It might be fruitful to wonder about this; but for the present we do not wish to disturb the existing consensus. His name does stand out on the death warrant. It would seem that he was a determined king-killer in January 1649.

There is an equal consensus that Cromwell had never voiced any thought of putting an end to Charles I's rule before October 1647. We can see no reason to doubt Cromwell's commitment to monarchy in some form before that date, and no evidence to suggest that he may have had regicide on his mind.

But historians do not agree at all about Cromwell's intentions in the intervening period. On one wing are those like Charles Firth, David Underdown, Blair Worden and Barry Coward[6] who see him as a reluctant regicide, as a very late convert. They rely principally on his recorded words at Putney, on a speech in the Commons at the passage of the Vote of No Addresses (on 3 January 1648), on a sequence of letters to Robert Hammond throughout the year 1648, on royalist newsletters, and above all on his actions in the three weeks that followed his return to London on 6 December and ended with his meetings with those lawyers who had taken their seats in the Rump – especially the Tweedledum and Tweedledee of commonwealth jurisprudence, Whitlocke and Widdrington; and they paint

---

3   A cross-section of recent writing can be found below, note 6.
4   There is probably no great significance in this. It is probably a function of the fact that he had now returned to London and was in daily oral communication with all the principals with whom he had been in regular contact by letter over previous months (Lenthall, Fairfax, St John, Hammond, etc.).
5   *The Letters and Speeches of Oliver Cromwell*, ed. T. Carlyle, rev. S. C. Lomas (3 vols., London, 1904), I, letter lxxxvi. For its significance see p. 35.
6   C. H. Firth, *Oliver Cromwell and the Rule of the Puritans in England* (Oxford, OUP, 1900), pp. 156, 168, 172–80, 185, 206–12; D. E. Underdown, *Pride's Purge: Politics in the Puritan Revolution* (Oxford, OUP, 1971), pp. 76–89, 119, 167–8, 183–5; A. B. Worden, *The Rump Parliament 1648–1653* (Cambridge, CUP, 1974), pp. 47–9, 67–9, 77, 179–81; B. Coward, *Cromwell* (London, Longman, 1991), pp. 58–68.

a picture of a man desperate not to fall into a republican abyss, to move every which way to pressurize Charles into accepting the army's bottom line. On the other side are historians such as Veronica Wedgwood, Ian Gentles, Peter Gaunt and Robert Paul,[7] who interpret some of the same material (especially the letters to Hammond and those after the battle of Preston) differently; who place less reliance on royalist newsletters as tainted by too much wishful-thinking; who rely more on tantalizing army documents and memoirs, which are often graphic but always tainted with the wisdom of hindsight; and who rummage around more in the events of the weeks immediately after the Putney debates. The resulting narrative sees Cromwell as steeling himself much earlier for a confrontation with Charles, and as someone willing to look at a variety of means of achieving that end. For these scholars, Cromwell's manoeuvres after Pride's Purge were intended not to prevent a trial but to ensure that it had the widest possible support and the best possible outcome. In the middle, inscrutable as he can be, stands the towering figure of Samuel Rawson Gardiner, reviewing the evidence with a care others have eschewed and with much still to teach us – and sitting inscrutably on the fence.[8]

We believe that it is possible to get closer to the truth; and we hope to demonstrate this by a more careful discrimination between several questions. We want to distinguish much more clearly between Cromwell's attitude to Charles himself and his attitude to monarchy; and to assess his view of the role of that king and of the monarchy itself in the settlement of the nation. We want to focus most sharply on his own words, to subject them to a keener biblical hermeneutic than hitherto and to interrogate other sources as and when that process requires it.

We are assisted by the fact that for the period from the meeting of the General Council of the army in Putney Church in late October 1647 to the purge of the parliament on 6 December 1648 we do possess plenty of Cromwell's own words. We have 43 of his letters, several of them more than 1000 words long and many of them to close friends, what we can take to be fairly full transcripts of 28 speeches and significant interventions during the recorded parts of the Putney debates, again several of them meaty and substantial contributions of several hundred words each. In addition, we have less full summaries of several speeches made in the House of Commons and written down by others. No similar period gives us such a balanced blend of Cromwell's public and private utterance. However, beyond that we enter a quagmire of fragmentary material, all of a treach-

7   C. V. Wedgwood, *The Trial of Charles I* (London, Collins, 1964), pp. 25–6, 321, 77–80, 232 n.30; I. Gentles, *The New Model Army in England, Ireland and Scotland 1645–1653* (Oxford, Blackwell, 1992), pp. 283–307; P. Gaunt, *Oliver Cromwell* (Oxford, Blackwell, 1996), pp. 85–91; Paul, *Lord Protector*, pp. 158–60, 168–9, 175–6, 183–4.
8   Gardiner, *Civil War*, IV, pp. 27, 31, 56–9, 175–6, 191–2, 232–9, 281–97.

erous kind, too much of it subject to much wisdom of hindsight, and much else to deeply partisan perspective. Although so much of this contextual material contradicts other evidence, most historians (Gardiner apart) have chosen to decide what is reliable and what is not on more or less *a priori* grounds. This more than anything else explains the quite sharp range of interpretations of Cromwell's part in events. We wish to suggest that a closer attention to his own words and tighter comparison of the contextual material can yield a projection of Cromwell's ideas and intentions that is more convincing than any previous account.

Most of the letters from 1647–8 investigated for this paper contain retrievable quotations or paraphrases from books Cromwell had read. We can see he had read 34 books – 21 of them from the Old Testament and 13 from the New. There is not a shred of evidence from this period that Cromwell read anything other than the Bible. His political theory derived exclusively from his understanding of God's willingness to work with and through a variety of forms as recorded in the Old Testament. The nearest he ever came to a historical disquisition on the basis of government was at Putney:

> [Consider the case of the Jews]. They were first [divided into] families where they lived, and had heads of families [to govern them], and they were [next] under Judges, and [then] they were under Kinges. When they came to desire a Kinge, they had a kinge; first elective and secondly by succession. In all these kinds of government they were happy and contented. If you make the best of it, if you would change the government to the best of it, it is but a moral thing. It is but as Paul says [Philippians 3.8] 'dross and dung in comparison of Christ.'9

Nowhere does Cromwell draw in any comparable way on classical or modern historical reading or knowledge. If we are to understand Cromwell's ruminations about what was possible and what was right to be done about the king in 1647–49 we must follow him through the Bible and the Bible alone.

II

The story begins at Putney, and – from Cromwell's point of view – it begins with the very last and longest of his 28 contributions. We need to begin by revisiting the conclusions of a separate joint paper published recently

9   *The Clarke Papers: selections from the papers of William Clarke*, ed. C. H. Firth, Camden Society, new series, vols. 49, 54, 61, 62 (1891–1901), I, pp. 369–70.

under the title *The Case of the Armie Truly Restated.*[10] In that paper we concluded:

> First, that the franchise debate at Putney was important because of its later resonance not because it changed anything at the time or helps us to understand the dynamics of politics in the later 1640s or the failure of the Putney Debates and the subsequent political recriminations. After the fury of the debate on 29 October, agreement was reached by all present – from Ireton on one wing to Rainsborough on the other – on a revision of the franchise, an agreement that was subsequently put out of mind by all present. Secondly, there was a running skirmish throughout the debates at Putney between the proponents of the *Case of the Armie* and the proponents of the *Agreement of the People.* The latter is far from a digest of the former and is not penned by the same hands, the *Case* being the work of Sexby and the *Agreement* of Wildman. This debate, we suggest, split officer from officer and adjutator from adjutator. Thirdly, the only 'Levellers' present at Putney were those spotted by historians. There were men present *later* associated with the name Leveller. Sexby, we have shown, was never a Leveller, and Wildman and Pettus were welcomed at Putney as men associated with the radicalisation of London politics not as the soulmates of Lilburne and Overton. Fourthly, the issue that really divided the General Council, and which led to its collapse amongst bitter recriminations of bad faith on all sides was not the franchise or even the detail of the Agreement; it was the Agreement's eloquent silence – the future role of the monarchy. It was bitter disagreements about that which caused Clarke to stop reporting; that caused Ireton to storm out on 5 November of all days; and which dominates the subsequent recrimination. And again it was an issue that split the senior officers amongst themselves, the officer-adjutators and soldier-adjutators amongst themselves and the new agents amongst themselves.

Three issues relating to the kingship came up at Putney. The first was the allegation in *The Case* that the grandees had entered into a personal treaty with the king that would lead to the betrayal of the cause for which the soldiers had fought and many of them died. To this Ireton and Cromwell robustly replied that everything they had done was rooted in the express will of the General Council, and it was the agents who were at fault for seeking to undermine army unity. This issue was tersely discussed at the outset of two days' debates, but in essence the agents withdrew the charge; and the grandees having protested their innocence dropped their complaint. The other debates related to the future settlement. Whether new arrangements for the making and administration of law, for civil government and for securing religious liberty for all sincere protestants were driven

10   Morrill and Baker, 'The Case of the Armie Truly Restated' in M. Mendle, ed., *The Putney Debates* (Cambridge, CUP, 2001).

through the existing parliament or formed into a paper constitution approved by the people at large, there remained the question as to whether the king would have any role in that settlement, and if so, at what point he would be consulted or invited to consent to it. Was there to be any *future* personal treaty with the king and if so with whom? And behind that lay a further question: whether *the* king, that is King Charles I, should be so consulted and invited; or whether *a* king should be so consulted and invited. Hard things were said about Charles I at Putney; and Sexby for one spoke against monarchy itself.[11] Captain Bishop and Colonel Harrison both called Charles 'a man of bloud',[12] and Cromwell for one assumed that Harrison was calling for the king's death, as we shall see.[13]

Personal animus against Charles was present from the beginning of the debates, with Sexby, in the first substantive contribution on the first day, saying that 'we have labour'd to please a Kinge, and I thinke, except we goe about to cutt all our throats wee shall not please him'.[14] Several speakers made clear their desire to ensure the outright abolition of the negative voice – something which had been a steady demand since the summer of 1646 of those soon to be called Levellers.[15] However, the *Case of the Armie* itself had called for a settlement of the people's rights and freedoms before there was any consideration of those of the king. It had not called for the abolition of monarchy.[16] In the words of William Allen: the *Case* had allowed kings to be set up 'as farre as may bee consistent with, and nott prejudiciall to the liberties of the Kingedome . . . which I thinke hee may and itt is not our judgement onely, butt of those set forth in the Case of the Army'.[17] If we read the silence of the *Agreement of the People* in the light of Wildman's *A Cal to all the soldiers of the Armie* of 29 October (which we can presume most of those present would have done), we would reach the same conclusion. For in *A cal*, Wildman exhibited an extreme hostility to Charles, demanded his impeachment and recommended that only a free parliament (in other words, one elected within a free constitution) should reach a

---

11 *CP*, I, p. 377.
12 *CP*, I, pp. 383, 417. For the significance of this phrase, see P. Crawford, ' "Charles Stuart. That Man of Blood" ', *Journal of British Studies*, XVI (1977), pp. 41–61.
13 *CP*, I, p. 417 and below, p. 25.
14 *CP*, I, pp. 227–8.
15 See the comments of Captain Allen (*CP*, I, p. 367), Col. Hewson (*CP*, I, p. 390) and Colonel Titchborne (*CP*, I, pp. 396, 405) and of the civilians Pettus (*CP*, I, pp. 351–2) and Wildman (*CP*, I, p. 386). Appearing in July 1646, *The Remonstrance of Many Thousand Citizens* was the first 'Leveller' pamphlet to manifest hostility to monarchy and the negative voice of the king: see D. M. Wolfe, ed., *Leveller Manifestoes of the Puritan Revolution* (New York, Humanities Press, 1967), pp. 109–15.
16 Ibid., p. 214. See also Morrill and Baker, 'Case of the Armie Truly Restated'.
17 *CP*, I, p. 377.

settlement with the king.[18] If monarchy were to be restored it would be by a free people conferring it onto a supplicant king – and not necessarily Charles I. This was a line of argument to which Wildman persisted in his heated exchanges with Ireton on 1 November,[19] where he concluded quite baldly that his argument was not about the survival of monarchy but about the need to call this king to account and to prevent future abuse of royal power: 'I onely affirme that [our settlement] doth affirme the Kinge's and Lords' interest surer than before.'[20] Such a programme was close to that previously articulated by some future Leveller leaders, by some officers and by some agents; but it was incompatible with what Lilburne had been urging most recently in print and in private, and with what many officers – Rainsborough[21] as much as Ireton – and some adjutators had been saying. It split the General Council vertically and not horizontally.

Beyond that, as the rhetorical temperature rose on 1 November, some people went further than they had previously. Thus Sexby asserted that 'wee are going to sett uppe the power of Kinges, some part of itt, which God will destroy; and which will bee butt as a burthensome stone that whosoever shall fall upon itt, will destroy him'.[22] But even this is compatible with a programme of extreme hostility to Charles and a delay in offering any role to some future monarch until every other aspect of the settlement was in place.

This, then, is the context for Cromwell's three major interventions in the debate on 1 November.[23] The sequence is important. He began by arguing that this was not the time or the place for the army to decide on a negative voice in the king or in the Lords. That belonged either to a parliament chastened and made wiser by the army's remonstrations or it belonged to a parliament elected under new and better electoral rules.[24] In a part of the speech apparently not recorded by Clarke but quoted directly by Colonel Goffe, he added that the General Council must beware of 'a lying spiritt in the mouth of Ahab's Prophets. Hee speakes falselie to us in the name of the Lord.'[25] Goffe rebuked Cromwell for cherry-picking the offerings of comrades from the Friday prayer meeting. Cromwell, clearly stung and hurt,

18 [John Wildman?] *A Cal to all the Souldiers of the Armie* ([29 Oct.] 1647, E412/10), pp. 2, 3, 5, 6, 8 [all second pagination].
19 *CP*, I, pp. 386–94.
20 *CP*, I, p. 377.
21 'Mr Rainsborough tooke occasion to take notice as if what Mr Allen spoke did reflect upon himself or some other there, as if they were against the name of Kinge and Lords': *CP*, I, p. 377.
22 Ibid.
23 For his views on kingship on the opening day see summary in Firth, *Oliver Cromwell*, pp. 177–8.
24 *CP*, I, pp. 368–71.
25 *CP*, I, p. 374.

responded by twice acknowledging his hastiness in running to judgement. Following Allen's call for all to keep an open mind on the king's future, and Sexby's meditation on the words of Jeremiah: 'we find in the worde of God: "I would heal Babylon but shee would not be healed". I thinke that wee have gone about to heale Babylon when shee would not',[26] Cromwell returns to Goffe's rebuke and pleads for caution against the too-ready appropriation of Old Testament typologies. But he then goes into a dramatic and clearly extempore meditation on the series of testimonies given forth as a result of the day of prayer.

> Truly wee have heard many speaking to us; and I cannott butt thinke that in many of those thinges *God* hath spoken to us . . . I cannott see butt that wee all speake to the same end, and the mistakes are onely in the way. The end is to deliver this nation from oppression and slavery, to accomplish that worke that God hath carried on in us . . . We agree thus farre.

He then makes a crucial admission: 'wee all apprehend danger from *the person* of the kinge'.[27] For several minutes he labours that point, reiterating that there is a problem with Charles himself – '[I] my self do concurre' with those who held that 'there can bee noe safetie in a consistencie with the person of the Kinge or the Lords, or their having the least interest in the publique affaires of the Kingedome'. But he argues that this does not mean that 'God will destroy these persons [ie kings in general] or that power'. Furthermore, God has clearly shown that they must not 'sett uppe' or 'preserve [kings]' where it threatens the public interest. But God has not yet made plain, he says, whether it would be hazardous to the public interest to 'goe about to destroy or take away' king and Lords or whether it would be more hazardous to retain them.[28] His plea is not to rush to judgement on this issue. The Council must not assume that even if God wills it, they are *ipso facto* the self-appointed instruments of God's will:

> [let] those to whome this is not made cleare, though they do but thinke itt probable that God will destroy them, yett lett them make this rule to themselves, though God have a purpose to destroy them, and though I should finde a desire to destroy them . . . Therefore let those that are of that minde waite uppon God for such a way when the thinge maye bee done without sin and without scandall too.[29]

---

26   *CP*, I, pp. 376–8.
27   *CP*, I, p. 379 [emphasis added].
28   *CP*, I, pp. 382, 380.
29   *CP*, I, p. 382.

It is our contention that this gives us the key to Cromwell's politics over the next 15 months: an ever-greater conviction that God intended Charles I to be struck down, and a continuing uncertainty about when and how that would be done and about the extent of his and the army's agency. This anger against a king who was duplicitous and who willed the nation back into blood, the principal author and progenitor of the second civil war, can be seen to mount steadily; and Cromwell's public and private letters are a chronicle of his introspective search for the connection between God's actions in the history of His first chosen people, the people of Israel, and of His new chosen people, the people of England. In a sense Goffe's rebuke at Putney took 15 months to reach fruition.

III

After 1 November, the generals reinforced the news blackout over events at Putney. The newspapers carried no reports, and Clarke and his team of stenographers laid down their quills. Fragmentary notes in his papers suggest that the mood got uglier by the day, but that the divisions remained vertical and not horizontal.[30] The debates seem to have been about whether the army should precipitate an immediate crisis by a confrontation with the parliament and king, or proceed more slowly, and this division underlay the bitter disputes about the nature of the rendezvous Fairfax had called, and whether the army as a whole would adopt the *Agreement* or the more orderly process laid out in what became the *Remonstrance*. According to a petition issued on 11 November by some – but not all – of the new agents, Ireton stormed out of the General Council, not to return, on 5 November when a vote was taken to send a letter to the Speaker declaring it was the army's desire that no further propositions should be sent to the king.[31] Significantly, although parliamentary duties may have kept Cromwell away on 5 and 6 November,[32] Cromwell remained active in the Council; and he was certainly present on 11 November, when Harrison called the king 'a Man of Blood' and demanded that 'they were to prosecute him'. Cromwell responded by reminding him that as in the case of David's refusal to try Joab for the slaying of Abner, there were pragmatic circumstances in which murder was not to be punished. The pragmatic circumstance was that 'the sons of Zeruiah were too hard for him'.[33] Zeruiah was David's sister, and Joab was just one of her many sons. Cromwell is saying that Joab's brothers were

30   Morrill and Baker, 'Case of the Armie Truly Restated'.
31   A. S. P. Woodhouse, *Puritanism and Liberty* (London, J. M. Dent & Sons, 1938), pp. 452–4. For the vote itself, see: *CP*, I, pp. 440–1.
32   *CP*, I, p. 440 discusses his absence on 5 and 6 November.
33   *CP*, I, p. 417.

too powerful for him to proceed against Joab. Joab/Charles was guilty of murder; *realpolitik* alone prevented his trial. It is worth speculating – we can do no more – who was who in Cromwell's application of this biblical passage. The difficulty of doing so does not detract from the shock. The reason for not proceeding against Charles was not that it would be unjust but they could not (yet) get away with it.

IV

Cromwell crossed some sort of Rubicon on 1 November, and events quickly strengthened his resolve. The next three weeks saw the king's escape from Hampton Court; the news reaching Cromwell from a variety of sources that Charles had initialled a treaty with the anti-Solemn Leaguers in Scotland followed fast on its heels, but – in the view of a number of observers from across the political spectrum – he was most affected by reading intercepted correspondence between the king and the queen which rejoiced in the way the army grandees were being bamboozled.[34] We do not have to believe the melodramatic tale of the letter containing Charles' plan to doublecross the army allegedly cut from a saddle-bag in the Blue Boar in Holborn by Cromwell and Ireton dressed as troopers, although Gardiner's careful analysis of its basis in fact is more impressive than the breezy dismissal of most modern scholars.[35] Certainly something as significant as this is needed to explain Ireton's dramatic volte-face between 5 and 21 November.[36] Perhaps the most important supplementary testimony comes in Sir John Berkeley's account of his encounter with Cromwell and Ireton on 28 November 1647 when Berkeley presented himself at Windsor with letters from the king. He found an army council meeting in progress: he records that 'I look'd upon Cromwell and Ireton and the rest of my acquaintance. Who saluted me very coldly, and had their countenance very changed towards me.' Berkeley was

---

34   Robert Ashton, *Counter Revolution: the Second Civil War and its Origins* (New Haven, Yale University Press, 1994), pp. 30–6; Austin Woolrych, *Soldiers and Statesmen: the General Council of the Army and its Debates 1647–1648* (Oxford, OUP, 1987), pp. 268–76; Gardiner, *Civil War*, IV, pp. 27–31.

35   See Gardiner, *Civil War*, IV, pp. 27–31, and especially pp. 27n.3, 28n.2. A strong piece of supporting evidence is the postscript in Ireton's letter to Hammond on 21 November which speaks of Cromwell being gone from headquarters up to London 'on scout I know not where' (ibid., p. 27). On the other hand, Patrick Little who has recently completed a thesis on the Boyle family and the politics of Britain and Ireland, tells us that the source of the story – Orrery's secretary Morrice recording a conversation he had with Orrery about a conversation Orrery had with Cromwell – is not to be trusted. So we will not pursue it.

36   Of course, the escape of the king and the immediate panic that he might have fled to the Scots (as the prioritizing of letters to Lambert in the North suggest) may be sufficient reason. This was the view of the bilious Robert Huntingdon in his unreliable *Sundry Reasons* (1648, E458/3), p. 11; see the comments of Gardiner, *Civil War*, IV, pp. 26–7 and 26n.2.

then told by an unnamed officer that at the afternoon meeting of the council, Ireton and Cromwell had called for the king to be transferred as a close prisoner to London 'and then br[ought] to a tryal'; and that none be allowed to speak to him' [i.e. negotiate with him] upon pain of death'.[37]

All this hangs together. A whole variety of separate and differently problematic sources see a transformation in Cromwell in the weekend of 19–21 November and the days that follow. Perhaps it was the escape of the king; but most of these accounts attribute it to the content of intercepted letters that revealed the king's initialled agreement with the Scots and intention to string the army along as far as maybe.[38] If Cromwell had had a regicidal epiphany at Putney, it became much firmer within the month.

Reliable material becomes very sparse for the next few months. We can be sure that Cromwell spoke strongly in favour of the Vote of No Addresses on 3 January 1648, and in that speech and in the first of a vital sequence of letters to Colonel Robert Hammond (a distant relation by marriage and the king's gaoler) a hardening of attitudes is clear. Cromwell's words as recorded by John Boys in his diary on 3 January are therefore important.[39] They seem to represent very clearly his conversion to the trial of the king but not to republicanism. Supporting the Vote of No Addresses, he said that they 'should not any longer expect safety and government from an obstinate man whose heart God had hardened'. This can only mean the end of Charles I. But it is perfectly compatible with his further statement that 'we declared our intentions for Monarchy unless necessity enforce an alteration'. Some historians, including Barry Coward and David Underdown, interpret 'necessity' here in a secular sense – 'the dictates of political reality' as Coward glosses it – while others, including Gaunt, gloss it in a religious sense – until God reveals it to be his will.[40] The latter is clearly the correct reading, as the incessant linkage of the words 'providence' and 'necessity' throughout 1648 and the speeches of the 1650s demonstrates.[41] Furthermore, Cromwell's reference in his letter to Hammond (written late on the evening of the same day) that the king's flight and subsequent developments represented 'a mighty providence to this poor kingdom and to us all' gives a rather chilling menace to his concluding words: 'we shall (I hope)

---

37   *The Memoirs of Sir John Berkeley* (1699), pp. 70–4.
38   Woolrych, *Soldiers and Statesmen*, pp. 305–6.
39   D. E. Underdown, 'The Parliamentary Diary of John Boys, 1647–8', *Bulletin of the Institute of Historical Research*, XXXIX (1966), pp. 156–7, 145–6.
40   Coward, *Cromwell*, p. 58; Underdown, *Pride's Purge*, pp. 88–9; Gaunt, *Oliver Cromwell*, pp. 89–91.
41   A. B. Worden, 'Providence and Politics in Cromwellian England', *Past and Present*, CIX (1985), pp. 55–99. See also Cromwell's charge to the Nominated Assembly in 1653 that their authority came to them 'by the way of necessity, by the way of the wise Providence of God (*LSOC*, II, p. 290), and his linking of providence and necessity (in having destroyed the name and title of king in 1649) when he declined the kingship in 1657 (ibid., III, pp. 56, 58, 70).

instantly go upon the business in relation to [the king], tending to prevent danger' and his request that Hammond 'search out' any 'juggling' by the king.[42]

There is tantalizing but unreliable evidence that Cromwell was seriously considering, in late January 1648, direct negotiation with the Prince of Wales which could have led to Charles' abdication or deposition. It consists principally of a letter of intelligence of the variably reliable Roman agent in London, written on 17 January, which names Cromwell and St John as the men behind the initiative.[43] But it is supported by a report home by the French ambassador Grignon.[44] He wrote on 31 January that there was a plan by people he does not name to send the Earl of Denbigh to France with letters for the Prince of Wales, but that Denbigh was reluctant to go; and this in turn is confirmed by a letter in the Hamilton papers (and Hamilton was Denbigh's brother-in-law), dated 1 February, that 'the Earl of Denbigh is to go over with some overtures to her Majesty and the Prince'.[45] It may be significant for what was to happen at the end of the year that the person who was supposed to raise the matter with the Prince was the Earl of Denbigh.[46] As the year wears on there is stronger evidence of Cromwell's involvement in plans to depose Charles in favour first of James Duke of York and then of Henry Duke of Gloucester. All this represents something more persuasive than the oft-quoted and more tainted evidence of the Ludlow manuscript that at that time Cromwell refused to join Ludlow in condemning monarchy, or to affirm it (the quotation is too well known and too unreliable to be repeated here).[47]

In essence, there were lots of insubstantial straws blowing around in the wind, and they were all blowing in the same direction. Cromwell was exploring all kinds of ways of moving to a reckoning with Charles I, but had yet to satisfy himself of the natural justice of any of them. He then set off on campaign, and was too preoccupied with the hydra with its variety of cavalier and Presbyterian heads to formulate any immediate practical solution. But his letters leave us in no doubt that his mind was as full of Isaiah as it was of the sound of musket and cannon.

---

42   *LSOC*, I, pp. 289–91 and top p. 290. Peter Gaunt, *Oliver Cromwell*, p. 90 makes more sense of the events of 3 January than any other recent historian.

43   Gardiner, *Civil War*, IV, p. 56, n.4.

44   Ibid., p. 57, n.1.

45   All the evidence is presented and weighed by Gardiner, *Civil War*, V, pp. 56–7 and p. 56, n.4, and evidence that St John 'hath made Cromwell his bedfellow' is in p. 57, n.1.

46   See the discussion of this in John Adamson's essay below, pp. 36–70 [in the original publication].

47   *The Memoirs of Edmund Ludlow*, ed. C. H. Firth (2 vols, Oxford, OUP, 1894), I, pp. 184–6. For three slightly contrasting commentaries on this meeting see: S. R. Gardiner, *Oliver Cromwell* (1900), p. 133; Firth, *Oliver Cromwell and the Rule of the Puritans*, p. 185; and Coward, *Cromwell*, p. 59.

V

The sweep of Cromwell's writings throughout 1648 suggests a man who feels guided by God and clear of the end though not quite of the means. He never again discussed the king except as someone who had put himself outside the protection of God's people. For the whole of 1648 Cromwell's concern was not whether to remove the king but when and how.

In the late spring, he set off on campaign first in South Wales, then to head off the Scottish invasion, then to pursue the retreating Scots almost to the gates of Edinburgh, and finally to mop up royalist resistance in the north. At every stage he wrote letters which have survived, several of them public or semi-public letters to Speaker Lenthall or General Fairfax, others private and confessional, as to St John, Wharton and Hammond.[48] His public rhetoric consistently calls for *all* (and all must include the king as principal author) responsible for the new war to be called to account for their treason and sacrilege; his private rhetoric adds to that a continuous engagement with the scripture and with very specific texts as he sought to discern the will of God for himself and for His people.

It is, of course, the case that the army council committed itself to the trial of the king at the conclusion of the three-day prayer meeting at the end of April. Or so William Allen maintained in a pamphlet written in 1659.[49] But we should not use this, as some have, as evidence of Cromwell's position. Allen *may* be recalling things accurately; Cromwell *may well* have been present for part of the meeting.[50] Even if both are true, it does not follow that this directly informed Cromwell's thinking. Allen alleged that at Windsor Charles Stuart was branded 'a man of blood' who should atone for his shedding of innocent blood in accordance with the requirements of the Book of Numbers [35 v.33]: 'So ye shall not defile the land wherein you are: for blood it defileth the land; and the land cannot be cleansed of the blood that is shed therein, but by the blood of him that shed it.' The army committed itself to putting the king on trial as soon as it was in a position to do so.[51] The application of this text to that man of blood Charles Stuart sustained many in the months that followed. But Cromwell himself never endorsed it; nor did he ever cite from the Book of Numbers before, during or for eight years after 1648.

His own thinking followed a different course. After each of the major episodes in the second war, unlike any of those in the first, the leaders were

---

48   *LSOC*, I, pp. 350–1, 353–4, 393–400.
49   W. Allen, *A Faithfull Memorial* in *Somers Tracts* (16 vols, 1748–52), VI, pp. 500–1.
50   Gentles, *New Model Army*, pp. 245–6; Gaunt, *Cromwell*, pp. 92–3.
51   Allen, *Faithfull Memorial*, pp. 500–1. At a less-well-remembered prayer meeting also at Windsor on 26 November this commitment was renewed: Gardiner, *Civil War*, IV, p. 235.

put on trial – either before a court martial or by reference to the High Court of Justice.[52] The first war had been a struggle between two parties who believed that they were fighting God's cause. God had shown which side he was on from the moment of the formation of the New Model. Anyone seeking to overturn 'so many evidences of a divine providence going along with it and prospering a just cause'[53] were in effect committing sacrilege, seeking to overturn the judgement of God. It was 'the repetition of the same offence against all the witnesses that God hath borne'. But, in addition, 'this is a more prodigious treason than any that hath been perfected before; because the former quarrel was that Englishmen might rule over one another, this is to vassalize us to a foreign nation'.[54] This comes from a letter written from Yorkshire to Robert Jenner and John Ashe on 20 November, the very day that the army's *Remonstrance* was being presented to parliament. That theme of the wickedness of the king in seeking foreign arms and giving undertakings to foreigners, starting with the Scots, was at the heart of the indictment of Charles in that *Remonstrance* and it was to reappear in the charge against him two months later.[55] The clearest statement that the time had come for Charles to account for his crimes came in the coda to Cromwell's long letter to Lenthall describing his victory over Hamilton at Preston on 20 August:

> Sir, this is nothing but the hand of God . . . You should take courage to do the work of the Lord in fulfilling the ends of your magistracy, in seeking the peace and welfare of the people of this land, that all who live quietly and peaceably may have countenance from you, and *they that are implacable and will not leave troubling the land* may speedily be destroyed out of the land.[56]

This cannot but be a reference to the king himself. We might note, however, that the phrase 'destroyed out of the land', for all its rhetorical strength, leaves open the possibility of exile rather than execution. A similar unambiguous if oblique reference to the king is to be found in a letter written to

---

52   Gardiner, *Civil War*, IV, pp. 202–6; S. R. Gardiner, *History of the Commonwealth and Protectorate* (4 vols, London, Longman, 1903), I, pp. 10–11, 41; Ashton, *Counter Revolution*, pp. 421–2; Gentles, *New Model Army*, pp. 255–7.
53   Cromwell to Lenthall, announcing the fall of Pembroke, 11 July 1648 (*LSOC*, I, pp. 324–5). Cromwell had the three principals of the South Wales revolt – Laugharne, Powell and Poyer – tried and convicted. They were sent up to London to draw lots as to which of them was to be shot. Poyer (literally) drew the short straw and was executed by firing squad in the Piazza of Covent Garden.
54   *LSOC*, I, p. 387 (cf. the comments of Firth, *Oliver Cromwell*, p. 206).
55   This is a point which is made all the clearer by the evidence of Anglo-Scottish dislikes presented in David Scott's paper below, pp. 138–60 [in the original publication].
56   *LSOC*, I, pp. 333–4 (emphasis added).

Fairfax which endorsed a petition from the officers of the regiments in the north, itself supporting the *Remonstrance*: 'I find . . . in [all the officers] a very great zeal to have impartial justice done upon *all* offenders; and I do from my heart concur with them.'[57]

Such language, sustained over six consecutive months, for judgement on *all* the authors of the war clearly extended to the king himself. The questions were when and how, not whether he should be tried and by implication deposed or executed. Cromwell spoke of providence throughout his life, but never with the persistence or confidence of 1648. Letter after letter speak of providence and (connected to it) of necessity as linked aspects of God's immanence and engagement with the affairs of men.[58] And providence is more and more invoked as the guarantor of action against the king.

Such were his musings on public events. But throughout the months of campaigning he was also clearly studying the Bible and looking for personal meaning in it. When we first planned this paper we thought we had identified a simple and powerful biblical parallel that guided Cromwell through the year. On four occasions in 1648 Cromwell makes references to the story of Gideon and we became convinced that he had come to see himself as Gideon *redivivus*.[59] Indeed his account of the battle of Preston written the day after the battle and sent to Speaker Lenthall, reads less like other accounts of the battle than it does of the biblical account of Gideon's defeat of the Midianites at Ain Harod.[60]

Let us recall the story of Gideon. He was called from the plough to lead the army of Israel. He winnowed the army, reducing it to a small, compact force made of Israel's russet-coated captains, and he destroyed the Midianites and harried their fleeing army for 200 miles as Cromwell did after Preston. He then executed the kings of the Midianites, denying them quarter because they had shed innocent blood on Mount Tabor. He refused to take the crown himself and returned, loaded with honours, to his farm. It is not surprising that Cromwell found this a powerful story and suitable to his condition in 1648. And he drew powerfully on it, nowhere more than in an extraordinary outburst to Fairfax in the middle of a letter full of nitty-gritty military matters as he swept through South Wales in June 1648:

> I pray God teach this nation . . . what the mind of God may be in all this, and what our duty is. Surely it is not that the poor godly people of this Kingdom should still be the objects of wrath and anger, nor that our God

---

57   *LSOC*, I, p. 391 (emphasis added).
58   See John Morrill, 'King Killing no Murder', *Cromwelliana* (1998), pp. 12–22, an early and much cruder version of this paper, but with a fuller analysis of the 1648 letters (printed as an appendix to the article in ibid., pp. 22–38).
59   Ibid.
60   *LSOC*, I, pp. 331–45.

would have our necks under a yoke of bondage; for these things that have lately come to pass have been the wonderful works of God; breaking the rod of the oppressor, as in the day of Midian, not with garments much rolled in blood but by the terror of the Lord.[61]

This passage draws on Galatians, Acts and 2 Corinthians, but the central image with its reference to the breaking of the Midianites is from Isaiah, and actually that turns out to be the crucial point. For Cromwell's allusions to Gideon are all passing ones; there is no sustained meditation on his story. On the other hand he spent much time and space in several letters in extended meditation on Isaiah chapters 8 and 9. Indeed he wrote to Oliver St John on 1 September 1648, a week after the battle of Preston, telling him that 'this scripture hath been of great stay with me, Isaiah eighth, 10. 11. 14. Read the whole chapter.'[62] That chapter and the next tell how most of the people have missed out on righteousness and that those who follow the idolatrous leaders of Judah and Israel will be destroyed. So

Associate yourselves, o ye people, and ye shall be broken in pieces . . . gird yourselves and you shall be broken in pieces . . . And I will wait upon the Lord, that hideth his face from the house of Jacob, and I will look for him, Behold I and the children whom the Lord has given me are for signs and wonders in Israel.

Cromwell was working out his own destiny in relation to God's plan, and God was no democrat. He had worked through a godly remnant in the days of Isaiah and he could and would do so again.

In November Cromwell wrote two letters to Hammond.[63] We do not have time here to demonstrate the many misunderstandings of the letter of the 6th such as Underdown's claim that it represents Cromwell's willingness to acquiesce in a settlement between parliament and the king 'if Charles accepted a permanent Presbyterian settlement'.[64] For Cromwell makes it clear that such an agreement could be approved of only if one followed 'carnal reasonings' – human expediency rather than divine imperatives. Instead we rely on Gentles' better reading of this letter: 'peace is only good

---

61   *LSOC*, I, p. 321.
62   *LSOC*, I, p. 350.
63   *LSOC*, I, pp. 393–400; and III, pp. 389–92.
64   *CP*, II, pp. 49–50, with a commentary by Firth and an attribution to Cromwell. This attribution is probable but not quite as secure as Firth maintains. Why was Clarke (in London) in possession of a letter of such a private nature written by a senior officer stationed in Yorkshire to a colonel stationed on the Isle of Wight? Could the letter have been by another senior officer who had been in Scotland with Cromwell? This is the only letter of Cromwell's for this period without any biblical allusions in it.

when we receive it from out of our father's hands . . . War is good when we are led by our Father.'[65] And peace with this king was not at God's hand.

Less enigmatic and more powerful was the follow-up letter Cromwell wrote on 25 November. It is a plea to Hammond to see how a critical mass of evidence points to God's manifest will being encapsulated in what the army proposes in the *Remonstrance*.

> Seek to know the mind of God in all that chain of Providence, whereby God hath brought thee thither, and that person to thee . . . and then tell me whether there be not some glorious and high meaning in all this, above what thou hast yet attained.[66]

Nowhere was the clustering of biblical gobbets more dense than in this letter. The opening paragraphs alone – some 700 words – contain 24 citations from 11 biblical books,[67] with especial focus on the Epistle of James [ch. 1 vv 2–6] with its exhortation to Christians 'to ask in faith, nothing wavering. For he that wavereth is like a wave of the sea driven with the wind and tossed' and from Romans 8, with its great cry that, freed from the law, the true Christian must look beyond present deprivations to the presence of the Holy Spirit. So Cromwell is pleading with Hammond to trust in providential reason and not in worldly, fleshly reasoning. By the time he wrote that letter Cromwell had seen the army *Remonstrance* approved by the army council on the 16th and presented to the parliament on the 20th and he knew that Hammond would have seen it. The letter is in fact begging Hammond to go along with the *Remonstrance*. Thus he told Hammond that while 'we could perhaps have wished the stay of it till after the treaty', in the end could the people of God expect any good from 'this man against whom the Lord hath witnessed'? The *Remonstrance* demanded unambiguously that 'the King should be brought to Justice, as the Capital cause of all'.[68]

VI

Space precludes any further exegesis. We hope that if our analysis of the development of Cromwell's thinking up to 25 November is convincing, then it provides the safe guide through the treacherous and incomplete shards of evidence for the month of December. It means that we can agree whole-

---

65 Gentles, *New Model Army*, p. 283.

66 *LSOC*, I, pp. 393–403.

67 As identified by Paul, *Lord Protector*, appendix V, p. 406, nn.1–9, p. 407, nn.1–11.

68 *A Remonstrance of his Excellency Sir Thomas Fairfax . . . and of the General Council of Officers* ([16 Nov.] 1648, E473/11), reprinted in *The Parliamentary or Constitutional History of England* (24 vols., 1761–3), XVIII, pp. 161–238.

heartedly with but recontextualize Ian Gentles' reading (itself pre-echoed in the work of Veronica Wedgwood and Robert Paul).[69]

The key to understanding Cromwell's actions over the seven weeks separating his return to London and the king's execution is to keep several questions separate. Did Cromwell want to see the king put on trial? *Yes.* Did he know what form the trial should take? *Yes and it was not the way it actually happened.* Did he want Charles to cease to be king? *Yes, either deposition or abdication.* Did he want to see the king dead? *Yes and no – yes in that he deserved it, no in that it might shipwreck the very civil and religious liberties it was intended to safeguard.* Did he want to see monarchy abolished? *Almost certainly not.* And underlying all his hesitancy was a dread that if the army pushed heedless on to regicide and a king-less commonwealth, the sons of Zeruiah would be too strong for him.

Let us remember that on 7 December, as Cromwell took his seat in parliament, the position was as follows. Even the purged Rump of the House of Commons had refused to take any action to reverse the decisions that had provoked Pride's Purge until Fairfax answered their demand for the release of the imprisoned members; the House of Lords was totally opposed to the Purge. The Presbyterian clergy were gargling in preparation for thunderous denunciations from their pulpits.[70] The Levellers were utterly opposed to trial of the king by parliament.[71] Lord General Fairfax was utterly opposed to the king's trial and as recently as 16 November all but six of the army council had voted that if the king agreed to the 'fundamentals' they would add to the Newport articles that he should be reinstated. His rejection of these terms outright had swung the majority behind the demands of the *Remonstrance* for his trial, but the army remained unpredictable. Cromwell was well aware that this was not an irrevocable conversion to regicide, rather it was evidence of volatility. Let us not forget that as late as 21 December 1648 the army council voted by a simple majority against the king's execution and even on 25 December, it voted by 6: 1 that if the king accepted the terms put to him by Denbigh his life should be spared. An unco-operative parliament, a divided and volatile army, a resentful, hostile and hungry populace, all of Scotland and 90 per cent of Ireland in the hands of men implacably opposed to the king's trial and deposition, and two of Charles' nephews ruling France and the Netherlands – all this must have made David's problems with the sons of Zeruiah look small beer indeed. No wonder Cromwell urged caution in moving to *the desired end.*

---

69   Wedgwood, *Trial of Charles I*, pp. 25–31; Paul, *Lord Protector*, pp. 183–4; Gentles, *New Model Army*, pp. 297–314.
70   See the argument and evidence presented below by Elliot Vernon, pp. 202–24 [in the original publication].
71   As demonstrated by Andrew Sharp in his essay below, see pp. 181–201 [in the original publication].

We have no shred of evidence from Cromwell's own lips or pen that he was keen to prevent the trial of the king, or that he doubted that the king deserved death, or that he believed he should remain on the throne. Indeed every piece of surviving strictly contemporary evidence – newspapers from across the spectrum, secret royalist intelligence reports, and German, French and Italian ambassadorial reports[72] support the following claims about his behaviour in December 1648.

1   Cromwell attempted to bring back anyone willing to accept the new situation created by the purge (to flatter and tame some of Zeruiah's sons).
2   He pushed on with a new paper constitution that might be brought in prior to a trial.
3   He attempted a private negotiation with Hamilton on 14/15 December.
4   He simultaneously worked to transfer the king to the custody of his most bitter and determined enemies, especially Thomas Harrison who had demanded his death as early as 11 November 1647.
5   He demonstrated a preference for the trial to be deferred until *after* the introduction of the new constitution and the holding of fresh elections on the new more equitable system and until *after* the trial of the other incendiaries who had shed innocent blood in the second civil war (trials which would demonstrate the depths of the king's duplicity).

We can go a step further. In January 1648, Cromwell had tried to persuade Denbigh to travel to France in order to persuade the Prince of Wales to accept the throne upon his father's deposition.[73] The army *Remonstrance* of November 1648 demanded that the Prince of Wales and the Duke of York surrender themselves for trial or stand debarred from the throne; which (in the absence of any statement in the *Remonstrance* against monarchy) would make Gloucester the heir to the throne. Cromwell was close to Isaac Dorislaus and wrote in December 1648 to the master of Trinity Hall asking him to use his position as master of Doctors' Commons to provide rooms for Dorislaus.[74] It was Dorislaus who co-authored the charges against the king, charges which specifically indicted the Princes Charles and James but not Henry in their father's treasons.[75] It was Denbigh who was sent to see Hamilton and the king at Windsor on 27 December with a secret offer which seems likely to have included an offer to the king: abdicate in favour of Henry and your life will be spared; refuse and you will die and the destruction of your House and of monarchy will be laid at your door.

72   All this material is discussed by Gardiner, *Civil War*, IV, pp. 276–92.
73   Above, p. 28.
74   *LSOC*, I, pp. 403–4.
75   Gardiner, *Documents*, p. 373.

This is certainly the view of the French ambassador in his report on 21 December, and he was more precise and accurate than most in his reporting throughout that month.[76]

Our argument is then that by 25 November Cromwell was resolved to see Charles I put on public trial. No more than Ireton had he committed himself to the abolition of monarchy. As the phrase in that letter to Hammond ('we could perhaps have wished the stay of it until after the treaty')[77] makes clear, Cromwell still preferred a different sequence of events: a breaking-off of the treaty; the purge or dissolution of parliament; an interim council on the model of the Scottish Commission of Estates; a high court or a commission of *oyer* and *terminer* consisting of Lords, Commons and military men; a trial of major royalist incendiaries culminating in the king; a conviction and then an ultimatum – abdicate in favour of your son and live, or refuse to abdicate and die. Prudence made him linger over the first; justice always pointed to the second. His return to London was timed to assist that process. He – like everyone else – was thrown off balance by the events of 5 and 6 December. Now the issue was whether to wait until the original sequence was re-established or whether to proceed straight to a trial. Ireton was drawn more to the latter, Cromwell to the former. Eventually, after the failure of the Denbigh mission, Cromwell fell into line. Whitelocke's teasing testimony that Cromwell invited Widdrington and himself to a meeting that presupposed the removal of Charles I, but for 'settling the Kingdom by Parliament, and not to leave all to the Sword' is perhaps the clincher.[78] The delays had little to do with cold feet over Charles. They represented the hesitations of a man who had a master plan at the end of November and was trying to work out how he could restore an orderly sequence to *necessary* events in the wake of the unplanned purge of 6 December. But events took on a momentum of their own, and Cromwell found that a flash flood required him to shoot the rapids in a raging torrent. When he muttered 'cruel necessity' over the corpse of Charles I, perhaps it was a reflection on the fact that it was not just the king who had experienced the harshness of divine decrees. As Cromwell said his prayers on 31 January 1649, perhaps he prayed: 'help me against the sons of Zeruiah who are *everywhere.*' Or to put it another way: 'help us in this time of cruel necessity.'

---

76   Gardiner, *Civil War*, IV, p. 282.
77   *LSOC*, III, pp. 389–92.
78   *The Diary of Bulstrode Whitelocke, 1605–1675*, ed. Ruth Spalding (Oxford, OUP, 1990), pp. 226–7. See the important gloss on this by Wedgwood, *Trial*, pp. 78–80.

2

Oliver Cromwell and the Sin of Achan

Blair Worden

Originally appeared as Blair Worden, 'Oliver Cromwell and the Sin of Achan' in Derek Beales and Geoffrey Best (ed.), *History, Society and the Churches: essays in honour of Owen Chadwick*. Copyright 1985 Cambridge University Press, Cambridge.

Editor's Introduction

In this essay, Blair Worden explores the implications of Cromwell's profound sense that God had a purpose for England and for himself, and that God's wishes were manifested through 'providences'. Worden traces the Biblical basis for the Puritan belief that worldly setbacks could indicate that God had withdrawn His favour and was punishing sinfulness. The conviction that individual iniquity might incur collective punishment prompted the characteristic Puritan response, when faced with defeats, of self-examination to identify what individual sins might have displeased God. A classic example of this pattern is found in William Allen's lengthy account of the Army officers' prayer meeting at Windsor Castle at the end of April 1648, in which the officers perceived their own 'cursed carnal conferences' with the Royalist party the previous year as a cause of the second Civil War.

Worden then shows how these issues reached a climax in the years 1655–7 following the defeat of the English expedition to the West Indies. He suggests that the collapse of the 'Western Design' dealt a severe blow to Cromwell from which it is possible he never fully recovered. In wondering what had brought God's displeasure upon England, he lapsed into a lengthy period of self-examination. This is a highly significant argument because it reveals that Cromwell followed through the logic of his own providentialism even when it was deeply painful and problematic for him to do so. In particular, the declarations for public fast days in 1655–6 referred explicitly to the story of Achan, told in the Book of Joshua, chapter 7. After the fall of Jericho,

Achan's greed led him to take 'of the accursed thing' by stealing 'a goodly Babylonish garment' and some gold and silver, thereby bringing down God's wrath on the people of Israel. Worden argues that Cromwell was haunted by anxiety that it was his own iniquities, like Achan's, that had caused England to lose God's favour. He shows, in particular, how Sir Henry Vane's *A Healing Question Propounded* (1656), which placed the blame for England's defeat on Cromwell's assumption of the Protectorate from motives of 'self-interest and private gain', deeply wounded Cromwell.

In the final section of the essay, Worden makes an important contribution to the debate over Cromwell's reasons for declining the kingship in May 1657. He places Cromwell's words in the context of his fears that his own ambition and selfishness might provoke God's anger against the English people. Worden charts his anguished indecision as he weighed these arguments, presented to him very forcefully by radical critics of the Protectorate, against those for stability and consolidation advocated by the proposal's supporters. In the end, it was Cromwell's fear of his own iniquity, and his belief that the fate of the people hinged on his decision, that convinced him that – in an explicit allusion to the story of Achan – he 'would not build Jericho again'.

Oliver Cromwell and the Sin of Achan

Blair Worden

Oliver Cromwell knew that God had a special and surpassing purpose in the civil wars. The Lord 'hath been pleased to make choice of these islands wherein to manifest many great and glorious things', 'such things amongst us as have not been known in the world these thousand years'.[1] For 'reasons best known to Himself', God had wonderfully raised up Cromwell, a 'weak instrument', 'not worthy the name of a worm'. Under his leadership 'the poor despised people of God', now miraculously delivered from the persecution of the 1630s, and 'by providence having arms', laid low the mighty in victories which, won as they were by 'an army despised by our enemies, and little less than despaired of by our friends', confounded all human calculations.[2] When Cromwell and the saints sought to comprehend the size and the meaning of those mercies, they turned to the Old Testament, which they knew so intimately. There they found the figurative models, the 'parallels', which came to dominate their political imaginations and to shape their interpretations of political and military events. In the divine plan of history, they believed, the deliverance of 'God's peculiar' in England might have a place equal in importance to the salvation of the people of Israel. They had passed out of an Egypt, through a Red Sea, towards a Promised Land.

Their progress constituted in Cromwell's mind a 'remarkable series' or 'chain' of 'providences'. The saints 'were never beaten; wherever they engaged the enemy they beat them continually. And truly this . . . has some instruction in it.'[3] There was Marston Moor, which Cromwell believed to have 'all the evidences of an absolute victory obtained by the Lord's blessing upon the godly party principally'. There was Naseby, where, inspecting the cavalry on the morning of battle, he 'could not . . . but smile out to God in praises, in assurance of victory, because God would, by things that are not, bring to naught things that are'. Then, in 1648, when royalist risings seemed certain to crush the godly party, the new Model was vouchsafed the spectacular triumphs of the second civil war. Cromwell cried out in astonishment at those 'wonderful works of God, breaking the rod of the oppressor, as in the day of Midian . . . Wherever anything in this world is exalted,

---

1   *A Declaration of his Highness the Lord Protector and the Parliament . . . for a Day of Solemn Fasting and Humiliation in the Three Nations* (London, [September] 1654); W. C. Abbott, *Writings and Speeches of Oliver Cromwell*, 4 vols. (Cambridge, Mass., 1937–47), III, p. 592 (hereafter cited as Abbott).
2   Abbott, I, p. 697, II, p. 483; Stephen Marshall, *A Sacred Record* (London, 1645), p. 30.
3   Abbott, IV, p. 471.

or exalts itself, God will put it down, for this is the day wherein He alone will be exalted.'[4]

Still greater mercies were to come. In 1649, the year when 'providence and necessity' directed Cromwell to kill the King, and when the Irish then threatened to destroy the infant Commonwealth, God bestowed 'astonishing', 'marvellous great', 'unspeakable mercies' at Dublin and Drogheda and Wexford. Those victories, wrote Cromwell to Parliament, were 'seals of God's approbation of your great change of government'. In a private letter he rejoiced that God still prospered

> His own work in our hands; which to us is the more eminent because truly we are a company of poor, weak and worthless creatures. Truly our work is neither from our brains nor from our courage or strength, but that we follow the Lord who goeth before, and gather what He scattereth, that so all may appear to be from Him . . . What can we say to these things? If God be for us, who can be against us? Who can fight against the Lord and prosper? Who can resist His will?

In 1650, now Lord General, Cromwell invaded Scotland. On the day after Dunbar, where the army together with the godly cause had seemed doomed to extinction, Cromwell wrote to Parliament to report 'one of the most signal mercies God hath done for England and His People, this war . . . It would do you good to see and hear our poor foot go up and down making their boast of God.'[5] The outcome was especially significant because both sides had 'appealed' to 'the God of battle' to decide between them.[6] 'The Lord hath heard us', proclaimed Cromwell, 'upon as solemn an appeal as any experience can parallel.' A year later the royalists were finally vanquished by that 'crowning mercy', the 'marvellous salvation wrought at Worcester'.[7]

How could the magnitude of those deliverances be measured? How could they be sufficiently praised? Cromwell said a great deal about the central place of providence in his life, in his victories, in the making of his decisions. Yet however much he said, he could never feel that he had done justice to his theme. How, amidst the lengthy and autobiographical 'narratives of matter of fact' which he visited upon so many audiences, was he to communicate 'those things wherein the life and power of them lay; those strange windings and turnings of providence' which gave a thread of meaning to 'the lowest historical narration . . . there being in very particu-

---

4   *Ibid.*, I, pp. 287, 365, 619, 638.
5   *Ibid.*, II, pp. 103, 124, 173, 235–6, 324–5.
6   *Original Letters and Papers of State . . . addressed to Oliver Cromwell*, ed. J. Nickolls (London, 1743), pp. 19, 25, 73 (hereafter cited as *Original Letters*).
7   Abbott, II, pp. 335, 463.

lar . . . a remarkable imprint of providence set upon it, so that he who runs may read it'?[8] He was unmoved when men questioned whether God's will could truly be known from the results of battles, or when they reminded him how unsearchable are God's judgements, and His ways past finding out; when they protested that Christ's kingdom is not of this world; or when they remarked that since in Scripture God often prospered the wicked but only for a season, his confidence in the Lord's approval might be premature. His knowledge of God's favour came not from logic but from experience, and not so much from the victories themselves as from the spiritual 'manifestations of His presence' among the saints in arms. The Lord declared His 'approbation and acceptance . . . not only by signal outward acts, but to the heart also'.[9] Victory was an aid to the sanctification of His elect: it strengthened the believer's assurance and assisted the workings of grace upon his heart. 'I think, through these outward mercies,' Cromwell told his friend Lord Wharton after the victories of 1648, 'faith, patience, love, all are exercised and perfected, yea, Christ formed, and grows to a perfect man within us.'[10]

Cromwell's trust in God's providence was the 'rock', the 'sure refuge', the 'sun and a shield' of his life. Even in adversity 'I can laugh and sing in my heart when I speak of these things.'[11] Through the fear of God he conquered the fear of men. When providence led him into unknown political territory he followed unflinchingly, and took his weaker brethren with him. And yet, within all the joy and confidence and wonder of his providentialism, there was always room for anxiety, perhaps even for doubt. What happened when, as in 1646–8 and again from 1651, peace afforded no military successes to fortify the saints, or to help them discern God's will amidst the complexities of political negotiation and compromise? What should His elect think when God 'mingled the cup' of triumph by dividing them among themselves, or by marking them out for private affliction and grief? And there was a further, graver possibility: that the God of battle, who had brought so many victories, would one day bring defeat.

Of course, the saints expected setbacks. They expected God to send them 'rebukes', 'trials' and 'corrections', in order to preserve them from the 'security', the 'drowsiness', the 'sloth' which unbroken prosperity might bring. Although God loved to melt the soul with mercies, He sometimes needed to scourge it with judgements. So adversity might be a sign of grace. Yet other, less assuring explanations were possible. God was known to abandon and exchange his imperfect 'instruments' when they began 'to fail, and fall off

8   *Ibid.*, III, pp. 53–4.
9   *Ibid.*, II, p. 190.
10   *Ibid.*, I, p. 646. Cf. *ibid.*, I, p. 698, II, p. 103; John Bond, *Ortus Accidentalis* (London, 1645), p. 34.
11   Abbott, III, p. 590.

like untimely fruit'.[12] Might not the saints' difficulties signify the withdrawal of His presence from them? Might He not be angry with them? That a wrathful God providentially punishes sin, and takes vengeance upon it in order to vindicate His honour, was a seventeenth-century commonplace, which Cromwell's mentor and friend Thomas Beard wrote a long and famous book to illustrate. 'Sin causes wrath', John Preston succinctly explained; 'sin and wrath are knit together, they are inseparable'. 'Wrath for sin! Who knows not that?' Henry Ferne asked the civil war royalists.[13]

God's punishments could visit communities and nations as well as individuals, and the sins which provoked Him must be repented collectively as well as individually, on days of solemn fasting and humiliation. Yet collective sins were the sum of individual sins; and just as the believer looked into his soul to divine the meaning of military success, so must he search inward to discern God's purpose in public adversity. The Puritan imagination observes a series of God-given correspondences and interactions between external events and the inward motions of faith: between the showers which end drought in the fields and the waters of grace upon the barren soul, or between the trials and deliverances of the traveller and the pilgrim's inner progress towards salvation. To the Puritan, reformation of the world begins with reformation of the heart. Politics are a public projection of the struggle which lust, will and passion wage against God's grace for dominion of the soul.

When God was provoked by transgression, He could be appeased only if the offending sin were identified and purged. The force of that conviction is evident in the belief, which justified much civil war killing, that an afflicted land must be cleansed of the blood which has been shed in it (Numb. 35, 33). But at least blood-guilt could be laid at the door of the saints' enemies. What if the sin was among the believers themselves? In the dread of that thought Cromwell and the saints, individually and collectively, devoted many hours and many days to intensive self-examination. We shall now see something of the politics of iniquity to which that preoccupation gave rise.

In late April 1648, as the second civil war approached, Parliament and army reflected on the imminent perils before them. On 25 April Parliament ordered a national fast day to be held. For

> whatsoever dangers are threatened or feared, either by divisions amongst ourselves, or practices from enemies abroad, we have assurance, out of the Word of God, that we are not in the least danger, if God Almighty be

---

12   *A briefe Relation*, 25 June–2 July 1650, p. 30. Cf. A. S. P. Woodhouse, *Puritanism and Liberty*, 2nd edn (London, 1974), p. 19; *The Parliamentary or Constitutional History of England*, 24 vols. (London, 1751–62), xix, p. 180.
13   John Preston, *The Saint's Qualification* (London, 1637), p. 252; H. F., *A Sermon preached at the Publique Fast, the twelfth day of April* (Oxford, 1644), p. 15.

not incensed against us for our sins and wickedness; which our consciences testify that He is exceedingly, against every one of us in particular, and the kingdom in general: yet we believe that, if we do heartily and sincerely humble ourselves, and turn to the Lord, crying mightily to Him in fervent prayer, with a lively faith in Christ, we shall certainly be delivered from all evils and dangers, and enjoy all needful blessings and benefit to the whole state and kingdom.

Parliament resolved to suppress the vice and the blasphemy wherewith the land was defiled, so that God's 'heavy judgements' might be 'diverted from us' and the Roundhead cause saved.[14]

Four days later, on 29 April, the New Model produced its own response to the crisis. The General Council of the army met at Windsor Castle 'to search out . . . our iniquities, which, we were persuaded, had provoked the Lord against us'. The army leadership often turned to prayer to help restore unity and direction to its counsels. In the Putney debates of 1647 the New Model had sought, through a 'prayer-meeting', to recover the spirit and the purpose which had sustained it in battle, but which in the post-war peace had made way for 'carnal' and 'fleshly strivings'. Cromwell spoke for his colleagues at Putney when he dwelt on the necessity 'to recover that presence of God that seems to withdraw from us', to root out 'false deceit', and to reflect that 'God will discover whether our hearts be not clear in this business'. 'I think the main thing', concurred Ireton, 'is for everyone to wait upon God, for the errors, deceits, and weakness of his own heart.'[15]

The army leaders were still divided and downhearted when they gathered at Windsor in April 1648. A party among them seems to have yielded to political despair and to have wanted the army to lay down its arms. The Windsor meeting lasted three days, of which the first evidently produced no answer to the army's prayers. On the second day, when 'many spake from the Word and prayed', Cromwell

did press very earnestly on all there present to a thorough consideration of our actions as an army, as well as our ways particularly as private Christians, to see if any iniquity could be found in them; and what it was, that if possible we might find it out, and so remove the cause of such sad rebukes as were upon us by reason of our iniquities.

William Allen, who was present and who later drew up a large account of the meeting, described how it then conducted 'a long search into all our

14   *Journal of the House of Commons*, 25 April 1648; Keith Thomas, 'The Puritans and Adultery: The Act of 1650 Reconsidered', in D. Pennington and K. Thomas (eds.), *Puritans and Revolutionaries. Essays presented to Christopher Hill* (Oxford, 1978), pp. 263, 277; *Several Proceedings in Parliament*, 16–23 May 1650.
15   Abbott, I, pp. 521, 523, 524; Woodhouse, *Puritanism and Liberty*, pp. 19, 22.

public actions as an army', to inquire why 'the presence of the Lord' was no longer 'amongst us'.[16] At length 'we were, by a gracious hand of the Lord, led to find out the very steps (as we were then all jointly convinced) by which we had departed from the Lord, and provoked Him to depart from us'. Those 'steps', it was agreed, were the 'cursed, carnal conferences' which 'our own wisdoms, fears, and want of faith had prompted us in the year before to entertain with the King and his party': in other words the negotiations which Cromwell and Ireton had held with Charles I in 1647 and which had aroused so much resentment among the army radicals.

At this stage of the meeting a decisive lead was given by William Goffe, who had instigated the prayer-meeting at Putney. He now 'made use of that good word, Prov. 1, 23, "Turn you at my reproof"'. In that chapter God threatens to 'laugh at your calamity; I will mock when your fear cometh; when your fear cometh as desolation, and your destruction cometh as a whirlwind; when distress and anguish cometh upon you'. But if the elect of Israel – and so of England – will 'turn at my reproof', 'behold, I will pour out my spirit unto you, I will make known my words unto you'. Goffe's speech

> begot in us great sense, shame and loathing our selves for our iniquities, and justifying the Lord as righteous in His proceedings against us. And in this path the Lord led us not only to see our sin, but also our duty; and this so unanimously set with weight upon each heart, that none was able hardly to speak a word to each other for bitter weeping.

Thus 'we were led and helped to a clear agreement amongst ourselves, not any dissenting'. Two historic decisions were taken. The army resolved, first, to fight the royalists; and secondly, 'if ever the Lord brought us back again in peace, to call Charles Stuart . . . to an account for that blood he had shed'.

The Windsor meeting was a critical moment in the Puritan Revolution – and in the career of Oliver Cromwell. His previous unhappiness, and his vulnerability to the reproaches of radicals, can be glimpsed at Putney, where his advocacy of moderation, of the practicable, was countered by men ready to match his claims to divine illumination, and to argue that there could be no half measures in the service of the Old Testament God: to claim that Cromwell's caution on the franchise betrayed a 'distrust of providence', or to report that God had 'providentially' indicated, through the medium of prayer, a liking for the Levellers' *Case of the Army Truly Stated*.[17] Cromwell

16   Allen's account, published in 1659, is reprinted in *A Collection of Scarce and Valuable Tracts . . . of the late Lord Somers*, ed. Sir Walter Scott, 13 vols. (London, 1809–15), VI, pp. 498–504 (hereafter cited as *Somers Tracts*). I believe that Allen's document, despite its late appearance, is likely to be broadly reliable. For the date of the Windsor meeting see S. R. Gardiner, *History of the Great Civil War*, new edn, 4 vols. (London, 1897–8), IV, p. 117.

17   Woodhouse, *Puritanism and Liberty*, pp. 70, 98–100, 439.

never supposed that radical programmes were necessarily more pleasing to God than moderate ones. He knew that the Lord required His instruments to work through political means and to be wise as serpents in His cause.[18] Yet he also knew God's way of blasting the 'politic contrivances' of men who, professing to serve Him but missing the path He had marked for them, stooped to 'carnal' political calculation. Within Cromwell's providentialism, which could lead him in such various political directions, there lay always a radical imperative, which asserted itself at times of crisis and uncertainty. In a swift and decisive change of course he would find sudden release from the strains and the doubts which negotiation and compromise invariably imposed upon 'my inward man'. So it was in April 1648. His decision to 'turn at God's reproof'[19] was to have massive consequences. The army recovered its unity and its fire; and the period which followed the Windsor meeting, the time of the second civil war and of regicide, proved in Cromwell's words 'the most memorable year . . . that ever this nation saw; . . . and this by the very signal appearance of God Himself, which, I hope, we shall never forget'.[20]

There were to be many more occasions when the army saints gathered to seek the root of iniquity among themselves.[21] In 1650 God 'mixed' their military successes in Ireland and Scotland with a series of afflictions: with grave demoralisation and acute division within the government; with differences within the army about the justice of invading Scotland;[22] with outbreaks of plague in garrisons in England and Ireland; with the deaths of 'many choice instruments'. The forces in Ireland, having earnestly 'inquired into' the 'meaning' of God's 'chastisements',[23] provoked the Lord by ceasing to interrogate themselves after Cromwell's departure for England in May. Fresh afflictions followed, until 'at last', as Cromwell later learned from Ireton and his colleagues,

> by all these sad strokes from heaven we were raised out of that sleepy secure condition to call upon His name, seek His face, and beg to know His mind in these His judgements, which while we were doing He both discovered the sin, which was our departure and backsliding from Him,

18   Cf. William Carter, *Israel's Peace with God* (London, 1642), p. 14; *Works of John Owen*, ed. W. H. Goold, Banner of Truth reprint, 16 vols. (Edinburgh, 1965–8), VIII, p. 348.
19   Cf. Abbott, II, p. 340 (l. 5); *A Collection of State Papers of John Thurloe*, ed. T. Birch, 7 vols. (London, 1742), VII, p. 367 (hereafter cited as *Thurloe State Papers*).
20   Abbott, III, p. 54; cf. *ibid.*, II, p. 20, III, p. 73. (Strictly speaking the 'year' to which Cromwell referred began in March; but see *Somers Tracts*, VI, p. 501 (ll. 32–3, 39–43).)
21   See e.g. *The Clarke Papers*, ed. C. H. Firth, 4 vols. (Camden Soc., 1891–1901), II, pp. 58–9; Worcester College, Oxford, Clarke MSS., XXI, fo. 73v, XXIV, fo. 98v.
22   For those differences see *Original Letters*, pp. 21, 29, 58, 73.
23   *A briefe Relation*, 1–8 January 1650; *A Perfect Diurnall . . . in relation to the Armies*, 7–14 January 1650; Bulstrode Whitelocke, *Memorials of the English Affairs*, 4 vols. (London, 1853), III, p. 151.

... and on a sudden, whilst He was discovering His mind to us, in answer to our desires, He was also pleased to abate ... that heavy stroke of the pestilence.[24]

As in England in 1648, so in Ireland in 1650, the army was promptly restored by its self-examination to its accustomed course of victory. Meanwhile army headquarters in England had circulated regiments and garrisons throughout the country to arrange a day of coordinated prayer, when the saints were to seek the cause of their travails. The Lord was besought 'to grant that this may be a cleansing day', and to 'enable us to turn at His reproof'.[25] Even Dunbar in September 1650 did not wholly assure the chosen of God's contentment with them. Oliver St John, rejoicing in the triumph but remarking too on the plague and the threat of famine, wrote to Cromwell that God, by 'mingling water with His wine, tells us that something is amiss amongst us, and calls upon us to search and try our ways'.[26]

The battle of Worcester in September 1651 brought a reversion to peace – and to its anxieties. Cromwell, who now returned permanently to civilian politics, warned Parliament not to permit 'the fatness of these continued mercies' to 'occasion pride and wantonness, as formerly the like hath done to a chosen nation'.[27] The regime must acknowledge its victories to have come from the Lord alone, for 'God will curse that man and his house that dares to think otherwise'.[28] And Parliament must 'improve' God's 'mercies' by righteousness and reform, for 'the eyes of the Lord run to and fro; and as He finds out His enemies here, to be avenged on them, so He will not spare them for whom He doth good, if by His loving kindness they become not good'.[29] The nation's want of gratitude for God's glorious dispensations, and its failure to give 'a worthy return of all the blessings and mercies you have received',[30] were to trouble Cromwell all his days. How often, in his speeches, he would recall the encouragement which after Worcester the army had given Parliament to reform, and the frustration which had eventually driven him to expel the Commons by force in April 1653. What had gone wrong?

No doubt the immediate blame lay with the notorious 'corruption' and 'self-seeking' of Parliament. But might not the failure of reform be a rebuke to the army saints themselves? Since Worcester, they observed in January

24   *Original Letters*, p. 72.
25   *Perfect Diurnall*, 20–27 May 1650; cf. *ibid.*, 10–17 June, 24 June–1 July 1650.
26   *Original Letters*, p. 26.
27   Abbott, ii, p. 463.
28   *Ibid.*, ii, p. 173. Cf. *ibid.*, i, p. 621, iii, p. 583 (ll. 4–8), 591 (ll. 18–22), iv, p. 707; Edmund Calamy, *God's Free Mercy to England* (London, 1642), pp. 14–15; Ps. 28.5; Jer. 17.5.
29   Abbott, ii, pp. 130, 433; cf. *ibid.*, ii, pp. 215, 325, 506, 588, iii, p. 56.
30   *Ibid.*, iv, p. 270; cf. *ibid.*, iv, p. 25.

1653, 'the work of the Lord' had 'seemed to stand still, and all the instruments thereof to have been of no might'. In that month they accordingly spent 'several days waiting at the throne of grace', where they 'humbled ourselves at His feet, for those evils which might cause Him to withdraw His presence from us, and to manifest tokens of His displeasure against us'.[31] Once more their self-examination produced vigorous action. They announced a bold reform programme, and made it clear that Parliament's survival depended on its implementation.

In the saints' new-found resolution lay a challenge not only to Parliament but to Cromwell himself. Since September 1651 he had sought to build bridges between Parliament and army, a policy which exposed him to suspicion and rebuke from the radicals. As early as December 1651 'the private churches begin to call his Excellency an apostate', while by the spring of 1653 he was 'daily railed on by the preaching party, who say they must have a new parliament and a new general before the work be done'.[32] Although such acute hostility is likely to have been confined to the extreme, the psychological pressure exerted on Cromwell by the army and the congregations was intense. They kept him informed of their constant prayers on his behalf; instructed him not to 'consult with flesh and blood'[33] or to succumb to the bait of compromise; listed the biblical heroes on whom they expected him to model his conduct; intimated to him his failure to meet their political hopes; and scrutinised his public statements for radical commitments or implications with which they could subsequently confront him.[34] In 1651 the officers in Ireland, Ireton among them, had urged him to 'remember Hezekiah's fate and judgement' and 'take heed of making it your own'.[35] Hezekiah, we may remember, had 'rendered not again according to the benefit done unto him; for his heart was lifted up: therefore there was wrath upon him, and upon Judah and Jerusalem' (2 Chron. 32. 25). The parallel made a point which was to acquire an added force once Cromwell became Protector in 1653: that a whole people might be punished for the sin of its leader.

Cromwell, whose bond with his radical followers was so important to him, was not well equipped to bear their admonitions. Why, he asked, had the godly cause become so dependent upon so weak an instrument as himself?[36] Although he had long known himself to be among the chosen, to have found 'acceptance' among 'the congregation of the firstborn', he retained a sense of spiritual inadequacy which can be glimpsed in his

31   *The Moderate Publisher*, 28 January–4 February 1653.
32   B. Worden, *The Rump Parliament 1648–1653* (Cambridge, 1974), pp. 291, 379–80.
33   *Original Letters*, p. 80. Cf. *Works of John Owen*, VII, p. 349; Gal. 1.16.
34   The best source for such pressure is *Original Letters*.
35   *Original Letters*, pp. 74–5.
36   See Abbott, II, p. 421, IV, p. 872.

private letters, in his artless acknowledgements there of 'my corruptions', 'my weaknesses, my inordinate passions, my unskilfulness and every way unfitness to my work'.[37] In 1651–3, as he manoeuvred among the parliamentary factions, he found politics a lonely business. He yearned to re-create the broad-based godly party which had been destroyed by Pride's Purge, and to persuade his intimate saintly friends among the parliamentary middle group, whom he believed to 'have helped one another to stumble at the dispensations of God', to return to the fold.[38] He missed other allies too. In September 1652, when the breach between Parliament and army was widening, he wrote to an intimate colleague, 'Have I one friend in our society to whom I can unbowel myself? You absent; Fleetwood is gone; I am left alone . . . Lend me one shoulder. Pray for me.'[39]

In April 1653 he bowed to radical pressure. Having 'sought the Lord day and night', he once more cut through 'carnal' politics, suddenly expelled Parliament by force, vituperatively attacked its members for their personal and political corruption, and assured his army colleagues after the coup that he had 'consulted not with flesh and blood at all'.[40] His action restored his position among the churches, who told him that his expulsion of Parliament had removed their 'fear of God's presence withdrawing from you'.[41] Yet the new mood did not last long. The members of Barebone's, that hand-picked assembly of the chosen which met in July 1653, were soon quarrelling among themselves, and in August, 'unbowelling myself' to Fleetwood, he confessed that 'I never more needed all helps from my Christian friends than now.' In December he took the title of Protector, 'which place I undertook not so much out of the hope of doing any good, as of a desire to prevent mischief and evil'.[42] He was to retain the position until his death in 1658.

Repeatedly he and his supporters would claim that providence had declared in favour of his elevation, and that the evidence of God's approval obliged the nation to accept the new constitution. Yet he faced a persistent chorus of accusation from men who had been among his closest and most trusted spiritual counsellors. Ousted from government by his 'usurpation', they held him to be a traitor who had sacrificed the cause on the altar of his own ambition, and without whose removal God's purpose could never be fulfilled. He was the scapegoat upon whom all future political failures and disappointments could be blamed. His problems were magnified in January

37 *Ibid.*, I, pp. 96–7, 696, II, pp. 289, 329, 400, 404–5, 483.
38 *Ibid.*, I, pp. 574–5, 577–8, 646, II, pp. 189–90, 328–9, 425–6, 453.
39 *Ibid.*, II, pp. 575–6.
40 Worden, *Rump Parliament*, p. 356; cf. Abbott, I, p. 698 (l. 21). I believe that in essence the explanation of the dissolution given in *The Rump Parliament* survives the searching and courteous criticism of it in Austin Woolrych, *Commonwealth to Protectorate* (Oxford, 1982).
41 *Original Letters*, pp. 91, 93.
42 Abbott, III, pp. 88–9, IV, p. 470.

1655, when the first Protectorate Parliament collapsed and when he sensed that the godly cause might collapse with it. In the months which followed, a siege mentality is evident in Whitehall. Cromwell now seems to have abandoned the conciliatory policies he had pursued, in politics and in religion, since December 1653. He had not lost his faith in God's approbation: indeed, he defiantly reaffirmed it in his magnificent angry speech at the Parliament's dissolution. In March 1655 'the good hand of God going along with us' enabled the government to put down Penruddock's rising, and in April the Lord 'was pleased to appear very signally' in Blake's victory at Tunis.[43] Three months later, however, in July 1655, news arrived of a catastrophe: of the abject defeat of the expedition sent by Cromwell to the Caribbean island of Hispaniola to launch the conquest of Spanish America. An ill-prepared, ill-disciplined force had been shamefully routed by a handful of Spaniards. There had been nothing in Cromwell's career to parallel that disaster. When the news came through he shut himself in his room for a whole day.[44] The defeat at Hispaniola was to have a profound and lasting effect on him. Indeed it may be that he never fully recovered from it.

Cromwell had sent the expedition to the West Indies because 'God has not brought us hither where we are but to consider the work that we may do in the world as well as at home . . . Providence seemed to lead us hither, having 160 ships swimming.' Spain, 'the great underpropper' of 'that Roman Babylon', was 'providentially' England's enemy. Citing Thessalonians and Revelation, Cromwell told the Parliament of 1656 that 'except you will deny the truth of the Scriptures, you must needs see that that state is so described in Scripture to be Papal and anti-Christian'. To those who questioned the justice of the war he opposed Genesis 3. 15, 'I will put enmity between thy seed and her seed', a text 'which goeth but for little among statesmen, but it is more considerable [than] all things'.[45] Yet could Cromwell be certain that God favoured his policy? In October 1656, when news of the capture of Spanish treasure ships had given an urgently needed boost to government morale, the Cromwellian preacher John Rowe told Parliament that the exploit had 'silenced the secret thoughts and reasonings of some, touching the engagement in this war; and who are too apt to say, that God never owned you since you undertook this business'.[46] In the same year Sir Henry Vane taunted Cromwell about the 'great silence in heaven' since 1653.[47]

43   *Ibid.*, III, pp. 672, 745.
44   S. R. Gardiner, *History of the Commonwealth and Protectorate*, 4 vols. (London, 1893), IV, pp. 142–3.
45   *Clarke Papers*, III, p. 207; Abbott, III, pp. 860, 879, IV, pp. 261–2, 274.
46   John Rowe, *Man's Duty Magnifying God's Work* (London, 1656), p. 20; cf. *A True Narrative of the Late Success . . . upon the Spanish Coast* (London, 1656).
47   Vane, 'A Healing Question Propounded', *Somers Tracts*, VI, p. 313; cf. Rev. 8. 1.

The debacle at Hispaniola could be blamed partly on 'instruments', on the leaders of the expedition, who were duly punished. But Cromwell knew the need to look deeper. Not only had the invasion force lost a battle: it had plainly been a godless army, untouched by the spirit of the New Model. Its cowardice was itself evidence of God's displeasure, for Cromwell knew that in the course of battle God gave and withdrew courage as it pleased Him.[48] He knew that sinful armies were their own worst enemies.[49] The expedition remained spiritually (and militarily) wanting even after it had proceeded to take Jamaica. 'The hand of the Lord hath not been more visible in any part of this rebuke', Cromwell told the commanders of the forces there in 1656, 'than in taking away the hearts of those who do survive amongst you, and in giving them up to . . . sloth and sluggishness of spirit.'[50] Whatever wickedness had been at work, it would not have been confined to the expeditionary force. When God humbled soldiers he also punished their rulers, or their countrymen, or both. What had provoked the Lord?

To find out, the government in November 1655 invited the nation to a day of solemn fasting and humiliation, when 'we may everyone be searching out the plague of his own heart' in the hope of discerning God's purpose in 'the late rebukes we have received'. Evidently the nation's prayers went unanswered in the months which followed, for in March 1656 the government tried again. The declaration for a further fast day acknowledged that 'the Lord hath been pleased in a wonderful manner to humble and rebuke us, in that expedition to the West Indies'. The disaster 'gives us just reason to fear, that we may have either failed in the spirit and manner wherewith this business hath been undertaken, or that the Lord sees some abomination, or accursed thing, by which He is provoked thus to appear against us'. In September 1656, after Cromwell's speech at the opening of Parliament had lamented the failure of the West Indian expedition, a declaration was passed by Protector and Parliament for another fast day, on which 'a people laden with iniquity', who had 'provoked the holy one of Israel to anger', was to strive 'to appease His wrath . . . that He will remove whatever accursed thing there is amongst us'.[51]

The Puritan readership of the declarations of March and September 1656 will have recognised, in their allusions to an 'accursed thing', a clear

---

48   Abbott, II, pp. 127, 164, 235, 324.
49   That, like much else in Cromwell's providentialism, was not a peculiarly Puritan or Roundhead view. Cf. William Chillingworth, *A Sermon preached to his Majesty at Reading* (Oxford, 1644), p. 13.
50   Abbott, IV, p. 193; cf. *ibid.*, p. 385.
51   *Ibid.*, IV, p. 274 (ll. 30–1); *A Declaration of his Highness, with the advice of his Council, inviting the People of this Commonwealth to a Day of Solemn Fasting and Humiliation* (London, [November] 1655); *A Declaration of his Highness, inviting the People of England and Wales to a Day of Solemn Fasting and Humiliation* (London, [March] 1656); *A Declaration of his Highness the Lord Protector and his Parliament for a Day of Solemn Fasting and Humiliation* (London, [September] 1656). The declarations will hereafter be cited by their dates.

signpost to the seventh chapter of the Book of Joshua. In 1650 the despondent forces in England had explored that text when they inquired into God's chastisements of that year.[52] Now Hispaniola gave the text a much sharper application. To appreciate it, we may need to reacquaint ourselves with the story which Joshua 7 relates. It concerns the catastrophe which afflicted the children of Israel after the fall of Jericho, that miracle to which the Cromwellian saints often compared their own mercies of 1642–51. After the victory 'the children of Israel committed a trespass in the accursed thing . . . and the anger of the Lord was kindled against the children of Israel'. The consequence was the shattering defeat of an expedition which had been confidently dispatched by the Israelites from Jericho to the east side of Bethel. The troops 'fled before the men of Ai', who (like the Spaniards on Hispaniola) were 'but few'. Joshua was devastated. He 'rent his clothes, and fell to the earth upon his face before the ark of the Lord until the eventide, he and all the elders of Israel, and put dust upon their heads'. To what purpose had God brought His people over Jordan, only 'to deliver us into the hand of the Amorites, to destroy us'? What could Joshua say to neighbouring nations 'when Israel turneth their backs before their enemies'?

> And the Lord said unto Joshua, Get thee up; wherefore liest thou thus upon thy face? Israel hath sinned, and they have also transgressed my covenant which I commanded them: for they have even taken of the accursed thing, and have also stolen, and dissembled also, and they have put it even among their own stuff. Therefore the children of Israel could not stand before their enemies, but turned their backs before their enemies, because they were accursed: neither will I be with you any more, except ye destroy the accursed from among you. Up, sanctify the people, and say, Sanctify yourselves against tomorrow: for thus saith the Lord God of Israel, There is an accursed thing in the midst of thee, O Israel: thou canst not stand before thine enemies, until ye take away the accursed thing from among you.

One particular man, God intimated, had 'taken of the accursed thing'; and for his wickedness all Israel was punished. He was identified by an investigative process which, in its ritual, revealed the extension of guilt from the sinner to his household, from the household to the tribe, from the tribe to the nation. The sinner was Achan, the son of Carmi, the son of Zabdi, the son of Zerah, of the tribe of Judah. His confession identified the accursed thing:

> When I saw among the spoils a goodly Babylonish garment, and two hundred shekels of silver, and a wedge of gold of fifty shekels weight, then I coveted them, and took them; and, behold, they are hid in the earth in

52   *Perfect Diurnall*, 20–27 May 1650.

the midst of my tent, and the silver under it. And they took them out of the midst of the tent, and brought them unto Joshua, and unto all the children of Israel, and laid them out before the Lord.

Achan, as God instructed, was stoned and burned to death in the valley of Achor. Only now that the accursed thing had been found and cast out was the hand of God's blessing laid once more upon His chosen people. The men of Ai were duly smitten, and the conquests of the Israelites resumed.

The saints did not expect the parallels between Israelite and English history to be exact.[53] But when there were so many literal and figurative parallels, divine instruction was clearly visible. Civil war Puritans had traditionally equated the sin of Achan with the ceremonialism of Archbishop Laud.[54] After Hispaniola there was a closer target. In 1656 Sir Henry Vane, who had been one of Cromwell's most intimate friends until in 1653 Cromwell bitterly accused him of betrayal, circulated a treatise, A Healing Question Propounded,[55] for which he was brought before Cromwell and the Council. Vane's document answered the passage in the fast-day declaration of March 1656 concerning the 'accursed thing'. The 'accursed thing', he suggested, was the motive of 'self-interest and private gain' hidden beneath the Protectorate. Cromwell's elevation sprang from the 'private and selfish interest of a particular spirit . . . which sin (Joshua 7) became a curse in the camp, and withheld the Lord from going any more amongst them, or going out with their forces'. The 'Babylonish garment' which Achan 'saved from destruction' signified the 'tyrannical principles and relics' of government by a single person.[56] Cromwell after the civil wars, like Achan after Jericho, 'brought not in the fruit and gain of the Lord's treasure, but covetously went about to convert it to his own use'. 'This' observed Vane, his eye turning to Hispaniola, 'caused the anger of the Lord to be kindled against Israel, and made them unable to stand before their enemies.' So only when England had been purged of Cromwell's selfishness would God again 'become active and powerful in the spirits and hearts of honest men, and in the works of his providences, when . . . they go out to fight by sea or by land'. Vane's Healing Question was not the only saintly tract to portray Hispaniola as God's punishment upon the cause for Cromwell's usurpation, and to tell the Protector that 'you are not able to bear the reproofs of the Lord';[57] but to Cromwell it must have been the most disconcerting of them.

53 See e.g. John Arrowsmith, England's Eben-ezer (London, 1645), p. 21.
54 Paul Christianson, Reformers and Babylon (Toronto, 1978), pp. 141, 186, 190. Cf. William Hunt, The Puritan Moment (Cambridge, Mass., 1983), pp. 188–9.
55 Somers Tracts, VI, pp. 303–15.
56 That may have been a shrewd blow, for there are hints that the disturbing image of the 'spotted garment' may have made an impression on Cromwell's mind: Abbott, I, p. 619 (cf. Isa. 9. 5), IV, p. 473.
57 The Proceeds of the Protector (so called) against Sir Henry Vane, Knight (London, 1656), p. 8; A Perfect Nocturnall of Several Proceedings, between Hiel the Bethelite, and . . . Madam Policy (n.p., n.d.), pp. 4, 6.

Cromwell responded uneasily and defensively to the charges which the defeat at Hispaniola elicited against him. He acknowledged, even more fulsomely than the proprieties of Puritan self-abasement required, that his own sins had 'justly . . . incurred' the disaster 'and much more'. He professed before the nation his desire 'first to take the shame to himself and find out his provocation'. Yet why should the blame lie with him alone? By what right, he asked, was the iniquitous people 'imputing the cause only to the work of the magistrate' and 'charging sad miscarriages upon instruments . . . when every individual hath helped to fill up the measure of those sins'?[58] Cromwell, belonging in this as in so much else to the mainstream of the Puritan tradition, was certain that God punished nations for vice and for blasphemy.[59] In March 1654 he had summoned a fast day to implore an end to 'the present rod of an exceeding and unusual drought', an affliction provoked, he ruled, by 'the common and notorious sins so boldly and impenitently practised amongst us'. He was to respond almost identically when God visited the nation with sickness in 1657 and again in 1658.[60] Why, in 1655–6, should the sin of Achan not be supposed to lie in the same moral territory?

Of one thing, at least, Cromwell professed himself confident. At Hispaniola God had punished the English, not declared 'in favour of the enemy'. Although England's rulers should, like Joshua, 'lay our mouths in the dust, yet He would not have us despond', for 'undoubtedly it is His cause . . . Though He hath torn us, yet He will heal us . . . After two days He will revive us, on the third day He will raise us up.'[61] Did Cromwell remember, when he thus alluded to Hosea 6, how in 1650, after Dunbar, he and his friends had derided the very similar biblical explanations of defeat which were then advanced by the Presbyterians?[62] We cannot say. Yet there are indications that Hispaniola taught Cromwell to think less boldly and less simply about the ways in which God reveals His purposes to men. In the days of Cromwell's triumph, providence had been 'clear and unclouded'; but in the later Protectorate he came to refer to 'the dark paths through the providence and dispensations of God'.[63] Although the Lord might still appear in battle, as in the 'very signal' and 'very wonderful' mercy vouchsafed to Blake off Santa Cruz in 1657, Cromwell's reading of such events became more tentative. 'We have been lately taught', he reminded Blake in April 1656, 'that it is not in man to direct His way. Indeed all the dispensations

58   Declarations of March and September 1656 (above, n.51); cf. Abbott, III, p. 858 (l. 33).
59   Abbott, II, p. 110, IV, p. 237 (ll. 23–4). For Cromwell as a zealous 'godly magistrate' see too *ibid.*, I, p. 278, III, pp. 400, 436, 589, 845, IV, pp. 25, 112, 274, 493–4.
60   Abbott, III, p. 225 (cf. *ibid.*, pp. 290–1); *Mercurius Politicus*, 13–20 August, 10–17 September 1657, 29 April–6 May 1658.
61   Abbott, III, pp. 859–60, 874. Cf. *Original Letters*, p. 26.
62   *Original Letters*, p. 23; Abbott, II, p. 335.
63   Abbott, I, p. 697, IV, pp. 472–3.

of God, whether adverse or prosperous, do fully read that lesson.'[64] The dynamic providentialism of the civil wars had become a part of Cromwell's past, to be remembered and praised and yearned after in speech after speech, but finding no parallel among current events. When he now reflected upon the present or the future, his tone was distant from army providentialism. It resembled instead the more conventional and more stoical approach to providence taken by moderate and Court party politicians like John Thurloe and Henry Cromwell. He came to speak, as they did, of the need to become 'submitted' or 'resigned unto' providence.[65]

Did God forgive His people in England for the accursed thing? Cromwell's anxiety on that subject is indicated by his preoccupation, during the last two years of his life, with Psalm 85, which on three occasions he urged upon the consideration of his second Protectorate Parliament. In September 1656 he recited it almost in full before the Commons, whose members he encouraged to 'peruse' that 'very instructive and significant' Psalm, which 'I wish . . . might be better written in our hearts'. It seems at first a Psalm of wholehearted thankfulness. The Lord 'hast been favourable unto thy land', 'hast forgiven the iniquity of thy people', 'hast taken away all thy wrath', 'hast turned thyself from the fierceness of thine anger'. Yet a sudden change of tense and of mood makes the meaning of the Psalm ambiguous. The Psalmist begs God to 'cause thine anger toward us to cease. Wilt thou be angry with us for ever? Wilt thou draw out thine anger to all generations?' While Cromwell is glad to infer from the Psalm that 'sometimes God pardons nations', and hopes for a time when Englishmen can 'say as David, thou . . . hast pardoned our sins, thou hast taken away our iniquities', he evidently believes the nation to remain under the penalty of its wickedness.[66]

I shall suggest in the concluding part of this essay that Cromwell's concern with iniquity – with his own and with the nation's – may help us to understand what was perhaps the most important (and perhaps the most disastrous) decision he made as Protector: his refusal in May 1657 of Parliament's offer of the title of King.

Cromwell could have taken the Crown had he wanted to. It is true that, by his hesitations and delays over three months, he gave the opposition in the army and the churches the chance to mobilise resistance. Yet even when it had done so, the challenge to Cromwell looked no stronger, and was probably weaker, than opposition which he had brushed aside before. The title

64   Abbott, IV, pp. 148, 549. Cf. *An Order in Parliament . . . for a Day of Thanksgiving . . . the third of June next* (London, 1657).
65   *Thurloe State Papers*, VI, p. 243, VII, pp. 153, 376, 579, 680; Abbott, IV, p. 148.
66   Abbott, IV, pp. 277–8, 706–7, 720.

was an attractive prospect. It would give his rule the parliamentary sanction he had long wanted for it, and would boost the hopes of settlement and stability. Yet those arguments, pressing as they were, might be 'carnal'. Had God led His chosen of England through the Red Sea of civil war merely in order to effect a change of dynasty? Had not 'the providence of God', asked Cromwell, 'laid this title aside'?[67] As Protector, he did not like to think of himself as King in all but name. He had accepted his elevation in 1653

> well looking, that as God had declared what government He had delivered over to the Jews, and placed it upon such persons as had been instrumental for the conduct and deliverance of His people; and considering that promise in Isaiah, that God would give rulers as at the first, and judges as at the beginning, I did not know but that God might begin, and though at present with a most unworthy person, yet as to the future it might be after this manner, and I thought this might usher it in.[68]

Parliament in 1657 had an altogether less biblical purpose. It aimed to break the army's hold on Cromwell, and to surround him with *politique* courtiers.

While Cromwell prayed for guidance, the radicals 'wearied him with letters, conferences, and monitory petitions'.[69] One letter was from Colonel Thomas Wilkes in Scotland. In the black month of January 1655 Cromwell had written to Wilkes a letter[70] which discloses the anxieties so often evident at Cromwell's times of trial: his dismay at his 'wounds' and 'reproaches' from 'such as fear the Lord, for whom I have been ready to lay down my life, and I hope still am';[71] his concern to convince the saints that in becoming Protector he did not 'make myself my aim';[72] his awareness that, but for the strength which his adherence to God's path gave him, 'the comforts of all my friends would not support me, no not one day'.[73] Now Wilkes urged him to 'stand fast, in these . . . apostatising days', and, rather than yield to parliamentary persuasion, to await 'that crown which the Lord of righteous judgement gives' in heaven.[74] The congregations of Gloucestershire, ever ready with advice to Cromwell, warned him to keep 'close to God, His cause and His people', and to resist the 'temptations' wherewith 'you are encompassed'. Acceptance of the title would 'rejoice the hearts of the profane party', and expose the saints to the charge 'that they fought not for the

67   *Ibid.*, IV, p. 473.
68   *Ibid.*, III, p. 589; Isa. 1. 26.
69   *Ibid.*, IV, p. 448 (from Bate).
70   *Ibid.*, III, pp. 572–3.
71   Cf. *ibid.*, I, p. 429, III, pp. 89, 756 (ll. 5–6), IV, p. 272.
72   Cf. *ibid.*, III, pp. 289, 452.
73   Cf. *ibid.*, IV, p. 146.
74   *Thurloe State Papers*, VI, pp. 70–1.

exalting of Jesus Christ, as they pretended, but themselves'. The crowning of Cromwell would 'generally sadden, and endanger your losing room in the hearts of, the saints in England'. He should 'search your heart', and beware that 'such as have prayed, wept, fought, followed on with you . . . may never have occasion to sit down by the rivers of bitter waters, lamenting for your sake'. In London the Baptists, the religious group which had been so close to Cromwell, alerted him to 'the fearful apostasy which is endeavoured by some to be fastened upon you, upon plausible pretences, by such who for the most part had neither heart nor head to engage with you'. The Baptists ventured an allusion, which Cromwell would not have missed, to the words of Mordecai to Esther: 'Think not with thyself that thou shalt escape in the King's house, any more than the Jews' (Esther 4. 13).[75]

In his diffuse and anguished speeches to Parliament during the kingship crisis, Cromwell longingly recalled the certitudes of civil war: the victories, and the manifest presence of God with his saints. The opponents of the title were eager to keep his memories alive. John Owen, a firm enemy to kingship, had once remarked that the rhetorical question 'Where is the God of Marston Moor, and the God of Naseby? is an acceptable expostulation in a gloomy day.'[76] In 1657 the saints expostulated accordingly. 'We beseech you in the bowels of Christ', the London Baptists warned Cromwell, 'remember what God did for you and us, at Marston Moor, Naseby, Pembroke, Tredah, Dunbar and Worcester, and upon what grounds.' William Bradford, writing as one who had 'gone along with you from Edgehill to Dunbar', urged that 'the experiences you have had of God at these two places, and between them, . . . should often make you shrink' from the title. Cromwell should 'remember you are but a man, and must die, and come to judgement . . . Those that are for a Crown, I fear you have little experience of them: the other, most of them, have attended your greatest hazards.'[77]

The opponents of kingship did not have all the providentialist arguments. John Thurloe and Henry Cromwell encouraged the Protector to make his decision as God directed him. It was their hope that God had given him 'the clearest call that any man had' to accept the title.[78] Throughout the Protectorate Cromwell had been described as the instrument of providence by men who welcomed the return to relative political stability under

75 *Original Letters*, pp. 139–43. John Lilburne, likewise alive to Cromwell's susceptibilities, had reminded him of the same text when Cromwell frustrated the Levellers in 1647: Abbott, I, p. 434.
76 *Works of John Owen*, VIII, p. 88. Cf. Obadiah Sedgwick, *A Thanksgiving Sermon, preached . . . April 9* (London, 1644), p. 21; Mathew Barker, *The Faithful and Wise Servant* (London, 1657), pp. 14–15.
77 *Original Letters*, pp. 141–3.
78 *Thurloe State Papers*, VI, pp. 183, 219, 222–3; cf. *Original Letters*, p. 144.

his rule. God had given England 'those lovely twins, peace and plenty (the unexpected issue of cruel wars)'.[79] A part of Cromwell concurred with that view. The arrival of peace seemed to him a 'miracle', while liberty of con-science, which in his eyes was a tangible and precious gain of civil war, could take root only beneath the shelter of stability. Had not a time come for consolidation rather than advance? In 1655 Cromwell told Parliament that, before it had wrecked the Instrument of Government, 'we were arrived . . . at a very safe port, where we might sit down, and contemplate the dis-pensations of God and our mercies'. Next year he and Parliament concurred in lamenting the nation's sin 'in being more dissatisfied that we have not obtained all that we aimed at, than thankful that we have obtained so much as through mercy we now enjoy'.[80]

Images of rest and peace, of 'sitting down in quiet under our vines', could sometimes appeal powerfully to the army saints.[81] Yet the radicals soon became restless and unhappy when providence 'stood still'. At best, the England of the Protectorate was but half reformed. Surely God had not led His people out of bondage for so limited a purpose. The rivalry between that radical perspective and the outlook of the kingship party produced some contrasting biblical allusions. From the regiment of Henry Cromwell's favourite Anthony Morgan, the Protector learned that 'after our long and' troublesome and dangerous pilgrimage through the Red Sea of blood, and wilderness of confusion, we have obtained to some prospect, nay some taste and enjoyment of Canaan, the resting place of God's people'. The Glouces-tershire congregations were outraged by such parallels: 'surely He speaks to us (as once to His people in the wilderness), "This is not your rest". It is not for us to call our wilderness Canaan.' The choice before Cromwell in the kingship crisis was between the 'Canaan' view and the 'wilderness' view of the Protectorate.[82]

His speeches indicate the difficulty of the decision and the strain which days of fruitless prayer created in him. Ill, wretched with uncertainty, acknowledging 'the abundance of difficulty and trouble that lies upon me', he spoke repeatedly of the 'burden', the 'weight', on 'my back'.[83] Courte-ously conceding the political force of Parliament's arguments, he concluded

---

79   *Original Letters*, p. 134. Cf. *ibid.*, pp. 105–6, 138–9, 147, 150–2; *Thurloe State Papers*, VI, p. 431; *Mercurius Politicus*, 8–15 February 1655, 11–18 March, 17–24 June, 8–15 July 1658.
80   Abbott, III, p. 579; Declaration of September 1656 (above, n.51).
81   See e.g. Woodhouse, *Puritanism and Liberty*, p. 403.
82   *Mercurius Politicus*, 8–15 April 1658; *Original Letters*, p. 146. Cf. Richard Vines, *The Happinesse of Israel* (London, 1645), pp. 4–5; Richard Baxter, *True Christianity* (London, 1655), p. 204; George Smith, *God's Unchangeableness . . . wherein is clearly demonstrated and proved that Oliver Cromwell is by the Providence of God Lord Protector* (London, 1655), p. 55; Abbott, III, pp. 434–5, 442; *Thurloe State Papers*, VI, p. 401, VII, p. 295; Owen Watkins, *The Puritan Experience* (London, 1972), p. 167; Deut. 12. 9.
83   Abbott, IV, pp. 443, 482; cf. *ibid.*, III, p. 756.

that 'I am not able for such a trust and charge': that 'what may be fit for you to offer, may not be fit for me to undertake . . . At the best I should do it doubtingly. And certainly what is so [done] is not of faith; and whatsoever . . . is not of faith, is sin to him that doth it.' He must 'give an account to God' for a decision which, he said again and again, must be taken within his 'conscience'.[84] He must follow the guidance which providence gave him; 'and though a man may impute his own folly and blindness to providence sinfully, yet that must be at my peril'. If the title should 'fall upon a person or persons that God takes no pleasure in, that perhaps may be the end of this work': the end of the cause to which Cromwell and the saints had committed their lives.[85]

Was it possible that Cromwell had become 'a person that God takes no pleasure in'? Might the Lord be exchanging His instruments once more? Cromwell's first biographer, writing in 1659, recorded that near the end of his life the Protector 'twice a day . . . rehearsed the 71 Psalm of David, which hath so near a relation to his fortune and to his affairs, as that one would believe it to have been a prophecy purposely dictated by the Holy Ghost for him'.[86] What was it that drew Cromwell to Psalms which fail to sustain their initial confidence? The opening verses of Psalm 71, like those of Psalm 85, have a message of hope and strength and faith. With the Psalmist, Cromwell could call God 'my rock and my fortress', 'my trust from my youth'. Yet we must wonder whether he did not also follow the Psalmist's ensuing supplication: 'Cast me not off in the time of old age; forsake me not when my strength faileth. For mine enemies speak against me; and they that lay wait for my soul take counsel together, saying, God hath forsaken him . . .'

Cromwell's salvation was not alone at stake in the kingship crisis. The fate of God's people rested on his choice. He feared that if he took the Crown wrongfully he might be made 'a captain to lead us back into Egypt'. Beside the risk of sinful leadership he saw another and perhaps a greater danger: the danger of contagion. To take the Crown without the light of God's approval might, in the manner of Achan's iniquity, 'prove even a curse to . . . these three nations'. 'If I undertake anything not in faith, I shall serve you in my own unbelief, and I shall then be the unprofitablest servant that ever a people or nation had.'[87] It was in the knowledge of that peril that he alluded to the warning which Joshua had given to the Israelites between the fall of Jericho and the disaster wrought by the sin of Achan: 'Cursed be the

84   For 'conscience' see Abbott, IV, pp. 446, 454, 470, 472, 473, 513.
85   *Ibid.*, IV, pp. 446, 454, 472–3, 513; cf. *ibid.*, IV, p. 277 (ll. 20–3).
86   R. S. Paul, *The Lord Protector* (London, 1955: Michigan, 1964), pp. 300–1 (quoting Carrington).
87   Abbott, IV, pp. 263, 446, 472–3, 513, 729. Cf. *Works of John Owen*, VIII, p. 448; Numb. 14. 4.

man before the Lord, that riseth up and buildeth this city Jericho' (Josh. 6. 26). 'I would not seek', said Cromwell to Parliament, 'to set up that that providence hath destroyed and laid in the dust, and I would not build Jericho again.'[88]

88 *Ibid.*, IV, p. 473. For Cromwell and the 'accursed thing' see too *ibid.*, I, p. 677. For the hold of the story of Achan on the Puritan mind see also, e.g., *Diary of Thomas Burton*, ed. J. T. Rutt, 4 vols. (London, 1828), I, p. 39 (where James Nayler is compared to Achan), IV, p. 458; Chillingworth, *A Sermon preached*, p. 14; John Goodwin, *Theomachia* (London, 1644), pp. 2–4; *A Seasonable Word: or, Certain Reasons against a Single Person* (London, 1659), title-page; *The Complete Prose Works of John Milton*, ed. D. M. Wolfe *et al.*, 8 vols. (New Haven, 1953–82), VII, p. 328; *The Political Works of James Harrington*, ed. J. G. A. Pocock (Cambridge, 1977), pp. 629–31; *Mercurius Politicus*, 3–10 July 1651; Conrad Russell, in *London Review of Books*, 4–17 October 1984, p. 21. Cf. Deut. 17. 5.

3

The Cromwellian Protectorate: A Military Dictatorship?

Austin Woolrych

Originally appeared as Austin Woolrych, 'The Cromwellian Protectorate: A Military Dictatorship?' in *History*, 75. Copyright 1990 Blackwell Publishers, Oxford.

Editor's Introduction

Many historians have raised the question of how far Cromwell's regime should be regarded as a dictatorship or a period of military rule. During the 1930s and 1940s, some scholars compared the Protectorate to the dictatorships of Hitler, Mussolini and Stalin. Although more recent scholars have shied away from drawing such explicit comparisons, the issues of the authoritarianism of Cromwell's rule, of the nature of his powers, the limits upon them, and whether they were compatible with the rule of law, have all continued to generate considerable interest. These are the questions that Austin Woolrych addresses in this essay.

He offers a masterly survey of many different aspects of the Protectorate, and his central conclusion is that the regime lacked both the means and the will to become anything approaching a dictatorship. Among his most telling points are that when Cromwell had his best chance of taking dictatorial powers in the spring of 1653 he consciously avoided them; that the cases where Cromwell's rule denied or compromised the rule of law were extremely rare; that the regime dealt with the Royalist Penruddock's Rising in 1655 in a scrupulous and restrained fashion; and that Cromwell generally preferred persuasion to coercion, and in any case did not seek to impose ideological conformity on England.

The episode that might most obviously smack of military dictatorship is the Major-Generals experiment. Woolrych rebuts such a claim with several arguments. He notes that the Major-Generals only existed for about 15 months at the most (from the autumn of 1655 to the beginning of 1657), and that the period when they were fully operational was considerably shorter than that. He feels that just as the standing army in England was fairly small by continental standards, and the military presence in local government was very limited, so the Major-Generals should not loom unduly large in any balanced assessment of the Protectorate. In the main the Major-Generals remained within the bounds of law, and their long-term impact on local government was minimal, prompting Woolrych to conclude that they did not amount to a time of military rule.

On balance, Woolrych's answer to the question he poses in the title of his essay is 'No'. He suggests that the element of the dictatorial in the Cromwellian Protectorate has frequently been overstated. However, insofar as such an element did exist, it stemmed not from any military involvement but from Cromwell's commitment to the interests of the people of God. Woolrych suggests that Cromwell possibly never intended to accept the Crown, and this inclination was reinforced not only by his fear that it would betray the cause for which he and so many others had fought, but also by his sense that God had already delivered a clear verdict against kingship. Closest to Cromwell's heart was his belief that the 'end of magistracy' was to foster virtue and suppress vice, and it was this goal of reconciling the interests of the godly with those of the whole nation that ultimately eluded him.

The Cromwellian Protectorate: A Military Dictatorship?*

Austin Woolrych

During the dark years preceding the Second World War and for more than a decade after its end, the dictatorships of Mussolini, Hitler and Stalin lay so heavily upon the political consciousness of the west, either in present fact or in recent memory, that writers about Oliver Cromwell and his Protectorate were inevitably drawn into seeking parallels with them. In the earlier years, before the brutal and degrading aspects of fascism were fully revealed, the comparisons were not always detrimental. John Buchan, for instance, in a biography of Cromwell published in 1934, could write: 'A corporate discipline, of which quality is the watchword, seems to many the only way of salvation. Minds surfeited with a sleek liberalism are turning to a sterner code, and across the centuries Oliver speaks to us strangely in the accents of today.'[1] Clive Rattigan, in the *Saturday Review* in 1934, called him admiringly 'a 17th-century Hitler–Mussolini, rolled into one', and Sir Ernest Barker openly compared him with Hitler – presumably not disparagingly – before an audience in Hamburg in 1937.[2] After the war, however, any such parallels were invariably pejorative. H. N. Brailsford, for instance, was not paying the Protectorate a compliment when he called it 'a totalitarian dictatorship', or wrote that 'the efficient police state which Thurloe constructed was as highly centralized as any of the totalitarian regimes of our own century.'[3]

It would be easy to multiply examples, but pointless. The grosser ones were always to be found more in the work of journalists, publicists and popular biographers than in that of academic historians, and reputable textbooks have long been free of such distortions. The purpose of this essay is not to set up an Aunt Sally. Serious historical questions sometimes fall out

---

* This is a revised version of the James Ford Special Lecture delivered in the University of Oxford on 28 October 1988.
1 John Buchan, *Oliver Cromwell* (1934); quotation from p. 445 of the Reprint Society edition (1941).
2 Maurice Ashley, *The Greatness of Oliver Cromwell* (1957) [hereafter Ashley, *Greatness*], p. 18; cf. Ernest Barker, *Oliver Cromwell and the English People* (Cambridge, 1937). For other examples of such parallels see Ashley, *Greatness*, pp. 14–15, 17–18, and W. C. Abbott, *Writings and Speeches of Oliver Cromwell* (Cambridge, Mass., 1937–47) [hereafter Abbott, *Writings and Speeches*], iv. pp. 897–9. Abbott's 'Addenda to bibliography' for the years 1931 to 1944 contains many suggestive titles; Rattigan's article is item 3591.
3 H. N. Brailsford, *The Levellers and the English Revolution*, ed. Christopher Hill (1961), pp. 492; cf. pp. 15, 57, 458 and 556 for similar expressions. Brailsford died in 1958.

of fashion before they are fairly answered, and whether Cromwell ruled as a military dictator remains a question worth asking, especially now that it carries fewer emotive overtones than were still resonating a generation ago. Its answer will not be a simple yes or no but a reckoning of degree.

An element of dictatorship there certainly was. No man played a larger part than Cromwell in destroying the vestiges of legitimate authority between 1649 and 1653. He would never have become head of state if he had not been the general of a powerful army, and the only body that gave any meaningful assent to his elevation, at least until 1657, was his Council of Officers. Army officers played a conspicuous part in both central and local government throughout the Protectorate, which never ceased to depend on the army for its survival. Yet a dictatorship is not identifiable solely by its origins or by its command of the means of enforcement, though both are obviously relevant. In common usage, and as a useful historical concept, dictatorship implies a whole mode of government, describable partly in legal, partly in physical and partly in qualitative terms. Here it is taken to mean a regime that acknowledges no constitutional restraints, that openly subordinates the rights of the individual to the interests of the state, that denies or at least compromises the rule of law because the law lies ulti-mately in the dictator's will, that commands absolutely whatever means of coercion – armed forces, police, bureaucracy, judiciary – the state possesses, and that can control such means of persuasion and propaganda as the current technology affords. An ideology that puts the claim of the dictator (whether an individual or a collective) to total obedience beyond question or criticism is not perhaps an essential characteristic, but it is generally found in post-classical dictatorships.

All these criteria must of course be scaled to the resources that were available in Cromwell's time, and in a country so singularly unaccustomed as England was to a standing army or a salaried bureaucracy, or to taxation remotely adequate to sustain either. Yet one has merely to state them to make the Protectorate look less clearcut a dictatorship than its irregular origins and its military *mise-en-scène* might first suggest. The question of how far it was dictatorial, in its constitution and in its actual exercise of power, is partly separable from that of how far the army was involved in its government, and will be considered first. Discussion is confined to England and Wales, for although the Protectorate's written constitution laid down 'The government of the Commonwealth of England, Scotland and Ireland',[4] and established a parliament representing all three countries, Scotland and Ireland were clearly different cases. In both countries, but especially in Ireland, the element of dictatorship was obviously stronger and the military presence, relative to population, much greater.

4   S. R. Gardiner (ed.), *Constitutional Documents of the Puritan Revolution* (Oxford, 3rd edn, 1906) [hereafter Gardiner, *Constitutional Documents*], p. 405.

How Cromwell acquired the office of Protector and how its powers were defined on paper are matters well known, and can be dealt with here quite summarily. But it is worth remarking that if Cromwell had aimed at dictatorship he had his best chance of achieving it in the spring of 1653, after he had expelled the Rump. Some sectarian voices did urge him to assume the mantle of a second Moses, but he had no such thoughts; indeed, he seems to have laid no plans at all. When he and his Council of Officers eventually decided to vest the supreme authority for a limited period in a sort of quasi-parliament nominated by themselves, they conspicuously refrained from nominating each other or (with negligible exceptions) any of their fellow-officers.[5] It was only when Barebone's Parliament was showing signs of collapse, through its own internal dissensions, that Major-General Lambert devised a written constitution, much in the spirit of the army's Heads of the Proposals that he had helped to draft in 1647, and designed like them to define the terms of a limited monarchy – though this time with Cromwell as king. Lambert and half a dozen fellow officers presented this 'Instrument of Government' to him at about the end of November 1653, but Cromwell would not hear of the royal title, nor would he dissolve another parliament against its will. It was only after Barebone's Parliament unexpectedly resigned its authority back into his hands (through what looks like a conspiracy between Lambert and the leaders of the moderate majority in the house) that Cromwell was persuaded to accept power under the terms of the Instrument of Government, though as Lord Protector, not as King Oliver I.[6] He did so because it was the only readily available way of terminating the brief dictatorship with which he had been saddled, the second within a year, and he positively welcomed the limitations which the Instrument imposed upon him.[7] But initially he did not regard his office as necessarily permanent. 'I have not desired, I have no title to the government of these nations', he said later, 'but what was taken up in a case of necessity, and temporary, to supply the present emergency.'[8]

According to the official apologia written by Marchamont Nedham, which Cromwell himself commended to parliament, the new constitution represented the acme of mixed government, a perfect Polybian blend of monarchy, aristocracy and democracy, embodied respectively in the Protector, the council and the parliament.[9] Compared with the traditional powers and prerogatives of the monarch within the older trinity of king, privy council and parliament, Cromwell's were far more circumscribed. He was

5   Austin Woolrych, *Commonwealth to Protectorate* (Oxford, 1982), ch. 4.
6   Ibid., pp. 343–7, 353–61.
7   Abbott, *Writings and Speeches*, iii. pp. 454–5.
8   Ibid., iv. p. 481.
9   [Marchamont Nedham], *A True State of the Case of the Commonwealth* (1654; facsimile edn, Exeter, 1978), pp. 9–11, 51–2; Abbott, *Writings and Speeches*, iii. p. 587.

required to 'govern . . . in all things by the advice of the council', and he had to obtain the consent of the *majority* of the council for decisions of peace and war and for his dispositions of the army and navy when parliament was not in session. He was not free to appoint or dismiss his councillors at pleasure, as kings had been, and on his death the council was to elect his successor. He and the council were given a purely temporary power to legislate by ordinances until a new parliament was scheduled to meet in September, but it did not extend to the intervals between parliaments thereafter. A parliament was to be elected at least every three years and to sit for at least five months. Opportunities for government influence over elections were greatly reduced by a radical change in the proportion of borough to county seats, from more than four to one to barely one in three. Parliament's approval was required for appointments to the higher offices of state and for the disposition of the armed forces during sessions, and upon a declaration of war a parliament had to be summoned immediately, if one were not already sitting. Bills passed by this single-chamber parliament were to go to the Protector for his consent, but they could become law without it after twenty days if they did not contravene what was written into the Instrument itself.[10]

So much for the restraints, but in two very important respects – arms and money – the Protector was given an advantage over his royal predecessors. The Instrument entitled him to a sufficient annual revenue to maintain an army of 10,000 horse and 20,000 foot, and what it called 'a convenient number of ships for guarding of the seas', though it named no sum and left the ways and means largely open. It also assured him, less munificently, of £200,000 a year for the whole cost of civil government, including the administration of justice and the Protectoral household. The sum of £200,000 was far less than the royal household alone had cost in the 1630s. Charles I would naturally have been very glad of a standing army of 30,000, but such a number by no means sufficed in the 1650s to secure the recently conquered kingdoms of Scotland and Ireland and at the same time to protect the English commonwealth against its internal and external enemies. When Cromwell became Protector he had at least twice that number of men under arms in all three countries, including local garrisons. After a year in office he had reduced the field armies to just over 53,000 in all, and progressive further reductions brought the overall total down to about 36,500 by the time that the Protectorate was overthrown in 1659.[11] Yet despite the paper provision for it in the Instrument, the army posed a financial problem that remained unsolved to the end. How far it sustained Cromwell's rule politically will be considered shortly.

10   The text of the Instrument is in Gardiner, *Constitutional Documents*, pp. 405–17.
11   H. M. Reece, 'The Military Presence in England, 1649–1660' (unpublished D.Phil. thesis, Oxford, 1982) [hereafter Reece, 'Military Presence'], p. 287. I am grateful to Dr Reece for permission to make use of his valuable thesis.

The Instrument imposed an oath on the Protector to 'govern these nations according to the laws, statutes and customs thereof',[12] and in England at least Cromwell made an honest attempt to keep to it. The whole system of the common law, from the central courts at Westminster through the assizes to the quarter sessions of the justices of the peace, continued to function almost without interference, except at a local level during the brief regime of the major-generals. Two Commissioners of the Great Seal resigned rather than implement a Protectoral ordinance of 1654 which attempted the long overdue reform of the Court of Chancery, but so far from penalizing them Cromwell promptly made them Commissioners of the Treasury.[13] Chief Justice Henry Rolle was the only other judge to resign during the Protectorate. He did so over the case of George Cony, a merchant who refused to pay customs duties because they lacked the authority of an act of parliament, and then violently evicted the customs officers who came to impound the goods concerned. Cony went to prison rather than pay the fine that a committee of the council imposed on him, and so for a day or two did the three distinguished counsel who argued for his release before the sympathetic Rolle, on the ground that the Protectoral ordinances that had continued the customs had no binding force. Cony and his counsel submitted and were freed, but Rolle resigned his office. Another such case was that of Sir Peter Wentworth, an old adversary of Cromwell's in the Rump, who refused to pay his monthly assessment after the parliamentary Assessment Act had lapsed, and had its local collectors arrested and prosecuted. He was summoned before Cromwell and the council, made his submission, and went free.[14] Cony's and Wentworth's cases were regrettable, but the reason why historians have mentioned them so often is that they seem to have been the only ones of their kind. No government that has come to power in revolutionary circumstances has ever been able to ignore those of its subjects who publicly impugn its whole legitimacy or go on a personal tax strike.

Another problem under such a government was that juries might not convict those who opposed or defied it. The Commonwealth had resorted fairly freely to High Courts of Justice, in which both judge and jury were replaced by nominated commissioners; five such were erected between 1649 and 1653, beginning with the one that tried Charles I. But throughout the Protectorate there were only two: one set up in 1654 solely to try three men who plotted to assassinate Cromwell; the other four years later, to deal with the organizers of what would have been a widespread royalist rising, had it not been unmasked. This court was so scrupulous in requiring watertight evidence that only five men suffered death by its sentence;

12   Gardiner, *Constitutional Documents*, p. 417.
13   S. R. Gardiner, *History of the Commonwealth and Protectorate* (3 vols, 1894–1901), iii. pp. 154–5.
14   Ibid., pp. 150–3.

indeed the most active of all the conspirators, John Mordaunt, went free because a key witness had escaped from custody, helped by Mordaunt's wife.[15] In between those plots came Penruddock's rising in March 1655, the one occasion under the Protectorate when royalists actually got under arms. After its suppression the leading participants were tried by due process of the common law, and a jury convicted thirty-nine of them of treason. But less than half that number were actually executed; and though rather more were transported to Barbados, most of the rebels and conspirators against the Protectorate were far more fortunate than the hundreds who were hanged or butchered for rising with the northern earls in 1569, or with Monmouth in 1685.[16] None of them were tried by court-martial, as the Earl of Derby and his fellow-insurgents had been in 1651, by order of the Rump;[17] only the army was subject to martial law under the Protectorate. Torture, which had been inflicted by order of Charles I's privy council on the leader of an anti-Laudian riot as recently as 1640,[18] was never employed at all, nor did anyone suffer death for any political offence short of high treason.

As for that other perennial resort of dictators, the imprisonment of dissidents without trial, it was used remarkably sparingly, considering how freely and virulently the Protectoral regime was attacked in press and pulpit. Most of those who did suffer it were committed only after they had refused to give an undertaking to live peaceably under the government, and one senses that in many cases the unwillingness to bring them to trial arose because if they were indicted before a court of law the charge would have had to be a capital one; sedition was a felony. Cromwell strongly preferred persuasion to coercion, and he was strikingly patient of criticism in long face-to-face confrontations with Fifth Monarchist firebrands like Thomas Harrison, John Carew, Vavasor Powell and Christopher Feake, and with rigid republicans like Edmund Ludlow. Only his treatment of Major-General Robert Overton, imprisoned for over four years (a term without parallel) on suspicion of hatching a conspiracy in the army in Scotland, looks untypically harsh; but Overton had promised Cromwell to his face that he would surrender his commission if a time came when he could no longer conscientiously serve him, and Cromwell believed that he had broken his word.[19]

Although Cromwell held the typical puritan conviction that the civil magistrate should inculcate godly conduct and punish vice, including blas-

---

15   Ibid., ii. pp. 459–62; C. H. Firth, *The Last Years of the Protectorate* (2 vols, 1909) [hereafter Firth, *Last Years*], ii. pp. 76–9. David Underdown, *Royalist Conspiracy in England 1649–1660* (New Haven, Conn., 1960) [hereafter Underdown, *Royalist Conspiracy*], pp. 227–9.
16   Underdown, *Royalist Conspiracy*, ch. 7; A. H. Woolrych, *Penruddock's Rising* (1955).
17   Gardiner, *Commonwealth and Protectorate*, i. pp. 461–3. On that occasion Cromwell strongly (but vainly) supported Derby's appeal for pardon.
18   S. R. Gardiner, *History of England 1603–1642* (10 vols, 1883–4), ix. p. 141.
19   See C. H. Firth on Overton in *The Dictionary of National Biography* [hereafter DNB].

phemy, he was deeply opposed to the imposition of any kind of ideological conformity. A wide religious liberty was entrenched in the Instrument of Government, and he upheld it as one of the four 'fundamentals' in that document that should be unalterable. Calling the nation to a day of fasting in March 1654, he asked: 'Have we a heart prepared as willingly to communicate the said freedom and liberty to one another, as we were industrious to get it?' 'Liberty of conscience is a natural right', he told parliament six months later, 'and he that would have it ought to give it.'[20] A serious source of friction between him and his parliaments was that he desired a much broader religious liberty than they did. His personal rapport with that much feared and hated man George Fox, his encouragement of the resettlement of the Jews in England, his quiet protection of practising Roman Catholics from serious persecution (though not from fines for recusancy), and the blind eye that he turned to much Anglican worship (except when serious royalist conspiracies were discovered), all testify to a range of sympathies far wider than that of most of his contemporaries. Nor was there much political strait-jacketing in a regime which had Milton as a defender and under which Hobbes, Harrington and scores of lesser political writers lived and published freely.

Contemporaries and historians alike have tended to see Cromwell's relations with his parliaments as a touchstone of his constitutionalism. No one would count them a success, though they were not such a total failure as Professor Trevor-Roper assumed in a famous essay.[21] Cromwell certainly lacked a Cecil's skill as a parliamentary manager, but the root cause of conflict went much deeper. He assumed that parliament's powers and functions were defined by the Instrument of Government, whose central aim was a balance between the executive and the legislature; it specified that all election returns should expressly state 'that the persons elected shall not have power to alter the government as it is hereby settled in one single person and a parliament'.[22] Most of the members, on the other hand, felt that no piece of paper concocted by a few army officers could impose limitations on the people's elected representatives or debar them from redrafting the constitution as they thought fit. Cromwell rid the 1654 parliament of its more

---

20   Abbott, *Writings and Speeches*, iii. pp. 226, 459; Gardiner, *Constitutional Documents*, p. 416. For the limits to the religious liberty permitted by the Protectorate, see Blair Worden, 'Toleration and the Cromwellian Protectorate', in W. J. Sheils (ed.), *Studies in Church History*, xxi (1984), pp. 199–233.

21   H. R. Trevor-Roper, 'Oliver Cromwell and his Parliaments', in R. Pares and A. J. P. Taylor (eds), *Essays Presented to Sir Lewis Namier* (1956). For less dismissive accounts, see Peter Gaunt, 'Law-making in the First Protectorate Parliament', in C. Jones, M. Newitt and S. Roberts (eds), *Politics and People in Revolutionary England* (Oxford, 1986), and Ivan Roots, 'Law-making in the Second Protectorate Parliament', in H. Hearder and H. R. Loyn (eds), *British Government and Administration* (Cardiff, 1974).

22   Gardiner, *Constitutional Documents*, p. 410; Abbott, *Writings and Speeches*, iii. p. 457.

doctrinaire republicans by requiring all members to sign a promise that they would be faithful to the Protector and would not seek to alter the government as it was settled in a single person and a parliament, but that did not deter the rest from spending most of the session in rewriting the constitution in a manner that threatened both religious tolerance and the security of the regime. The council purged his second parliament more crudely by abusing a temporary power that the Instrument had given it to disallow the returns of members who were royalists, papists, or not 'of known integrity, fearing God and of good conversation'. With nearly a quarter of the house thus arbitrarily disqualified, it is no wonder that Cromwell got on much better with the parliament of 1656–7 than with its predecessor – but only until the return of the excluded early in 1658 led to another angry dissolution.

Yet seven of the eight parliaments that the Stuarts had summoned prior to the Long Parliament had been dissolved more or less in anger, and so would the Long Parliament doubtless have been if it had not deprived Charles I of the power to do so. By that comparison (admittedly a forced one) Cromwell's score looks more like par for the course. If he had lived a little longer, he would almost certainly have improved it. The third parliament of the Protectorate, which was elected in January 1659 without any significant pressures and was subject to no arbitrary exclusions, contained majorities in both houses that were well disposed towards Richard Cromwell's government and hostile to its republican and military opponents. That, it might be argued, was because Oliver was safely dead and buried, and it is true that Richard accentuated a number of conservative trends that his father had kept in check. But that is too simple and personal an explanation. Without altogether excluding it, a broader one is that the political nation was settling fairly contentedly under the Protectoral regime as redefined by parliament in 1657, and was registering its satisfaction that the political balance had been swinging against the army for at least two years.

Before returning to the political changes from 1657 onward it will be useful to take stock of the military presence at various stages, and as far as possible to quantify it. The total strength of the army is less relevant than the numbers stationed in England, for much the greater part of it was always on duty in Ireland, Scotland, and latterly Flanders.[23] In December 1654 there were just over 11,000 officers and men in England, excluding small and purely local garrison companies, and that was fewer by more than 2,000 than the Rump had been maintaining two years earlier. By October 1655, after Penruddock's rising, the number had risen insignificantly by about 500, but that does not include the new mounted militia that

---

23   For the figures in this paragraph I am again indebted to the table in Reece, 'Military Presence', p. 287.

the major-generals commanded. In July 1657, after that militia had been stood down, the total of home-based troops, including officers, came to about 13,500, and when Richard Cromwell was overthrown it was nearly a thousand more. These slight increases do not denote any overall military expansion, for the total establishment was progressively reduced; they reflect simply a steady withdrawal of regiments from Scotland, as that country became more peaceful and settled.

Now by European standards a home-based standing army of between 11,000 and 14,400 officers and men amid a population of around five and a half million was rather on the light side. How happy (for instance) the Great Elector's subjects would have been to support so modest a proportion! For an English comparison, James II had 15,710 regular troops in England when Monmouth was defeated in 1685, nearly 20,000 by the end of the same year, and nearly 30,000 when William of Orange invaded – not counting thousands of soldiers in garrisons or under training, and thousands more of Scottish and Irish troops on English soil.[24] If forces of that size could not save an anointed king from deposition, it is worth asking how much of a military dictatorship could be sustained by less than a third as many in Cromwell's England. James, moreover, regularly concentrated a large part of his army close to London, to overawe the capital, whereas the regiments that Cromwell kept in England were always widely dispersed, so that the military presence in London was relatively light.[25]

James of course alienated his own senior officers, Churchill especially, to an extent that Cromwell never did, for when disaffection stirred in his army Cromwell was prompt to cashier the offenders. But there was a more vital difference. James's army, though he used it for political ends, remained a military instrument; Cromwell's had been a major force in politics for six and a half years before he became Protector, and its officers continued to be directly involved in both central and local government throughout his rule. The extent of their involvement is what next needs to be considered.

Inevitably the army was represented on the council of state, to which the Instrument had accorded such large powers, but its strength there has often been exaggerated. Of the eighteen councillors who had been appointed by June 1654, ten were civilians[26] and only four – Lambert, Fleetwood, Desborough and the semi-retired Skippon – were unequivocally regular officers. Of the remaining four, Colonels Sydenham and Mackworth owed their rank to local rather than national military service and now, as governors of the Isle of Wight and Shrewsbury respectively, commanded purely local gar-

24   John Childs, *The Army, James II and the Glorious Revolution* (Manchester, 1980), pp. 2–4, 184, and the same author's '1688', *History* lxxiii (1988), pp. 398–424, esp. p. 413.
25   Reece, 'Military Presence', pp. 76ff., 144.
26   Ashley Cooper, Fiennes, Lawrence, Lisle, Major, Mulgrave, Pickering, Rous, Strickland, Wolsey.

risons; Mackworth died in December 1654. Colonel Philip Jones's sole military responsibility was for a company of fifty men in Cardiff Castle, and he had long been much more of an administrator than a soldier. Edward Montagu was still styled colonel, but he had resigned his command of a foot regiment back in 1645, though he was to be appointed General-at-Sea in 1656.[27] Military titles of the 1650s are often deceptive, and the civilian preponderance in the council increased further in 1657, as will shortly be shown.

Of the highest officers of state below the council, the Commissioners of the Great Seal were all eminent lawyers, quite unconnected with the army, and the only Commissioners of the Treasury with any military links were Sydenham and Montagu. There were naturally some servicemen among the Admiralty and Navy Commissioners and on the Army Committee, but those bodies did not busy themselves outside their own proper spheres. A major central commission of a very different character was the one 'for approbation of ministers', commonly known as the Triers, whose task it was to approve candidates presented to livings in the broad national church of the Protectorate. The Triers numbered thirty-eight, and just two of them were army officers; but Colonel William Goffe and Major William Packer, both prominent Particular Baptists, were probably chosen more for their standing among the gathered churches than as bastions of an army interest.[28] There were no officers among the important Trustees for the Maintenance of Ministers, who wielded a large control over ecclesiastical revenues and augmented inadequate clerical stipends.

But most government in seventeenth-century England was of necessity local government, and for most of the people the face of authority bore the features of county magistrates and parochial or manorial officials, rather than of great officers of state in distant Westminster. The most important at the county level were of course the justices of the peace, who had been restored to their historic functions in the early 1650s, though with many changes of personnel. The proportion of army officers among them is vital evidence for any estimate of the weight of the military presence in local government. Fortunately, Dr H. M. Reece has carefully listed all the officers who served on the commission at any time between 1649 and 1660, and his total comes to 123.[29] Here, discussion must be confined to the period of the Protectorate, and we have two *libri pacis* – contemporary official lists of all

---

27   On the council and its membership in 1654 see Woolrych, *Commonwealth to Protectorate*, pp. 379–80.
28   Murray Tolmie, *The Triumph of the Saints* (Cambridge, 1977), pp. 157–8, 168.
29   Reece, 'Military Presence', tables on pp. 296–301. Again I am deeply indebted to Dr Reece's work, and if I appear to draw somewhat different conclusions from it than he has done, this is partly because I am considering a much shorter period (five and a half years, against nearly twelve) and I am not asking quite the same questions.

the justices in all the English and Welsh counties except Lancashire – that fall entirely within it.[30] One was made in about September 1656 and updated until the next, which was made in March 1659 and corrected for about a year thereafter.

The *libri pacis* enable one to estimate the total number of JPs in the country at any one time. Each contains almost exactly the same number of names – just under 3,500 – though 480 are struck out in the first and 294 in the second. Death or disaffection were the commonest reasons for their removal, and many other entries are plainly additions to the original lists. This turnover has to be allowed for, and so do the many pluralists who figure in more than one county. But at a very conservative estimate there were fully 2,500 JPs alive and qualified to act at any one time under the Protectorate. How many were willing to act is another question, and for the country as a whole an unanswerable one; though the major-generals had been in post for almost a year when the earlier of our *libri pacis* was first drawn up, so most of the seriously ill-disposed justices had probably been removed by then.

Of the 123 officer-JPs listed by Dr Reece, three died before Cromwell became Protector, and at least fifteen more had either left the army or were about to be cashiered. Most of these, so far from being pillars of his regime, were strongly opposed to it – so strongly in some cases, such as those fanatical Fifth Monarchist ex-colonels Henry Danvers, Thomas Harrison and Nathaniel Rich, that they were struck off the commission of the peace. Scarcely less hostile were those staunchly republican ex-officers Algernon Sydney and Sir Arthur Hesilrige. Four more senior officers, Colonels Okey, Saunders and Alured and Major-General Overton, were cashiered for their overt opposition within a year of Cromwell becoming Protector, and a further dozen more of the 123 were in Scotland or Ireland or overseas during all or most of his rule, so they cannot have contributed to the military presence in English local government.[31] We are now down to fewer than ninety serving officers who were actually in a position to act on the commission of the peace, and eleven of these were not appointed until 1657. We should further subtract the military grandees on the Protector's

30 Public Record Office, C193/13/6, C193/13/5; microfilm copies in the Institute of Historical Research.
31 Dead before Dec. 1653: Maulyverer, Henry Ireton, Thomas Ireton (first names are given only where necessary to avoid confusion). No longer in the army (besides those named above): Nathaniel Barton, Duckenfield, Evelyn, Hubbard, Joyce, T. Mason, Richard Price, Rede, Syler, Swift, George Twisleton. Out of England during all or most of Protectorate: Thomas Cooper, Charles Fairfax, Hewson, Jephson, Knight, Monck, Pearson, Reynolds, Sankey, Talbot, Thomlinson, Venables (cashiered in 1655 after the West Indies expedition). Information drawn mainly from *DNB*; C. H. Firth and G. Davies, *The Regimental History of Cromwell's Army* (2 vols, Oxford, 1940) [hereafter Firth and Davies, *Regimental History*]; *Calendar of State Papers, Domestic Series*; Reece, 'Military Presence'.

council who were named on numerous county commissions for honorific reasons, and allow for other officer-JPs who were on duty outside England for shorter periods than the dozen already referred to. This done, the ratio of military to civilian justices available for service at any one time falls to about one in thirty. Some of the civilians too were honorific appointments, but however generously one reckons the number of these and of the simply inactive, the proportion of army officers on the bench looks rather a mild threat to civil liberties.

Furthermore these officer-JPs did not represent a monolithic interest. A distinction is worth drawing between those who held general or regimental commands in the field army, the national force that was lineally descended from the army of Fairfax as reorganized in 1647–8, and those whose authority was restricted to local garrisons. It will be convenient, if not strictly correct, to call the first type regulars and the second garrison officers. Of all the officer-JPs in service during the Protectorate after the early weeding-out of the disaffected, and normally resident in England, only fifty-five were regulars, and before 1657 only forty-four. The rest were garrison officers, and they were not homogeneous. A few governors of important towns and strongpoints were colonels with a distinguished war record who certainly contributed to the military presence, even though they were no longer (if ever) of the field army: men such as Robert Bennet of St. Michael's Mount, Thomas Croxton of Chester, Wroth Rogers of Hereford and Adrian Scrope of Bristol (though Bristol was completely disgarrisoned in 1655, so that its governorship became honorific).[32] But they shade off into figures like John Bingham and Richard Norton (Cromwell's 'idle Dick'), who must have thought of themselves, and been thought of by their fellow justices, more as the heads of ancient county families than as the governors of Guernsey and Portsmouth, let alone as agents of an army interest. They were not the only ones whose commitment to their county or regional communities must have been at least as strong as their ties with central authority. Then there were the captains who governed places like Chepstow, Cowes Castle, Upnor Castle, Pendennis and Landguard Fort, and disposed of military forces as modest as their rank;[33] surely their presence on the bench was more an administrative convenience than a threat to the ascendancy of the local gentry magistrates.

As for the 'regulars' who constituted the core of the military element in the commission of the peace, it should not be assumed that they represented just one interest, whether of the central government or of the army as such. Charles Howard, for instance, was well on the way to becoming the magnate

32   For Bristol see Reece, 'Military Presence', pp. 172ff. The whole of ch. 6 of Reece's thesis is devoted to garrisons.
33   Captains J. Nicholas, W. Baskett, T. Harrison, J. Fox and Benjamin Gifford were the governors of the places named; they are examples only.

that he was to be as earl of Carlisle under Charles II, and men bearing such names as Constable, Fleetwood, Ingoldsby, Whalley, Winthrop and Worsley (to take only colonels and above) had on social grounds as good a claim to be included as most of their gentry neighbours, especially now that the exclusion of royalists and other opponents of the regime had lowered the barriers of birth and property that hedged the commission. Officer-JPs like these must have felt the two-way pull between court and country that England's local governors experienced throughout the early modern period, and they would have been much surprised at the notion that the profession of arms should debar them from taking their place among their counties' natural rulers.

Officers were also appointed to another county-based commission, that for the collection of the monthly assessment. Though its functions were obviously narrower, it too helps one to gauge the degree of army involvement in local government. Cromwell dissolved his first parliament before it confirmed his ordinances or passed an act for the continuances of the assessment, though his progressive reductions of the amount levied, from £120,000 a month to eventually only half that sum, probably reconciled most of his subjects to having to wait until 1657 before parliamentary sanction was renewed. The year 1657 was, however, the only one of the Protectorate in which assessment commissioners were appointed by statute.[34] There would have been cause for complaint if army officers had played a dominant role in apportioning and collecting the tax that was specifically allocated to the maintenance of the army, but clearly it was not so. The total number of commissioners, allowing for the many pluralists who were named more than once and for the non-functional grandees at the head of the county lists, was around 3,000. The number of serving army officers among them was seventy-two: fifty-one regulars and twenty-one garrison types.[35] The total comes down to little more than sixty when one subtracts those who were out of the country or fully occupied in the central administration, so that over the country as a whole about one assessment commissioner in fifty was an officer, and in most cases he was a local man. Again, one cannot know how many of these 3,000 men engaged actively in their duties,[36] and there seems to be little information available as to whether soldiers were employed at all often to enforce payment of taxes

34 *Acts and Ordinances of the Interregnum*, ed. C. H. Firth and R. S. Rait (3 vols, 1911) [hereafter *Acts and Ordinances*], ii. pp. 1058–97, 1234–49. Two assessment bills were passed in June 1657, the first a retrospective one to cover the three months from 25 March onward, the second to be in force for the ensuing three years. The second continued the commissioners named in the first and added a few more, who are included in the total considered above.
35 Reece, 'Military Presence', pp. 296–301.
36 Perhaps only a fraction: see David Underdown, 'Settlement in the Counties, 1653–1658', in G. E. Aylmer (ed.), *The Interregnum: the quest for settlement 1646–1660* (1972) [hereafter 'Settlement in the Counties'], esp. pp. 180–1.

during the Protectorate. There may be more to be discovered, but if taxes *were* collected at all widely at sword's point, and if the very small military element in the assessment commission was widely resented, it is surprising that more has not been heard of it.

Army officers played a slightly larger relative part in the very different commission that was set up, again on a county basis, by an ordinance in August 1654 to remove any scandalous, disaffected or simply inadequate parish clergymen who had not already been ejected during the Civil Wars or under the Commonwealth. The Ejectors, as they were commonly called, were all laymen; there were about 750 in England and Wales, and fewer than fifty were serving officers.[37] Subtracting those who remained in the army only very briefly or were usually out of the country, the effective total was forty-four, of whom only twenty-four were regulars. Considering the reputation of Cromwell's officers for strong religious commitment and the general antipathy of conservative men of substance towards the broad comprehension and the evangelizing ideals of the Cromwellian national church, a ratio of about one military to seventeen civilian Ejectors seems neither surprising nor sinister. The evidence suggests moreover that the officer-Ejectors were selected for their standing and reputation as Christians rather than as representatives of the army, because in the ordinance the great majority of them are styled 'esquire' or (much more rarely) 'gentleman', and not accorded their military rank.[38] Their proportional share in the actual work of the commission must have been even smaller than these figures suggest, because the ordinance named about 500 ministers to act as coadjutors to the Ejectors; for instance, no beneficed clergyman or schoolmaster could be removed for ignorance or insufficiency without the concurrence of at least five Ejectors and five of these designated ministers.[39]

Notoriously, the governance of England took on a more overtly military character during the regime of the major-generals. In the autumn of 1655, following upon Penruddock's rising and the discovery of royalist plans for a nationwide rebellion, the country was divided into 10 districts, in each of which a major-general, assisted by a named body of commissioners, took command of a specially raised mounted militia and assumed a wide range of duties, of which keeping check on royalist activities was only one. Just how large a change in the spirit and practice of local government the major-generals introduced, and how long they were fully operative, are currently matters of controversy. The most generally held view is that Cromwell set out as Protector with the aims of 'healing and settling' the rifts in the nation and

---

37 Ibid.; *Acts and Ordinances*, ii. pp. 968–77. A crude count gives just over 850 names, but many appear in more than one county.
38 Except for some reason in the commission for Yorkshire; was this Lambert's influence?
39 *Acts and Ordinances*, ii. pp. 978–84; a crude count gives 517 ministers, but a very few were named to more than one county.

winning back the confidence and co-operation of its traditional governing class, but that the extent of the royalist conspiracy uncovered in 1655 made him change his policy drastically. Since the cavaliers were bent on rebellion, he thought, they must submit to military control, and pay for it through the 'Decimation', a tax of one tenth of the income from all royalists' estates worth £100 or more a year. When, however, he discovered how widely and deeply unpopular this regime was, and when his one manageable parliament threw out the Decimation tax in January 1657, he ditched 'the disastrous experiment of the major-generals'[40] and reverted to his former policy of reconciliation. Against this interpretation, it has recently been argued that the military presence in local government was so strong and pervasive throughout the Protectorate that the establishment of the major-generals marked much less of a break than has generally been supposed; it brought a difference in degree rather than in kind.[41] The evidence for this revisionist view has yet to be published, so any attempt to adjudicate between it and the widely accepted three-phase interpretation of the Protectorate would be premature, as well as beyond the scope of this broad survey. Nevertheless there are some indications, in the present state of knowledge, that the two versions are not as irreconcilable as they might seem.

Whether or not the major-generals' regime was nasty and brutish it was undeniably short, so it should not bulk too large in a balanced view of the Protectorate as a whole. Although about fifteen months elapsed between October 1655, when most of them went out into their districts, and parliament's rejection of the Decimation which furnished their essential financial support, they were in full operation for much less long. Professor Aylmer sees their activities winding down after September 1656, when most of them returned to Westminster to attend parliament.[42] Professor Fletcher maintains that they had passed their peak by May 1656, when Cromwell called them in for a review of their work; for although most of them returned to their districts in late June or July they were soon mainly occupied in trying to manage the parliamentary elections. He concludes that 'the scheme had clearly collapsed in most areas several months before the vote' that pronounced a final verdict on it.[43]

40   The description is David Underdown's in 'Settlement in the Counties', p. 181; his whole essay is a succinct and cogent exposition of the interpretation here summarized. 'Healing and settling' was the keynote to Cromwell's opening speech to his first parliament: Abbott, *Writings and Speeches*, iii. pp. 434–43, esp. p. 435.
41   Reece, 'Military Presence', pp. 201–11. The book that Dr Reece is preparing on the subject-matter of his thesis is keenly awaited, and will do his argument better justice than is possible in the brief and doubtless oversimplified summary above.
42   G. E. Aylmer, *The State's Servants: the civil service of the English republic 1649–1660* (1973), pp. 314–17.
43   Anthony Fletcher, 'Oliver Cromwell and the Localities: the problem of consent', in C. Jones, M. Newitt and S. Roberts (eds), *Politics and People in Revolutionary England* (Oxford, 1986) [hereafter Fletcher, 'Cromwell and the Localities'], pp. 187–204; quotation from p. 189.

Although historians differ as to how strongly the major-generals' regime was disliked when it was actually in operation, rather than in retrospect, there is some consensus that the most unpopular part of it was the Decimation. It was not only quite unconstitutional but a breach of the Rump's Act of Oblivion, and it was hated by many besides those who had to pay it. But it was not the only cause of resentment. The new militia must have been a visible reminder of the state's command of military force to hundreds of small towns and villages that had not seen a redcoat for years. The close check on their movements to which former royalists had to submit, and the bonds that were demanded of them for their own good behaviour and that of their servants, were serious interferences with personal liberty, though the number of bonds actually taken varied from 1,089 in Staffordshire to a mere 8 in Warwickshire.[44] Indeed, the major-generals differed so much among themselves in their zeal, their priorities and their attitudes to the local communities within their areas of responsibility that it is hazardous to generalize about their impact. But what inevitably made them unpopular, at least among most of the gentry, was that their duties made them encroach on the authority and cramp the initiative of the county justices, the town corporations and other local officials. They were outsiders, they were swordsmen, and many of them and their deputies were of inferior birth. It was all very well for Cromwell to assure the city fathers of London, and by implication all the magistracy of England, that his purpose was 'not at all to supersede them, or at least to diminish any of their rights, privileges or liberties'.[45] It is true that there was never a 'rule of the major-generals' in the sense that they supplanted the traditional agencies of local government, for all those agencies went on functioning; but they were rather crudely superimposed upon them.

If the major-generals had been restricted to their primary task of stamping out royalist conspiracy they would have been more readily tolerated, and their drive against highway robbers may even have been popular. Their enforcement of the ban on country sports and city pleasures was *not* popular, nor was their suppression of alehouses; and Cromwell himself was probably responsible for giving them a general brief to spur easy-going jus-

Fletcher's is now the best general survey of the major-generals' regime, but see also Ivan Roots, 'Swordsmen and Decimators', in *The English Civil War and After* (1970) [hereafter Roots, 'Swordsmen and Decimators'], pp. 78–92; Stephen Roberts, 'Local Government Reform in England and Wales during the Interregnum: a survey', in Ivan Roots (ed.), *'Into Another Mould': Aspects of the Interregnum* (Exeter, 1981) [hereafter Roberts, 'Local Government Reform'], pp. 24–41; Derek Hirst, *Authority and Conflict: England 1603–1658* (1986) [hereafter Hirst, *Authority and Conflict*], pp. 335–41, 345; and the authorities cited in notes 42, 44 and 45. Dr Paul Pinckney is writing a large-scale book on *Cromwellian Politics and the Major-Generals*.

44   Toby Barnard, *The English Republic 1649–1660* (1982), p. 53.

45   Abbott, *Writings and Speeches*, iv. pp. 112–13; his instructions to the major-generals are in ibid., iii. pp. 844–8.

tices into enforcing the puritan laws against drunkenness, swearing, sabbath-breaking, celebrating Christmas and Easter, and other breaches of the godly code. He probably caused some jaws to drop, even in 1656, when he publicly set 'the suppressing of vice and encouragement of virtue' on a par with 'the security of the peace of the nation' as 'the very end of the magistracy' and the major-generals' *raison d'être*.[46] He had not erected them in a deliberate plan to extend the control of central over local government systematically and permanently, though one or two of his most senior officers, Lambert especially, may have played with such a design. To Cromwell they represented an *ad hoc* reaction to the threat of royalist conspiracy and a means of reducing general taxation by shifting the cost of security on to the cavalier gentry who endangered it. Once they were there, however, he saw no harm in using them, even for purposes far beyond their original ones. In the local communities, however, only the godly interest shared his attitude, and they were everywhere a minority.

Yet it will not do to take the major-generals at the valuation of their critics and enemies. So far from acting like the satraps and bashaws to whom republicans and royalists likened them, they mostly tried hard to operate within the bounds of the law. They were added to the commissions of the peace in their districts at their own request, to bind them closer to the local magistracy and confer as much legitimacy as possible on their own actions. Far from descending on those districts as the imperious agents of a centralizing dictatorship, they showed much anxiety about their reception, they were often different about the daunting range of their duties, and they frequently sought advice and reassurance.[47] They did not always get the support from the government that they expected, for Cromwell's attitude towards them became revealingly ambivalent. He praised them to their faces and justified their activities to parliament, yet he showed so much sympathy to individual royalists who remonstrated to him against their treatment that they sometimes felt let down. He chided them for inviting their own overthrow by seeking parliamentary approval – 'Who bid you go to the house with a bill', he asked, 'and there receive a foil?' – but he probably felt some relief when the bill was rejected.[48] He did not cease to believe in the duty of a Christian commonwealth to promote what he called a reformation of manners, and he personally saw nothing wrong in employing soldiers in the good work, but he drew back from paying the

---

46   Ibid., iv. p. 112; cf. pp. 274, 493–4.

47   Much of their correspondence is printed in *A Collection of State Papers of John Thurloe* (7 vols, 1742) [hereafter *Thurloe State Papers*], mainly in vol. iv. See also Roots's remarks in 'Swordsmen and Decimators', pp. 85–6.

48   Abbott, *Writing and Speeches*, iv. p. 417, and cf. pp. 273–4; Fletcher, 'Cromwell and the Localities', p. 203; Roberts, 'Local Government Reform', p. 38; Hirst, *Authority and Conflict*, p. 336. The rejection of the bill was moved by Cromwell's son-in-law John Claypole, who was widely assumed to be expressing the Protector's own attitude: Firth, *Last Years*, i. pp. 110–11.

price, which was what was left of the goodwill of most of the old governing class.

Not that the major-generals were universally unpopular, or mere agents of central power. They were soon feeling that two-way tug of loyalties that conscientious district administrators tend to experience always and everywhere. As Derek Hirst has put it, 'They were soon acting as mediators, speaking for their localities to the central government, as well as *vice versa*.'[49] In strongly puritan territory the godly interest that welcomed and supported them included many of the county elite; in Suffolk, for instance, it was headed by the magnate Sir Thomas Barnardiston, though his party's co-operation with Major-General Haynes probably caused its setback in the 1656 parliamentary elections.[50] The twenty-odd active commissioners, including Barnardiston, who assisted Haynes in Suffolk were men of considerable substance, and so they were in some other counties. In old royalist territory, however, and particularly in the north and in Wales, commissioners of gentry status were much harder to come by, and many of those appointed proved unwilling to act. No complete nationwide lists of the major-generals' commissioners survive to compare with those of the JPs, the Ejectors and the assessment commissioners, but the names of over 430 of them, representing thirty-two counties, are to be found among the Thurloe State Papers, and these were mainly the active and willing commissioners. From the same source Dr Reece has identified thirty-eight serving army officers among them,[51] but four of these were deputy major-generals – principals rather than assistants – and five or six more were garrison officers. From such incomplete figures one can deduce no more than an order of magnitude, and there is often no means of knowing how many of the apparently civilian commissioners held commands in the local militia, but it does look as though professional army officers of all types were outnumbered by ten to one or more, even in a commission with so much of a military function as that of the major-generals' assistants.

A paid militia, commanded by a major-general and backed by commissioners embodying the leadership of the godly interest in each county, could in theory have been a powerful instrument of dictatorship, but that is not the way it worked out. For one thing the Decimation never yielded enough to pay the militia, except in Kent, where the number of indigenous gentry, including royalist gentry, was exceptionally large. After a few months they had to be reduced nationwide by a fifth, and still Cromwell was forced to

49   Hirst, *Authority and Conflict*, p. 338.
50   *Thurloe State Papers*, iv. pp. 225, 272; Paul Pinckney, 'The Suffolk Elections to the Protectorate Parliaments', in C. Jones, M. Newitt and S. Roberts (eds), *Politics and People in Revolutionary England* (Oxford, 1986) [hereafter Pinckney, 'Suffolk Elections'], pp. 205–24, esp. pp. 214ff.
51   Reece, 'Military Presence', pp. 296–301.

have the assessment from December 1656 to June 1657 collected in advance. Major-General Haynes would dearly have liked to enlist the local militia's interest in swaying the 1656 elections in Suffolk, but he could not, since it had never been paid; he found himself thwarted by a hostile grand jury and a 'malignant' sheriff.[52] Indeed, money apart, it was the coolness and inertia, if not the outright hostility, of most of the gentry magistrates and of other old local institutions that most limited the initiative and effectiveness of the major-generals. Faced with the ingrained preference for traditional ways and traditional authority that he found in Lancashire, Cheshire and Staffordshire, Major-General Worsley pulled strenuously against the tide and worked himself literally to death at the age of thirty-four. But most of the rest seem slowly to have succumbed, to a greater or lesser degree. Historians are now agreed that their long-term influence on the development of local government was minimal. What used to be called the rule of the major-generals looks now less like a thought-out experiment than an untidily improvised expedient; less akin to Colbert's Intendants than to the county committees of the 1640s.

Perhaps, therefore, the three-phase picture of the Protectorate – two conciliatory, 'civilianizing' periods separated by a sharply defined plateau of military domination – needs to be modified, though without abandoning it in favour of a continuous and heavy military presence, varying only in degree. The major-generals' regime did mark a sharp change of policy, arising from an over-reaction to the royalist conspiracies uncovered in 1655, which temporarily gave the military faction in the council of state an influence out of proportion to its numbers. The scheme was potentially dictatorial, within limits; but it proved in practice less oppressive and less effective in most parts than was feared, and in less than a year – much less in some regions – it entered upon a long diminuendo. There were various reasons for this: inadequate financing, despite the heavy toll of the Decimation in both money and goodwill, the quiet determination of county magistrates not to let go of their authority, the discouragement that overcame some at least of the major-generals, the equivocal attitude of Cromwell himself, and the gradual discovery that most royalists would rather nurse their estates back to health than plot against his government. The Protectorate could do without the major-generals and their militia, so that when parliament's condemnation delivered the *coup de grace*, the waters closed silently over their whole organization.

Their establishment was not the only over-reaction to the royalist threat, for in the wake of it the dissemination of news was brought strictly under Secretary Thurloe's control. In September 1655 eight weekly newspapers appeared on the bookstalls, but from October until the end of the Protec-

52   Pinckney, 'Suffolk Elections', p. 215.

torate only the government-controlled *Mercurius Politicus* and *Publick Intelligencer* were permitted.[53] This was an unhappy anticipation of modern dictatorial practice, but the presses in general were not subject to rigid control. The output of pamphlets diminished slowly, but rather because the times were becoming more settled than because writers feared the censor.[54] Only those who openly incited readers to reject Cromwell's government, as Sir Henry Vane did in *A Healing Question*, or called upon them to assassinate him, as Edward Sexby did in *Killing No Murder*, incurred the wrath of the council.

In other spheres the brief military ascendancy achieved in 1655–6 was well on the wane by the early weeks of 1657. Cromwell showed his exasperation with the army's clumsy politicking in a speech he made to about a hundred officers at Whitehall on 27 February. They had come to protest against the draft of a new constitution that parliament had just presented to him, proposing that he should assume the title of king and that a new upper house should be established. This had already incurred much opposition from the major-generals, to his intense irritation. He told the hundred officers, 'that it is time to come to a settlement and lay aside arbitrary proceedings, so unacceptable to the nation'.[55] The whole speech was an angry and occasionally unfair castigation of the army leaders' political incompetence. Cromwell was for a while seriously at odds with the military members of his council and their allies Sir Gilbert Pickering and Walter Strickland, who would have liked to keep the Protectorate in its present form and to perpetuate the army's prominent role in central and local government. He was more and more sympathetic, though not uncritically so, to the party which was promoting the Humble Petition and Advice (as the new constitution came to be called) – a party no less loyal to the Protectorate than the army was, but anxious to hasten its transference from a military to a civilian basis and to give it a more traditional cast. Its leaders included the great lawyer-officials Bulstrode Whitelocke, Sir Thomas Widdrington, Nathaniel Fiennes, John Glyn and William Lenthall, and patricians like Lord Broghill, Edward Montagu, Charles Howard and Sir Charles Wolseley. They were not all civilians, for Howard had lately been a deputy major-general, Montagu was now General-at-Sea and General Monck was a strong ally, but several of them

53   *Catalogue of Pamphlets . . . Collected by George Thomason, 1640–1661*, ed. G. K. Fortescue (2 vols, 1908), ii. pp. 433–5. A third paper, *The Publick Adviser*, ran briefly from May to September 1657.

54   See the table in ibid., i. p. xxi. The pamphlet output was always high in years of rapid or violent political change, most of all in 1642–3 and 1647–8, and to a lesser extent in 1653 and 1659–60. The pamphlets (excluding newspapers) collected by the bookseller Thomason in each year from 1650 to 1653 numbered 481, 402, 427 and 598; from 1654 to 1658 the annual harvest was 526, 443, 402, 306 and 282, rising to 652 in 1659 and 976 in 1660.

55   Abbott, *Writings and Speeches*, iv. p. 417, and see pp. 412–19 *passim*.

had a royalist background, and most of the army was deeply suspicious of the whole group.

At first sight it might look as though victory went to the military faction, since Cromwell, after much opposition by the army to the royal title, eventually refused it, while the senior officers gained an enhanced status and an entrenched political position as life members of the new upper house. But appearances are deceptive, and it should not be assumed that the army's hostility was the reason why Cromwell refused the crown. His motives were almost certainly more complex. He had never been opposed to monarchy in principle, and he was keenly aware of what the constitutionalists' proposals had in their favour: the greater legitimacy of a frame of government devised by parliament, the firmer basis that it would give to the rule of law, recognition of the political nation's continuing attachment to monarchy, a better prospect of solving the problem of the succession, and (not least) a means of checking the swollen political pretensions of some of the army grandees. About the latter, Henry Cromwell wrote to Thurloe from Ireland:

> I look upon some of them as vainly arrogating to themselves too great a share in the right of his Highness's government, and to have too high an opinion of their merit in subverting the old . . . And therefore I am so far from a tender sense of their dissatisfaction, that I rather esteem [this] a providential opportunity to pull out those thorns, which are like to be troublesome in the sides of his Highness.[56]

As for the royal title, it was in itself a thing indifferent to Cromwell – 'but a feather in a man's cap', he called it.[57] Two considerations, however, weighed heavily with him against accepting it. First, he knew what a betrayal of the old cause it would seem to hundreds of russet-coated captains and thousands of brave, God-fearing soldiers who believed that he and they had fought the Lord's battles together.[58] But it was respect for their convictions that moved him, not fear of their resistance. Secondly, although kingship might thrive elsewhere with God's blessing, he could not but suspect that God had pronounced against it in Britain. 'I would not seek to set up that that providence hath destroyed and laid in the dust', he said; 'I would not build Jericho again.'[59]

He is usually depicted as hesitating for weeks over the offer of the crown, but a good case can be made out that he never intended to accept it. If one reads his first real answer to the parliament-men (on 3 April 1657) without

---

56   *Thurloe State Papers*, vi. p. 93, quoted in Firth, *Last Years*, i. p. 162.
57   *The Memoirs of Edmund Ludlow*, ed. C. H. Firth (2 vols, Oxford, 1894) [hereafter Ludlow, *Memoirs*], ii. p. 24; Abbott, *Writings and Speeches*, iv. pp. 417, 509. He seems to have used the expression repeatedly.
58   Ibid., pp. 471–2, 481–2.
59   Ibid., p. 473.

hindsight, its natural sense is surely that he was definitely declining the royal title, though in terms as respectful to parliament's authority as possible, and without reference to the other proposals in the Petition and Advice.[60] It was only when the house refused to take no for an answer – and it was admittedly a rather muted 'no' – that he entered upon a negotiation that in the event lasted five weeks, his hope being that despite parliament's all-or-nothing stipulation he would eventually be allowed to accept its new constitution without changing his title. During this time he kept very close counsel, but when he did unbutton it was in very familiar fashion with a small group of 'kinglings', including Broghill, Wolseley, Thurloe, Whitelocke and William Pierrepont.[61] Of these, only Wolseley was as yet a councillor. The question is what one makes of the confident reports by Thurloe and others in late April and early May that he was about to accept the whole package, crown and all.[62] It is possible that for a week or two he really did hesitate, doubting perhaps whether he had read the will of providence aright; but it is at least as likely that he was testing the loyalty of his senior officers, while attaching the kinglings to himself by his relaxed intimacy to the point where (he hoped) they would relent over the title, as they eventually did. Certainly the opposition of the army grandees became much more subdued, and he skilfully manoeuvred them (with the exception of Lambert) into believing that the best solution would be to adopt the Petition and Advice, if he could, without changing his title. That had been his own preferred solution throughout. Lambert was still much against it; he did not care to see his handiwork, the Instrument of Government, superseded, and he almost certainly had his eye on the succession. Under the Instrument the next Protector would have been elected by the council, and he stood a chance, but by the Petition and Advice Cromwell was to name his own successor, whether he took the crown or not, and after all that had passed it was inconceivable that he would name Lambert.

When the more determined army officers finally mustered their opposition to kingship in a famous petition to parliament, the grandees – even Lambert – fought shy of it. Little more than thirty officers signed it, half of them mere captains, and only two as senior as colonel. Fleetwood, the senior commander below Cromwell himself, personally persuaded the house not to have the petition read.[63] It was one of his rare displays of good political judgement. When Cromwell was installed afresh as Lord Protector and the new constitution promulgated, Lambert alone declined to take the

---

60 Ibid., pp. 445–6.
61 Bulstrode Whitelocke, *Memorials of the English Affairs* (1682), p. 647. The word 'kingling' is much used in (e.g.) *A Narrative of the late Parliament* (1658).
62 Abbott, *Writings and Speeches*, iv. pp. 508–10; Firth, *Last Years*, i. pp. 188–90.
63 Ludlow, *Memoirs*, ii. p. 27; Firth, *Last Years*, i. pp. 191–3. Firth's masterly account of the transactions over the offer of the crown is unsurpassed among modern authorities.

councillor's oath that it prescribed, and was stripped of all his commissions. Lambert had probably been the most popular commander after Cromwell, 'deservedly so after his brilliant services in the Preston, Dunbar and Worcester campaigns, but there was not a murmur of protest from the army at his going; indeed the officers in and about London hastened to reaffirm their loyalty to the Protector. So far from muddling through weeks of indecision to a renunciation forced by military pressure, as some historians and biographers would have it, Cromwell seems to have played his hand with considerable finesse and to have achieved as nearly as possible what he wanted – including important modifications of the Petition and Advice and an addition of nearly fifty per cent to the regular revenue that it first proposed for him.[64]

The questions that concern us here are whether the changes of 1657 made Cromwell any more or less of a dictator, and whether they strengthened or weakened the army's influence in civil government. On paper the Protector's powers were on balance slightly enlarged. The financial provision that he received was specific and relatively generous (though it still did not meet expenditure), and he was no longer required to 'govern . . . in all things by the advice of the council'; but henceforth privy councillors (as they were now called again) could not be appointed or dismissed without the approval of both houses of parliament, who also had power to approve or reject an enlarged range of officers of state. No member of either house could in future be excluded except by a decision of the house itself. In practice Cromwell's personal powers remained very much as before, except for his new right to name his own successor. The emphasis of the Petition and Advice was on parliamentary rather than conciliar restraints on his authority, as was to be expected from its authorship.[65]

Cromwell was entrusted with selecting the members of 'the other house', and among the sixty-three whom he summoned were seventeen army officers.[66] But they included his sons Richard (a civilian until he was made a colonel of horse in December 1657) and Henry, as well as Monck and Howard, all members of the anti-military party, and since Colonel Humphrey Mackworth never took his seat the true army interest numbered no more than a dozen. The civilian constitutionalists had a clear majority. One also has to ask whether these career officers gained or lost in political authority by accepting seats in the other house, thereby excluding themselves from the Commons, and the answer must be that they lost; the

64   Compare his requests to the parliamentary committee on 21 April 1657 (Abbott, *Writings and Speeches*, iv. pp. 490–7), with the 'Additional Petition and Advice' of 26 June (Gardiner, *Constitutional Documents*, pp. 459–64), which gave him all he asked.
65   Text in Gardiner, *Constitutional Documents*, pp. 447–64, including the Additional Petition and Advice.
66   Full list in Abbott, *Writings and Speeches*, iv. p. 951.

experience of Richard Cromwell's parliament in 1659 would drive it home to them. In the privy council the military faction suffered a decisive setback when Lambert was dismissed and Thurloe admitted on the same day, for it never recovered its former influence. Further afield it was the same story, though unfolded over a longer time-span. In November 1657 Henry Cromwell's long delayed appointment as Lord Deputy of Ireland in succession to Fleetwood set the seal on a slow transition from military and sectarian ascendancy to a more moderate and broadly based civil government. In Scotland, Monck continued with little change the civilizing regime established by Broghill, with its emphasis on conciliation, impartial justice and honest administration.[67]

One more tremor disturbed the Protectorate during Cromwell's lifetime. When parliament reassembled for a second session in January 1658 after a seven-month recess, his most reliable supporters had been elevated to the other house and his most embittered opponents, whom the council had hitherto excluded, flocked back to the Commons. The republican politicians soon made the lower house unmanageable and tried at the same time to subvert the army, where just enough republican sentiment lingered to be worrying. Suddenly there appeared a new threat: that the army might react against the partial eclipse of its political influence at the hands of conservative civilians by turning against the Protectorate itself. But it was a very slight threat while Cromwell lived, and he quashed it by promptly dissolving the parliament and cashiering six officers in the army's most disaffected unit, which was his own regiment of horse. As Protector he had seen little of it, and its *de facto* commander Major William Packer, a Particular Baptist and republican, had surrounded himself with troop commanders of like mind – and 'a light chaffy mind' Packer's was, in George Fox's judgement.[68] Cromwell then held a sentimental reunion with two hundred of his officers at a feast in the Banqueting House at Whitehall, where enough wine was poured to help them sit happily through a two-hour speech from him.[69] All was quiet during the remaining seven months of his life, but a regime to which a parliament could give such an unpleasant shock and whose army needed such managing was some way short of an autocracy.

Richard Cromwell's brief rule showed how vulnerable it was under a Protector who had no standing among his father's comrades in arms and no idea how to hold the balance, as Oliver had done, between the older military Cromwellians and the newer constitutionalist ones; he leaned altogether too far and too tactlessly towards the latter. His government was far from unpopular in the country at large, and it had the support of a clear

67   T. C. Barnard, *Cromwellian Ireland* (Oxford, 1975); F. D. Dow, *Cromwellian Scotland 1651–1660* (Edinburgh, 1979), esp. ch. 10.
68   Quoted in Firth and Davies, *Regimental History*, i. p. 71.
69   Abbott, *Writings and Speeches*, iv. pp. 736–7.

majority in the fullest and freest parliament to sit since 1642. But the army grandees were having the worst of both worlds, not much listened to by 'the young gentleman' (as Richard was called in military circles), who preferred the advice of suspect civilians, inside and outside the privy council, yet distrusted for their association with the court by the mass of more junior officers, who were being persuaded by a spate of emotive rhetoric in press and pulpit that the Good Old Cause (a catch-phrase whose content, when specified, varied widely) was being betrayed.[70] In an unholy half-alliance with the republican opposition, which would have been powerless without the army's support, the grandees organized the military coup that toppled Richard; his own brother-in-law and most senior officer, Lieutenant-General Fleetwood, gave the orders. They did not intend to depose him, but they could not control the situation that they created when they led the army in first defying and then dissolving the parliament, and their own excited subordinates called the tune. In little more than two weeks the Rump was back at Westminster, the Commonwealth re-established, and Britain was set inexorably on the road to the Restoration. The Protectorate, which had offered the only viable alternative to that road, had fallen not because it had been antagonizing the nation with a military dictatorship but because government and parliament had proceeded too fast and too clumsily in reducing the political role that this always-political army felt to be its due.

Ironically, the restored Rump, despite its lip-service to the supreme authority of the representatives of the sovereign people, felt the need for a much greater military establishment than ever the Protectorate had done. The forces in England were rapidly built up until by the end of 1659 they numbered almost double what they had been when Richard was over-thrown in April.[71] But they did not save the Rump, which immediately began to provoke the army again, and to be provoked by it. Lambert's brief alliance with the republicans ended almost as soon as he got his command back, and he led part of the army in a second coup which turned the Rump out again in mid-October. What followed for the next two months, under the so-called Committee of Safety, was nearer to a military dictatorship than anything that the country had yet experienced, and may have done more than anything under the Protectorate to leave the English people with a lasting aversion to standing armies. But it was utterly sterile and inherently unstable, for the generals had lost all sense of political direction, and the soldiery were demoralized by lack of pay, public hatred, divided loyalties, and the massive changes in the officer corps in recent months. When the

---

70   A. Woolrych, 'The Good Old Cause and the Fall of the Protectorate', *Cambridge Historical Journal*, xiii (1957), pp. 133–61; Barbara Taft, 'That Lusty Puss, the Good Old Cause', *History of Political Thought*, (1984), pp. 447–68; Derek Hirst, 'Concord and Discord in Richard Cromwell's House of Commons', *English Historical Review*, ciii (1988), pp. 339–58.
71   Reece, 'Military Presence', pp. 287, 297–301.

men frankly declared that 'they would not fight, but would make a ring for their officers to fight in',[72] it was time to quit.

Against such a rapid breakdown within months of his death, and such unbridled strife between military and civil authority, the achievement of Cromwell's Protectorate can be seen in perspective. How much sooner the Commonwealth might have collapsed if he had not taken on the headship of the state is anyone's guess, but he deserves to be taken seriously in his claim that 'I undertook [it] not so much out of the hope of doing any good, as out of a desire to prevent mischief and evil, which I did see was imminent upon the nation. I saw we were running headlong into confusion and disorder.' He said this to the MPs who were pressing the crown on him in 1657, and he was probably no less sincere when he told them that he was 'ready to serve not as a king, but as a constable'; for he could only justify his office to himself by 'comparing it with a good constable, to keep the peace of the parish'.[73] He did keep the peace, and in most respects that matter it was not an oppressive peace. A constable is of course an officer of the law, and he cared profoundly about upholding the rule of law as far as he could in such disturbed times – 'very fickle, very uncertain', he called them.[74] He would dearly have liked to see the laws comprehensively reformed and made more humane, but he was frustrated by the conservatism of the legal profession and by parliament's constant preoccupation with other matters.[75] Unlike most dictators, he was not convinced that any one mode of government or political philosophy was inherently better or truer than others. He was a pragmatist in his politics, not 'wedded and glued to *forms* of government', he said, but prepared to believe that 'any of them' – monarchical, aristocratic, democratic – 'might be good in themselves, or for us, according as providence should direct us'.[76]

But throughout his rule he was subject to two tensions which set his instinctive constitutionalism in conflict with other forces and ideals. The more obvious one was between his obligation to the army through which he rose to power and his desire to achieve a lasting settlement by winning back the confidence and co-operation of the political nation as a whole. He embarked on his aim of 'healing and settling' with a military presence in central and local government that was notably modest in the circum-

72   *The Clarke Papers*, ed. C. H. Firth (4 vols, 1891–1901), iv. p. 300; A. Woolrych, Historical Introduction to *Complete Prose Works of John Milton* (8 vols, New Haven, Conn., 1953–82), vii. pp. 118–55; Ronald Hutton, *The Restoration* (Oxford, 1985), pp. 64–83.
73   Abbott, *Writings and Speeches*, iv. p. 470.
74   Ibid., p. 473.
75   Nancy L. Matthews, *William Sheppard: Cromwell's law reformer* (Cambridge, 1985), chs 3 and 4.
76   A. S. P. Woodhouse (ed.), *Puritanism and Liberty* (London, 1938), p. 36 (my italics); Ludlow, *Memoirs*, i. pp. 184–5.

stances, but the exasperating experience of the first Protectorate parliament and the shock of the royalist conspiracies revealed in 1655 made him change course for a while and give the army men their head. But to describe even the major-generals' regime as military rule is an overstatement, and it did not last long. From early in 1657 the military element in local administration reverted almost to its former level, while the influence of the army grandees on the policies of central government fell far below what it had been in earlier years. If Cromwell unduly enhanced the army's political role in 1655–6, it is arguable that he reduced it further in 1657–8 than was healthy for his successor.

Yet he was never disposed to eliminate the army from politics altogether, even if he could safely have done so, because he clung to so many of the values for which it stood in the heyday of the New Model. There lies the second major tension that strained the Protectorate. His later speeches are full of his desire to balance civil and Christian liberty, and to reconcile what he called the interest of the nation with the more particular interest of the people of God. By the interest of the nation he meant the rights and desires and susceptibilities of the unregenerate majority, and especially those of the gentry magistracy. The interest of the people of God, on the other hand, demanded the enforcement by public authority of a strict moral code and the sanctity of the sabbath, plus the toleration of a range of sects and religious practices that to traditionalists seemed downright heretical. To a puritan of Cromwell's stamp the people of God came first, and it may be that lingering misgivings about the legitimacy of his authority were a spur to his promotion of their interest, to whose defence he thought that providence had called him. But he would never acknowledge that the two interests were necessarily in conflict. 'He sings sweetly that sings a song of reconciliation betwixt these two interests', he said, 'and it is a pitiful fancy, and wild and ignorant, to think they are inconsistent.'[77] And again: 'If anyone whatsoever think the Interest of Christians and the Interest of the Nation inconsistent, I wish my soul may never enter into his or their secrets!'[78] But in a wicked world they did not consist at all easily. I suggested earlier that whether the Protectorate was a dictatorship and whether it was a military dictatorship are partially separable questions. The conclusion I offer is that what there was of the dictatorial in Cromwell's rule – and there was such an element, often though it has been overstated – stemmed not so much from its military origins or the participation of army officers in civil government as from his constant commitment to the interest of the people of God, and his conviction that suppressing vice and encouraging virtue constituted 'the very end of magistracy'.

77 Abbott, *Writings and Speeches*, iv. p. 490.
78 Ibid., pp. 44–5.

4

'The Single Person's Confidants and Dependents'? Oliver Cromwell and his Protectoral Councillors

Peter Gaunt

Originally appeared as Peter Gaunt, ' "The single person's confidants and dependents"? Oliver Cromwell and his Protectoral councillors' in *Historical Journal*, 32. Copyright 1989 Cambridge University Press, Cambridge.

Editor's Introduction

Most contemporary observers assumed that Cromwell wielded sweeping powers, especially during the Protectorate. Both the two written constitutions of these years, the *Instrument of Government* and the *Humble Petition and Advice*, established a Protectoral Council intended to restrain Cromwell's freedom of action, yet the activities of this institution have remained largely mysterious. Insofar as it has been studied at all, the Council has been depicted as Cromwell's puppet. In much the most detailed study to date of the membership and workings of the Council, Peter Gaunt argues that such a view is fundamentally incorrect.

Gaunt begins by showing that in most areas of government the Lord Protector could only act with the consent of the Council. The written constitutions ensured that Cromwell was more tightly bound to his Council than the early Stuarts had been to their Privy Council. These powers were especially extensive during the intervals between Parliaments, which were often lengthy given that Parliament did not have to meet for more than a minimum of five months in every three years. No aspect of government lay outside the Council's scope, and although Cromwell always retained ultimate control, the

Council's official records reveal that it was well able to press ahead with a considerable amount of business even during his absences.

Cromwell's own attendance at Council meetings fluctuated: he was present at over half the recorded meetings in 1655, whereas he attended far fewer meetings in 1654, or from mid-1657 until his death. He also seems to have attended assiduously the more informal meetings at Whitehall and Hampton Court. He apparently felt uneasy at the prospect of exercising wide – and possibly corrupting – powers, and willingly accepted the imposition of conciliar restraints. Sometimes, as with the purges of the first two Protectorate Parliaments in 1654 and 1656, he preferred to dissociate himself from a distasteful political intervention and to allow the Council to take responsibility.

Gaunt also argues persuasively that Cromwell's handling of the Council was not domineering or manipulative, and that his councillors were not mere ciphers. In the summer of 1656, for example, the Council was divided over whether the Protectorate's serious financial problems necessitated calling another Parliament. Cromwell was initially opposed to summoning Parliament, but the majority of his councillors thought otherwise and in the end Cromwell was persuaded to do so against his own wishes. Later, in 1658, as Cromwell's health declined and his grip on public affairs weakened, the Council played a central part in discussing the regime's continuing fiscal difficulties and possible solutions to them. The surviving evidence indicates that Cromwell respected the Council's independence and that he sometimes allowed councillors to deflect him from his preferred course of action. This is an important conclusion because it suggests that Cromwell was not the boundless tyrant portrayed in some older works, and that his councillors were not puppets who meekly deferred to the Lord Protector's will.

'The Single Person's Confidants and Dependents'? Oliver Cromwell and his Protectoral Councillors

Peter Gaunt

It is because they [the Protectoral Councillors] accepted Cromwell so thoroughly for their head, and made themselves so willingly his advisers only and the agents of his will, that History is now apt to forget what important men they were in the eyes of their contemporaries.[1]

Little has happened in the century since Masson wrote those words fundamentally to alter his assessment and both the operation of Protectoral central government 1653–8 and the role of the Council within it remain sadly under-studied. Although recent historians would doubtless deny that they have simply forgotten the Protectoral Councillors, in practice most surveys either ignore the Council or allude to it in a few passing and usually dismissive sentences. For example, the Councillors are mentioned only once in Kenyon's *Stuart England*, a reference to their 'clumsy decision' to exclude M.P.s in 1656.[2] And the assessment of the Council as a politically power-less vehicle for the Protector's will still generally prevails, albeit expressed in more cautious tones. Thus in his recent study of interregnum Britain, Barnard asserts that 'in practice the Council seldom deflected him [Cromwell] from his chosen courses' and that it is 'likely that the council-lors would usually defer to him'.[3] Barnard himself laments the dearth of surviving evidence about the Council's work, a dearth which has all but stifled serious examination of the operation of Protectoral central government and which may have led contemporaries and later historians alike to under-rate the role of the Council and correspondingly to inflate that of Cromwell. For despite the paucity of evidence, there are clear indications that the Council was not the impotent cypher nor Cromwell the boundless autocrat of so many histories and biographies.

1 D. Masson, *The life of John Milton* (7 vols., London, 1859–94), IV, p. 545.
2 J. P. Kenyon, *Stuart England* (London, 1978), p. 176.
3 T. C. Barnard, *The English republic 1649–1660* (London, 1982), p. 36. Although sceptical of the Council's political power, Barnard does suggest that it may have had an important administrative role.

I

That so much attention has focused on Cromwell is understandable, for he was by far the most visible element of the Protectoral establishment, almost to the exclusion of his supposed partners in government. From the inauguration ceremony of 16 December 1653 to his state funeral in autumn 1658, the Protector was consistently projected as the conspicuous figurehead of government, ensconced in palaces, surrounded by an increasingly elaborate court, appointing many officials and distributing honours, receiving ambassadors and dignitaries, opening parliaments and presiding on state occasions. In short, he was invested with most of the pomp and trappings, the public duties and ceremonials, of an early modern monarch. Most of the people for most of the time could see and recognize only one element of the executive – the Lord Protector – and in consequence contemporary commentators frequently assumed that in all important matters Cromwell *was* the government and that he possessed and exercised unlimited powers. Seventeenth-century accounts of the work of the Protectoral government tend to be sketchy and unbalanced and to most contemporaries Cromwell was simply an 'absolute Lord and Tyrant over three potent Nations'.[4] A mixture of ignorance, increasingly repressive censorship and the natural caution which it engendered effectively precluded the publication of detailed analysis during the Protectorate itself. The few accounts which did reach the presses generally comprised wild denunciations of the government, countered by a handful of empty eulogies. After the fall of Richard Cromwell in April 1659, and even more following the restoration of the Stuarts a year later, published attacks upon the Protectorate became far more numerous, but they remained noticeably shallow and ill-informed. Seventeenth-century narratives and biographies are searched in vain for reasoned assessments of the composition and operation of central government 1653–9 or detailed examinations of the powers and limitations of the executive.

Few contemporary authors looked beyond the person of the Protector and to most Cromwell was merely an all-powerful autocrat – 'tyrant' and 'oppressor' were the watchwords. The 1682 volume *Arbitrary government displayed to the life . . . of the tyrant and usurper Oliver Cromwell* defined such government as 'the rule of any Person or Persons by their own Will and Authority without being tyed to the rules, methods and directions of the Laws of the Land' and went on, after a typically bland account of events 1654–8, predictably to conclude that the Protectorate was a time of

---

4   *A declaration of the freeborn people of England* ([16 Mar.] 1655; B[ritish] L[ibrary, London], Thomason 669 f.19 (70)).

'Tyranny, Oppression and Injustice' perpetrated by Cromwell, who 'ruled by himself with greater power and more absolute Sway than ever any Monarch of England did'.[5] Of the attacks which appeared in Cromwell's lifetime, *Killing noe murder* and *A declaration of the freeborn people* amongst others portrayed the regime as government by a boundless tyrant who knew no limits to his powers and could be checked only by deposition or assassination. *The English devil*, published just after the restoration, claimed that the nation had been enchained and 'compelled to submit to this Tyrant Nol or be cut off by him; nothing but a word and a blow, his Will was his Law; tell him of Magna Carta, he would lay his hand on his sword and cry Magna Farta'.[6] But perhaps the most colourful assessment of Cromwell's sweeping powers as Protector survives in manuscript only, a bitter attack attributed to Anthony Ashley Cooper in the third Protectorate parliament: 'If Pope Alex 6, Caesare Borgia and Machiavelli should joyne in a platforme of an absolute Tyranny, they could not go beyond that which is held forth in that thing which is called the Humble Petition and Advice'.[7]

Ashley Cooper had at least recognized that Cromwell's office and government rested upon a written constitution. Most writers were apparently ignorant of the fact, or found it impossible or unnecessary to describe the provisions of that constitution. Those who did at least acknowledge the existence of the Instrument of Government and Humble Petition and Advice rarely progressed beyond a bald summary of the main provisions and fought shy of analysing their practical operation – the constitutions are irrelevant to most accounts of the events and policies of the Protectorate government. Accordingly, the limitations which the constitutions placed on Cromwell were usually ignored entirely or scathingly dismissed as inoperative after the briefest of discussions. Typical was *A declaration of the freeborn people*, which treated with the utmost scepticism the notion that the terms of the Instrument were observed in practice or placed strict limits on the Protector's powers, and enquired 'if he [Cromwell] pleases to throw away (or burne by the hands of the hangman) his Limits in his paper of Government, who can trouble him?'. Constitution or no, Cromwell is still the unlimited tyrant.

That a mere handful of contemporary commentators went on to look in any detail at the constitutional checks upon the Single Person, and particularly at the role of the Council, is understandable and was probably due to more than censorship or hostility. The concept that parliament should carry some influence with or over the executive, particularly in financial affairs, was not new in the mid-seventeenth century. It was the existence of a

5   *Arbitrary government displayed to the life . . . of the tyrant and usurper Oliver Cromwell* (London, 1682), pp. 3, 89, 142–3.
6   *The English devil* ([27 July] 1660; B.L., Thomason E1035 (3)), p. 2.
7   Bodl[eian] Lib[rary, Oxford], Tanner MS 51, fo. 25.

permanent and independent executive Council, established under a written constitution and entrusted with extensive powers to control the head of state – powers far wider than those ascribed to the legislature – that was the unknown and untried element. Moreover, the Councillors themselves did nothing to dispel such ignorance, for they met behind closed doors, their deliberations were secret and largely remained so and their dealings with the Protector were hidden from the public gaze. It is clear from the hundreds of petitions addressed to the Council that its existence was fairly well known, very brief reports of conciliar work appeared in some newspapers and the Councillors were often ascribed prominent parts in state ceremonies. But the twin hurdles of novelty and concealment fostered a profound ignorance of the way in which the Council operated, its relationship with Cromwell and its role in central government.

Of the seventeenth-century writers who gave any attention to the Protectoral Council, most portrayed it as a caricature of the king's privy council, a body of acquiescent servants existing to advise and flatter the Single Person and extend and execute his will rather than to curb or control his actions. Writers questioned the independence of the Protectoral Council and asserted that in practice it was either moulded or completely disregarded by Cromwell as he saw fit. *The Protector (so called) in part unvailed* of October 1655 described the Council as 'like a Nose of Wax, which will winde and turn which way the Single Person pleases' and which left the people 'in bondage and slavery to the will of a man'.[8] Even *The perfect politician* of February 1660, a remarkably balanced and generally favourable account of Cromwell's life, concluded that 'he never relyed so much on their [the Councillors'] counsels, as to have it said, England was governed by a Council and Protector; for he made the world know, it was by Protector and Council'.[9] But by far the fullest contemporary assessment survives in manuscript only, a paper written in late 1656 by John Hobart, a Protectoral politician and M.P. and a distant relative of Cromwell.

> It [the Instrument] seemeth all along to trappe and allay and balance the Single Person with this check of a Councill, without whose consent forsooth he is to do nothing of generall concernment, but when I look upon those that he hath gotten to him for that purpose, it makes me think of the Character given to the Cardinalls who were to be of the Pope's Councill: they sat in Councill to Assentari not Assentiri. Some want heads, as Skippon, Rous, Pickering, the others want hearts, as that condemned coward Fiennes, Whitelock, Glynn, Wolseley, &c, almost all want souls, so

8   *The Protector (so-called) in part unvailed* ([24 Oct.] 1655; B.L., Thomason E857 (1)), pp. 5–6; cf. *A looking-glass for, or an awakening word to, the officers* ([22 Oct.] 1656; B.L., Thomason E891 (1)).

9   *The perfect politician* ([Feb.] 1660; B.L., Thomason E1869 (1)), p. 348.

that the best quality you shall find in those who usually sitt is that they are the Single Person's confidants and dependants, perfectly awed by him and his 30,000 myrmidons.[10]

Surprisingly few contemporary publications defended Cromwell from accusations of unbounded tyranny or his Council from portrayal as a worthless puppet. Government propaganda invariably avoided detailed discussion of constitutional matters and focused instead on particular worthy policies or on the peace and stability which the new government had brought, in the hope of fostering a 'business as usual' attitude. Pro-Cromwellian accounts of the constitution rarely extended beyond an examination of the establishment of the Protectorate, stressing the disorder and confusion created by the resignation of the Nominated Assembly, an abdication which left the three nations without any form of government and placed sole and unlimited power in the hands of the Lord General and his army. In accepting the Protectorship and the terms of the Instrument of Government, Cromwell had not only saved the people from a 'torrent of blood and confusion' but also agreed to 'abridge himself' of his absolute powers and to 'circumscribe himself with such bounds and limits' as the constitution prescribed.[11] The commentators are silent on how these provisions worked in practice and do not move on to analyse Cromwell's role in government 1654–8. The most lucid defence of the regime published during the 1650s, *A true state of the case of the commonwealth*, analysed the Instrument in detail, though in attempting to demonstrate that 'the Foundation of this Government [is] laid in the People', the author played up the role of parliament and so gave little attention to that of the Council. Moreover, *A true state* was published in February 1654, just eight weeks after the inauguration of the regime, and was therefore a record of constitutional theories and ideals yet to be tested, not an account of the practical operation of that constitution.[12] Favourable accounts of the Protectorate,

---

10   Bodl. Lib., Tanner MS 52, fo. 159v. It is, perhaps, a reflexion of contemporary knowledge of the Council that two of the seven members named by Hobart – Whitelock and Glynn – were never, in fact, Protectoral Councillors.

Other published attacks on the constitution and unofficial and semi-official replies tend to concentrate on Cromwell alone or on parliament and devote little attention to the role of the Councillors or to the relative powers of, and relationship between, Protector and Council. See, for example, *The humble petition of several colonels of the army* ([18 Oct.] 1654; B.L., Thomason 669 f.19 (21)); *Some mementos for the officers and souldiers of the army* ([19 Oct.] 1654; B.L., Thomason E813 (20)); *A representation concerning the late parliament* ([9 Apr.] 1655; B.L., Thomason E831 (13)); and two editions of Nedham's shortlived newspaper *The observator*, 24–31 Oct. and 31 Oct.–7 Nov. 1654.

11   The quotations are from *Killing is murder* ([21 Sep.] 1657; B.L., Thomason E925 (12)), pp. 7–8, one of several tracts to follow this line.

12   *A true state of the case of the commonwealth* ([8 Feb.] 1654; B.L., Thomason E728(5)), pp. 21–46.

particularly those carried in biographies of Cromwell published soon after his death, are very bland and innocuous, concentrating on 'safe' issues such as wars overseas and failed royalist conspiracies at home, on the beneficial results of government policies rather than the mechanisms of policy-making.[13] Their coverage of the Protectoral Council ranged from non-existent, through a few shallow and uncritical references, to the mindless and excessive praise of *Historie and policie re-viewed*:

> . . . never was a more compleat body of Council, or more exquisite com-position, of so many excellent Tempers together in the World . . . they have by their great piety and prudence, kept this State so well united within the bands of concord, and charity, that it cannot but appear to for-reigners themselves, as it were a little Temple of Peace, though in the very heat and hurry of War . . . it seemed his late Highnesse had drawn so many Angels from Heaven, to fix them at the stern of his Estate. . .

and so on.[14]

Later accounts of the Protectorate have generally followed the well-worn path, concentrating on the Protector to the virtual exclusion of both the Council and serious analysis of the mechanics of government. Cromwell, firmly centre stage and frequently the only character in sight, is still occa-sionally portrayed as the unbounded tyrant and autocrat. Recent accounts, however, are usually more cautious and acknowledge some restraints upon Cromwell's actions, military, financial, even parliamentary. But the consti-tutional checks, and particularly the severe restrictions upon the Protector vested in the Council, are rarely examined in any detail. A notable excep-tion are the writings of S. R. Gardiner, who not only analysed the written constitutions, highlighting the restraints on the Single Person vested in the Council, but also proceeded to review the operation of Protectoral central government. Gardiner acknowledged that evidence is generally meagre and sometimes almost non-existent, but concluded that 'we know enough to convince us that the ordinary belief that Oliver was an autocrat and his councillors mere puppets is a very incorrect view of the situation'. Unlike a Tudor or Stuart monarch, the Protector was 'bound to do nothing without the consent' of his Council, and although Cromwell 'no doubt' possessed considerable personal influence over the members, ultimately 'he had to rely on influence, not on authority'; the Council was 'by no means a tool in his hands'. Thus in practice as well as in theory, the Councillors served as

13   See, for example, R. Flecknoe, *The idea of his highness, Oliver*, and S. Carrington, *The history of the life and death of his most serene highness Oliver, late Lord Protector*, both of which appeared in April 1659, shortly before the collapse of the Protectorate.
14   *Historie and policie re-viewed in the heroick transactions of his most serene highness, Oliver, late Lord Protector* ([Apr.] 1659; B.L., Thomason E1799 (2)), pp. 130–2.

'a real constitutional control' on the Protector, though the secrecy in which they met and acted rendered conciliar constraints almost invisible. Nonetheless

> the notion which prevailed at the time, and which has continued to prevail in modern days, that Cromwell was a self-willed autocrat impos- ing his commands on a body composed of his subservient creatures, is consistent neither with the indications which exist in the correspondence of that day, nor with his own character.[15]

Few historians have followed Gardiner's lead and the Protectoral Council remains in the shadows.[16] The most detailed account is that of E. R. Turner, whose study of the privy council included two chapters on the Protectorate. Turner based his account on the original council order books, so avoiding many of the pitfalls created by the often deficient and misleading printed calendars,[17] but the resulting study is brief and limited and the conclusions correspondingly shallow. Composition, organization, attendance and the

15 S. R. Gardiner, *Oliver Cromwell* (London, 1899), p. 151; *Cromwell's place in history* (London, 1897), p. 86; *History of the Commonwealth and Protectorate* (4 vols., London, 1893 edn), II, pp. 333–9.

16 For example, Harrison noted that 'the Instrument of Government was a constitution of a strictly limited type' under which the Protector was 'bound by the Council', but the author made no attempt to assess the practical effects of these restraints and instead contradicted himself by asserting that, as Protector, Cromwell 'was, and felt himself to be, a dictator, . . . a ruler invested with absolute power', F. Harrison, *Oliver Cromwell* (London, 1929), pp. 191–5. Kenyon's *The Stuart constitution* dismissed the Protectoral Council in a single sentence loaded with questionable innuendo – 'the Council of State was designed as a brake on executive authority, but 15 of its members were named in the Instrument, and subsequent vacancies were to be filled by a cumbersome method obviously open to manipulation' – and ascribed to a 'Council of Officers' key political decisions, such as the establishment of the major generals and the exclusion of M.P.s in 1656, which were, in fact, clearly taken by the executive Council and the Protector, J.P. Kenyon, *The Stuart constitution* (Cambridge, 1986 edn), pp. 300–5. Hill saw the Instrument founding a 'veiled dictatorship of the generals . . . by nominating to the Council the generals, their friends and relations'; the Humble Petition not only established par- liamentary control over the new Council but also 'liberated' Cromwell from the old military- dominated body 'imposed' upon him in December 1653, C. Hill, *God's Englishman* (London, 1970), pp. 148, 175, and *Oliver Cromwell, 1658–1958* (London, 1958), pp. 20–1. Coward rightly pointed out that, from the beginning, the membership included civilians and 'aristo- crats' as well as generals, but he largely ignored the Council's operation and described it mis- leadingly as merely 'an advisory body akin to the old privy council', B. Coward, *The Stuart age* (London, 1980), p. 226.

17 C[alendar of] S[tate] P[apers] D[omestic series], 1649–1660, ed. M. A. E. Green (12 vols., London, 1875–86). The introduction to each volume carries a table showing the attendance of Councillors at every recorded meeting. Although the dates of meetings and indications of attendance are frequently at fault, these tables do provide accurate lists of the members of Oliver Cromwell's Protectoral Council. The only error concerns Rous, for the editor seemed unclear whether Anthony or Francis sat during the Protectorate. It was, in fact, the aged Francis Rous who served from December 1653 to September 1658; his kinsman, Anthony, was never a member of the Protectoral Council.

like are described and the order books scanned for examples of the types of business handled by the council. But the crucial issue, the role of the council as a check upon the Single Person and its relationship with Cromwell, is all but ignored and the very hesitant conclusion is supported by no argument or cited evidence and was apparently lifted from Gardiner.[18] Some of the more recent accounts of the period have included valuable comments on the Council's role: Roots notes that the Council often met and worked in Cromwell's absence and apparently without his knowledge and he sees certain incidents, particularly the Councillors' refusal to admit the Jews, as illustrating the 'practical restraints' upon Cromwell;[19] Woolrych acknowledges that the constitutional restraints upon Cromwell 'would have meant little if the council had been an obedient rubber stamp or a junto of army officers, but it was neither. Its role in decision-making has often been underestimated. . .';[20] and Hirst sees in Cromwell's later comments to parliament strong indications that the Instrument's conciliar restraints had 'proved effective'.[21] Useful as they are, such brief assessments are no compensation for the lamentable absence of a detailed study of the Protectoral Council and its role in government. History is still apt to forget or ignore the Councillors.

II

So how were the three nations governed during the Protectorate? We are concerned here not with routine administration or the execution of policy at the local level, but with the mechanics and operation of central government, the machinery in Whitehall and Westminster which formulated policy for the three nations – for Scotland and Ireland as well as for England and Wales. (Although Scotland and Ireland had a form of devolved administration, with a governor and Council sitting in Edinburgh and Dublin, and although in 1655–7 certain policies were implemented throughout England and Wales by influential regional administrations headed by the major generals, policy making and overall control in all vital matters – and

---

18   E. R. Turner, *The Privy Council of England in the seventeenth and eighteenth centuries, 1603–1784* (2 vols., Baltimore, 1927), 1, chapters xii–xiii, particularly p. 325.

19   I. A. Roots, *The great rebellion* (London, 1966), pp. 171, 179.

20   A. H. Woolrych, *England without a king* (London, 1983), p. 31. The comment quoted contrasts with Woolrych's rather dismissive view of the Council's effectiveness – that although 'at first sight' the constitution appeared to give the Council wide powers with and over the Protector, 'appearances were to prove deceptive' – in *Commonwealth to Protectorate* (Oxford, 1982), pp. 369–70.

21   D. Hirst, *Authority and conflict. England, 1603–1658* (London, 1986), p. 318.

apparently in many trivial areas, too – always remained with the Protector, the Whitehall Council and the parliament.) The starting point for such a study must be the written constitutions, for they not only established the new regime but also laid down certain rules governing the roles and relationships of its constituent elements. The Instrument of Government of December 1653 and the Humble and Additional Petitions of May and June 1657 set forth a model system, the theoretical yardstick against which the practical operation of central government – and particularly of Protector and Council – can be assessed.

The Instrument of Government ended a decade or more of rather *ad hoc*, improvised government, during which a parliament or representative assembly, almost continually in session, had exercised both legislative and executive functions, the latter in part through a series of relatively weak parliamentary councils and committees. The new constitution separated the two arms of government once again, establishing a permanent, well-defined and largely independent executive and an assured, regular succession of parliaments entrusted with wide but far from boundless legislative powers. In an attempt to avoid renewed clashes between the two, the Instrument also laid out a series of checks and balances to encourage co-operation and to stop one arm exercising too much power by itself or attacking the foundations of the other. The two arms of government were drawn together by the Chief Magistrate, the Lord Protector, who worked with and oversaw both. Thus the first article of the Instrument laid down that 'the supreme' legislative authority . . . shall be and reside in one person, and the people assembled in Parliament' and article ii that 'the exercise of the chief magistracy and the administration of the government . . . shall be in the Lord Protector, assisted with a council'. Although the Humble and Additional Petitions later modified certain powers and procedures and generally placed more emphasis on the role of parliament, in these respects the foundations of government remained unaltered until 1659. Protectorate Britain was to be ruled by a separate legislature and executive, working in tandem under a Lord Protector.

Under the written constitutions parliaments were to meet every three years at most, to remain in session for at least a set minimum period, and to exercise apparently supreme and extensive legislative functions. During the session, the Single Person could exercise many of his powers only with parliament's approval and the legislature would have a prominent role in the future selection, approval and dismissal of Councillors. But despite the fine phrases and reassuring tone, even on paper parliament was to be far from omnipotent. The Instrument placed restrictions on electors and elected and gave the executive sweeping powers to exclude M.P.s from the house. Both the Instrument and the Humble Petition implicitly gave the Protector unlimited power to dissolve parliament whenever he chose, once the assured minimum period had expired, and the constitutions went on to make detailed arrangements for executive government during the intervals of parliament, which under the Instrument could amount to 31 in any 36 months. Even the appearance of legislative omnipotence was illusory, for not only were Protector and Council given wide powers to legislate during the opening months of the Protectorate, but also parliament itself possessed distinctly limited legislative rights. The Instrument empowered the Protector to veto any bills which in his sole and unquestionable opinion ran counter to the constitution, a potentially massive restriction on parliament's legislative powers. The Humble and Additional Petitions made no mention of the negative voice, presumably leaving Cromwell an unlimited veto. In short, the Protectoral parliaments were to hold only limited legislative powers, were set about by potentially severe restrictions and held a rather weak position within government, markedly inferior to the executive.

The Protectoral executive was headed by a Single Person, the very conspicuous Chief Magistrate of the three nations. Cromwell's deliberately projected image as a powerful and at times dazzling Lord Protector, an image which encouraged accusations of despotism and tyranny, was based on sound foundations. Certainly, parliament could have limited control over an officer appointed for life, removable only by death and possessed of a large standing army and a reasonable annual income, neither of which could be reduced by the legislature. He was largely beyond the reach of a body which he could dissolve at whim after its minimum lifespan had expired, which need be in session for only a few months every three years and whose legislation he had an absolute power to veto. Moreover, Cromwell's position as Lord General of a large standing army gave him a huge power base which, although at times proving something of a mill-stone, could enable him to over-ride constitutional niceties should need arise.

Yet despite the immense military potential of his position, Cromwell's constitutional role was far from unfettered; despite the glitter and appearance of unlimited power surrounding the office of Protector, the written constitutions gave Cromwell anything but absolute power. According to the Instrument all documents were to run in the Protector's name and all magistracy and honours were 'derived' from him; he could pardon most crimes and delay or veto parliamentary bills; the final choice of a new Councillor would be his, though from a shortlist of two selected by others; existing public lands were 'vested' in him and his successor; a drafting error seems to have given him sole power to 'dispose and order' the regular armed forces in the intervals of parliament; and the power to dissolve parliament was presumably his. The Humble and Additional Petitions modified some of these provisions, though in the end the powers of the Chief Magistrate remained almost as limited as before. Cromwell was to name his successor, nominate and summon the founder-members of the 'other house' and select the first members of the new privy council; the Protector was to summon parliament 'whenever the affairs of the nation shall require', provided one was called every three years at most; the powers to pardon offences, dissolve parliament, veto legislation and command the trained bands were not mentioned but presumably were vested in the Protector. Crucial as some of these powers were, many vital areas of government, particularly control over finance, the armed forces or appointment to senior offices of state, lay almost entirely beyond the reach of the Chief Magistrate alone. The Protector could dominate the legislature, but elsewhere the impressive outward appearance was scarcely matched by constitutional substance. The powers which the constitutions bestowed upon the Lord Protector and which he could exercise alone do not amount to an adequate, workable executive; still less did they anoint Cromwell the unbridled tyrant of tradition.

Just as co-operation between Protector and parliament was essential for the legislature to function effectively, so the constitutions stressed that the Protector would have to work very closely with the Council if there was to be a powerful or adequate executive. The Council, 'the keystone of the newly-flung-up arch of government',[22] filled the void left by the weakness of both the legislature and the Single Person, enabling the system not merely to operate but, the drafters hoped, operate safely. Under the Instrument the Council possessed a few important powers of its own – to examine and exclude M.P.s, reduce a shortlist of candidates for Council vacancies and elect a new Protector on the death of the old – which it later lost under the Humble Petition. But the Council's principal role throughout the period was as a check upon the Single Person and its real power lay in its ability to prevent the Protector acting in a whole range of fields unless he first obtained its advice and consent. Some conciliar checks operated at all times, others only during the intervals of parliament.

Like the king's privy councillors before them, the Protectoral Councillors were to serve as general advisers to the Single Person, offering counsel and assistance in all aspects of government. But they were to be very much more than that, for in many areas of government the Protector could not act unless he first obtained their consent. Some of these were quite minor – the allocation of parliamentary seats in Scotland and Ireland, for example – and others, particularly the 'extraordinary' powers given to the executive during the opening nine months of the regime, were temporary and soon lapsed. The Humble and Additional Petitions laid less stress on the Council's restraining role than the earlier constitution and some of the powers formerly given to Protector and Council jointly, including the declaration of

22   Roots, *The great rebellion*, p. 171.

war and peace and control over the local militias during the intervals of parliament, were left to the Protector alone. The precise intentions of several provisions are obscured by vague or contradictory phraseology. Nonetheless, the principal aim of the constitutions is quite clear and remained consistent throughout the period. The Protector alone was to possess limited and narrowly defined powers and in most areas of government, from fairly minor matters to the crucial functions of controlling finance, the regular forces or the militias and appointing senior officers of state, he could act only with the consent of his Councillors. It was left to Protector and Council to work out detailed procedures and routines and to establish the daily mechanisms by which conciliar advice and consent would be sought, tendered and received.

The Protectoral Council was to be a stable, permanent and very powerful body, almost entirely independent of the legislature and at the height of its powers during the intervals between parliamentary sessions. Thus it was entirely different from the succession of committees and councils of state of the decade up to December 1653, weak and short-lived bodies, dependent for their powers and very existence upon the ever-present legislature. It more closely resembled the royal privy council, the permanent body which advised the monarch in almost every aspect of government and was independent of the parliaments which met from time to time. But there were crucial differences, for where the king was free to ignore his council altogether or to disregard its advice, the Protector was often constitutionally bound to seek and obtain conciliar consent. Moreover, the king could appoint and dismiss privy councillors at will and thereby build up a group of like-minded malleable servants. If the Protector could have done likewise, the whole restrictive, supervisory role of the Council would have been meaningless. In fact, the constitutions went to some lengths to ensure that the Council would be largely independent not only of parliament but also of the Protector's influence. True, Cromwell probably helped select the Councillors named in article xxv of the Instrument and the Humble Petition left him free to choose the founder-members of the new privy council, subject to a predetermined minimum and maximum size. Thereafter, however, the Instrument directed that the Protector fill any vacancies from a shortlist of two drawn up by Council and parliament, the Humble Petition that new appointees be examined, approved or rejected by parliament. Vacancies were in any case likely to be infrequent, for a Councillor held office for life and was removable only by death or conviction for 'corruption or other miscarriage', either proved before a joint board of Councillors and M.P.s on which the Protector had no seat or approved by both houses of parliament. On paper, at least, the constitutions placed Cromwell under the tight supervision of a powerful and independent body of Councillors with wide powers to control and constrain the Single Person.

III

Unfortunately, the practical implementation of these provisions is partly concealed by a shroud of secrecy and ignorance. 'In spite of all my diligence', complained the Venetian ambassador in autumn 1654, 'it is incredibly difficult to discover the secrets of this government'.[23] 'Certainly', wrote Sagredo in the following year,

> no government on earth discloses its own acts less ... than that of England. They meet in a room approached through others, without number, and countless doors are shut. That which favours their interest best is that very few persons, at most sixteen, meet to digest the gravest affairs and come to the most serious decisions.[24]

While Cromwell played out his official duties as Protector in the public eye, his actions well-recorded both in his own letters and speeches and in many other contemporary accounts, he and his Councillors, Sagredo's sixteen men sitting behind closed doors, met and conducted business in such secrecy that even experienced diplomats found it all but impossible to discover 'the true substance of their deliberations'.[25] The secrecy and corresponding dearth of evidence surrounding the Councillors' activities not only create the impression that they were politically insignificant, particularly when compared to the Protector, but also make it difficult to uncover the inner workings of Protectoral government and accurately to assess the role and relationship of Cromwell and his Council.

Unable to penetrate the cloak of secrecy, most contemporary commentators simply ignored the Council's work. Bereft of factual information concerning the inner workings of government, foreign diplomats in London often turned to wild and unsubstantiated rumour, blended with expressions of despair and ignorance, current scandal and frequently unreliable interpretation, if not pure invention. Bordeaux was something of an exception, better informed than most, and his dispatches to Paris, recording only the strongest rumours and occasionally containing accurate accounts of events in Council, may have been based upon inside information.[26] English commentators, including Ludlow, Whitelock and Clarke's correspondents, were generally as ignorant of conciliar affairs as their foreign counterparts, and

23 *Calendar of State Papers and manuscripts relating to English affairs in the archives and collections of Venice and other libraries of north Italy* [hereafter *C.S.P.Ven.*], xxix–xxxi, ed. A. B. Hinds (London, 1929–31), xxix, p. 251.
24 *C.S.P.Ven.*, xxx, pp. 142–3.
25 Ibid.
26 Nineteenth-century transcripts of Bordeaux's letters are at P[ublic] R[ecord] O[ffice, London], P.R.O., 31/3/92–102.

they merely noted the Council's public actions, reporting without comment the appearance of a printed ordinance or the reception of an ambassador, and becoming fuller only on the rare occasions when they or their colleagues were called before the Council for congratulation, condemnation or interrogation.[27] The London newspapers concentrated on 'safe' issues, mainly foreign and non-political domestic news, and their brief and uncritical accounts of political events in England reveal very little. Council meetings are frequently noted, sometimes with additional information such as the time or duration of the meeting or a bare list of the main decisions reached, but even *Severall Proceedings of State Affairs*, which contained by far the fullest and most regular reports of the Council, gave few details of its role or functions. The surviving letters and papers of the Councillors themselves are almost as uninformative, for they were all depressingly discreet on paper. Many have apparently left nothing more than a few papers, now widely scattered, and the collections which have survived – including those of Ashley Cooper, Jones, Lisle, Maijor, Montagu, Sydenham and possibly Strickland – are dominated by family and estate papers and contain very little of a political nature from the Protectorate period. Even Thurloe's massive and wide-ranging collection reveals far less about the Council than its sheer volume might suggest. The Councillors strictly upheld the secrecy which surrounded their office and their correspondence is searched in vain for 'behind the scenes' accounts of the Council at work.

With little information available elsewhere, we are forced to rely heavily upon the official conciliar records. Unfortunately, these provide a partial and distorted picture of the Council's work and its relationship with the Protector. Council meetings were recorded in a series of draft and fair order books, the notes of each session headed by the date, an indication of time and venue if appropriate and the names of those present, followed by a list of decisions reached and orders issued.[28] It is, however, quite clear that these books carry an incomplete record of meetings, business and decisions. Suspicions are aroused by references to Council committees whose initial appointment is nowhere recorded and by meetings at which only one or two very minor decisions are noted.[29] A wealth of evidence indicates that the Council was deeply involved in running foreign affairs throughout the Protectorate, in summoning parliament in 1656 and in excluding M.P.s in

27   *Memoirs of Edmund Ludlow*, ed. C. H. Firth (2 vols., Oxford, 1894); B. Whitelock, *Memorials of the English affairs* (London, 1682); the Clarke manuscripts at Worcester College, Oxford, particularly the newsletters in vols. xxv–xxx, available on microfilm (Harvester Press, 1979); many are printed in *The Clarke papers*, ed. C. H. Firth (4 vols., London, 1891–1901).
28   P.R.O., SP25/47–60, 73–8.
29   For example, the order books claim that Cromwell and ten Councillors met on the afternoon of 12 June 1655 merely to warrant the payment of £100 to a private individual, P.R.O., SP25/76, fo. 120.

1654 and 1656, but such matters are rarely mentioned in the official records. Presumably the Councillors deemed it unwise to commit to paper confidential or politically compromising decisions, particularly to one transcribed and viewed by numerous under-clerks. Many diplomatic and military directives, including a series concerning the western design and fleet movements in 1654–5, were deliberately omitted from the official records and survive only as fair copies on separate sheets of paper.[30] Although on one occasion the order books note that 'the orders of this day are all entered into the private book',[31] perhaps the 'secret book of Resolutions . . . by his Highnesse and the Council' referred to in 1654,[32] the official records usually give no indication that orders had been suppressed.

The confidential directives also reveal that records of whole meetings were omitted from the order books, for the survival of a secret order of 26 February 1655[33] is the only indication that the Council assembled on that day. The order books may occasionally point to their own deficiencies, noting an order for a further session that afternoon or on the following day but then carrying no record of this second meeting. Councillors occasionally completed and dispatched official letters, and on almost fifty occasions President Lawrence and six of his colleagues, a Council quorum, assembled to sign money warrants, on days when no meetings are recorded in the order books.[34] The newspapers, particularly *Severall Proceedings of State Affairs*, reported private and informal meetings of Cromwell and his Councillors, sometimes on days when the order books record no meeting, sometimes in addition to the official, recorded session. Although the demise of most newspapers in 1655 ends such reports, other sources, including the French and Venetian ambassadors and Clarke's correspondents, suggest that the informal meetings continued, noting that Cromwell and his Councillors met and transacted business at Hampton Court on several weekends during 1655–7; not until the last weeks of Cromwell's life do the order books begin recording official sessions at Hampton Court. Indeed, there were very many occasions – public functions, days of fasting and prayer, and daily life in and around Whitehall Palace – entirely unrecorded in the official papers on which Cromwell and his Councillors met and had the opportunity to discuss and transact business.

The order books are just that – records of orders passed at meetings, not minutes of those meetings – and there is no mention of the debates and divisions which preceded decisions or of discussions which failed to produce a specific order of some kind. There survives a single report of a Council

---

30   P.R.O., SP18/72/10, 30; SP18/94/95, 97; SP18/98/18; SP18/100/119; SP18/101/59a.
31   P.R.O., SP25/76, fo. 54. No such volume is known to survive.
32   Bodl. Lib., Rawlinson MS A15, fo. 105.
33   P.R.O., SP18/94/97.
34   The money warrants are at P.R.O., SP25/105–6.

meeting, a paper of dubious veracity relating a highly stylized and probably atypical exchange between Cromwell and Lambert,[35] and we remain in almost total ignorance of the content and manner of Council debates. Much business was transacted in committees which, with one exception,[36] have left no formal record of the proceedings. The other official records, including volumes containing warrants, lists of committees,[37] and notes on petitions,[38] and the copies of letters, proclamations and other conciliar documents entered in the fair order books and in separate copybooks,[39] throw further uncertain light on the Council's role. Out of these formal records and the mass of rough notes, semi-legible drafts, internal memoranda, scribbled endorsements and the like which passed through the hands of Cromwell and his Councillors and which are preserved in the Public Record Office,[40] it is possible to reconstruct much of their work, procedures and relationships. But it is a daunting task.

IV

Although the order books tend to portray the Council as an outwardly impressive body which spent its time in rather limited administrative duties, never quite fulfilling the role ascribed to it under the constitutions, other conciliar and non-conciliar records make clear that in reality no aspect of government, trivial or important, was beyond its scope. The Councillors played a large part in every field of Protectoral government and handled an almost overwhelming quantity and variety of business. Certainly, the Councillors oversaw routine administration and the day-to-day governance of the state and throughout the Protectorate they devoted a surprising amount of time to quite minor business, much of it of a private or local

---

35   The paper is in Montagu's nautical journal at Mapperton, Dorset, vol. 1, fos. 55–7, printed with minor errors in *The Clarke papers*, III, 207–8. Although it is in Montagu's hand, he was in fact absent from the meeting of 20 July 1654 which he purports to describe. A second paper, in vol. 1, fos. 49–55 of the journal and printed in *The Clarke papers*, III, 203–6, is a review of the causes of the western design and is dated 20 Apr. 1654; there is no record in the order books of a meeting on that day and, despite the title added by Firth, the original document nowhere claims to be an account or summary of a Council debate.

36   P.R.O., SP25/124.

37   P.R.O., SP25/121–2.

38   P.R.O., SP25/92–3.

39   P.R.O., SP25/73–8.

40   The miscellaneous papers have been arranged in chronological order and bound in a series of large volumes at P.R.O., SP18/42, 65–77, 94–102, 123–31, 153–57a, 179–82. These papers complement but are completely different in origin or nature from the order books and other official Council records at P.R.O., SP25. The *C.S.P.D.* not only calendars this material in a partial and sometimes faulty manner but also runs these two essentially different sources together in an often indiscriminate and potentially misleading way.

nature, supervising the actions of subordinate government departments and officials, receiving complaints and appeals from all quarters, handling difficult cases and dealing with an unending flow of petitions. But the Councillors also handled the very highest affairs of state, including the military and political settlement of Scotland and Ireland, state finance, the establishment or reform of religious and legal procedures, national security, the summoning, purging and management of parliaments and the development of foreign policy. When in March 1654 the Dutch representatives were presented with a paper agreeing to certain terms in the prospective peace treaty, signed by Cromwell alone, they indignantly returned it, 'not considering it valid, and insisting on having it signed in a clearer form by the Council of State'.[41] Despite their shortcomings, the surviving sources strongly indicate that all aspects of government, from the highest to the lowest, from national and international affairs to private and local issues, were discussed at the Council table.

From time to time illness or other causes forced Cromwell to miss all or most of the formal, recorded Council sessions for periods of a month or more. Very occasionally important business was deferred until Cromwell's return – the preparation of commissions and instructions for the major generals in August and September 1655, for example. Usually, however, Cromwell's prolonged absences had no perceptible impact on the range or quantity of business coming before the Council. Important Council directives had to gain the Protector's assent and there is no doubt that Cromwell retained ultimate control; decisions taken in his absence were often ineffective until so approved and he would return to find a backlog of orders awaiting approval. But the important point is that the Council nevertheless pressed on, examined an undiminished range of business and took important decisions, apparently unhindered by Cromwell's long absence; such decisions were invariably approved by the Protector on his return, without further delay, renewed discussion or any amendment. Again, the order books suggest that the task of initiating, drafting and amending the ordinances of 1653–4 was undertaken largely by the Council. Although Cromwell could and very occasionally did veto completed legislation or return it for further consideration, in practice he almost always accepted and passed the Council's ordinances without hesitation or alteration. Such conduct seems inconsistent with the representation of Cromwell as a boundless autocrat and his Council as a politically impotent puppet.

In marked contrast to these occasional periods of prolonged absence and indications of limited participation, during most of his 56 months in office Cromwell was clearly working very closely with his Council. He was present at 332 (or around forty per cent) of the 813 official sessions recorded in the

41   C.S.P.Ven., xxix, p. 197.

order books.[42] Although his attendance was surprisingly poor during 1654 and fell away markedly from mid-1657, presumably due to ill health, he attended well over half the meetings recorded in 1655, missing only eight of the 54 sessions held during the last three months of the year, and his attendance fell only slightly during 1656. Most formal sessions, morning or afternoon, lasted three to four hours, but the newspapers and other sources indicate that some went on far longer. For example, the single meeting on 1 June 1655 apparently lasted most of the day and Protector and Council 'sate late in the afternoon and did not rise to dinner'.[43] On 2 August 1655, when Cromwell and his Councillors held two separate meetings, they sat 'all day [with] only a very little time for dinner about 2 a clocke'[44] and must have been in session for a total of nine or ten hours. Several afternoon meetings attended by Cromwell went on well into the evening, to 9 p.m. or even later.[45] In addition, contemporaries indicate that Cromwell invariably attended the informal Council meetings at Whitehall and Hampton Court; indeed, one suspects that they were initiated by the Protector for the purpose of being briefed on current business or holding private and unminuted discussions with his Councillors. Evidence of Cromwell's long and frequent consultations with his Councillors does not, of course, prove that he accepted and acted upon their advice, still less that he was seeking conciliar approval or experiencing conciliar restraints. It is, however, a further strong indication that the image of the autocratic potentate ignoring or manipulating a set of pawns is fundamentally wrong.

Some of Cromwell's own comments on his constitutional position and the conciliar restraints have been preserved. Several times he referred to his unease when the departure of established governments in April and December 1653 left almost total and potentially very dangerous and corrupting power in his hands. Initially, at least, he welcomed the adoption of new systems which removed or reduced that power.[46] In a long oration to parliament on 12 September 1654 he reviewed recent history, stressing the tight restrictions placed upon him by the written constitution, which 'limited me and bound my hands to act nothing to the prejudice of the nations without consent of a Council until the parliament'. He was emphatic that these provisions had been strictly observed during

42　The tables of Council meetings and attendances printed in *C.S.P.D.* are often at fault; the figures quoted here are drawn from the fair and draft order books.

43　*Perfect proceedings of state affairs*, 31 May–7 June 1655.

44　Ibid. 2–9 Aug. 1655.

45　See, for example, the report of the meeting of 4 May 1654 in ibid. 4–11 May 1654.

46　For Cromwell's unease after the expulsion of the Rump see *Memoirs of Edmund Ludlow*, I, p. 358. The relief with which he handed over power to the Nominated Assembly in July and welcomed the advent of a firm constitutional framework in Dec. 1653 come over in his speeches to parliament in Sep. 1654, W. C. Abbott, *The writings and speeches of Oliver Cromwell* (4 vols., Cambridge, Mass., 1937–47), III, pp. 434–43, 451–63.

the opening months of the Protectorate – 'this government hath been exercised by a Council, with a desire to be faithful in all things' – and underlined the crucial role which the Council played, particularly when parliament was not sitting:

> the Council are the trustees of the Commonwealth, in all intervals of Parliaments, who have as absolute a negative upon the supreme officer in the said intervals, as the Parliament hath whilst it is sitting; . . . there is very little power, none but what is coordinate, in the supreme officer; . . . he is bound in strictness by the Parliament, out of Parliament by the Council.[47]

His speech at the opening of the 1656 parliament was concerned with policies, not the mechanics of government, and contained no explicit assertion of conciliar powers. Cromwell did, however, consistently use the first person plural when reviewing government actions, not in this case the royal 'we', but an almost unconscious recognition of the Councillors' close co-operation. Halfway through the speech, when discussing the imposition of decimation, he suddenly realised that his audience may not have understood the reference: 'We did find out – I mean, myself and the Council – . . .'.[48] Seven months later a parliamentary committee was treated to a second history lesson, in the course of which Cromwell commented, 'I was a child in its [the army's? the Instrument's?] swaddling clouts. I cannot transgress. By the government, I can do nothing but in ordination with the Council'.[49]

Such statements could have been hypocrisy and deception, convenient fictions to impress M.P.s and others. Similarly, Cromwell may have portrayed a false image of the power of the Council to cover his own failures to fulfil pledges, to remove obstructions from episcopal clergy in and around London – 'having advised with his Council about it . . . they thought it not safe for him to grant liberty of Conscience to those sort of men'[50] – and to abolish tithes by September 1654 – 'for his part, he could not do it, for he was but one, and his Council alledge it is not fitt to take them away'.[51] If so, the duplicity surrounding the Council's role ran very deep and apparently extended to self-deception. Two of the most important conciliar restraints imposed upon the Single Person by the 1657 constitution were not contained within the Humble Petition and Advice of 25 May. Instead they sprang from a 'paper of objections', a list of suggested revisions and additions to the constitution, submitted to parliament, accepted by the house and embodied in the Additional Petition of 26 June. The paper is in

---

47   Abbott, *Writings and speeches*, III, pp. 455, 460.
48   Ibid. IV, p. 269.
49   Ibid. IV, p. 488.
50   R. Parr, *The life of the most reverend father in God, James Ussher, late Lord archbishop of Armagh* (London, 1686), p. 75.
51   *The Clarke papers*, II, pp. xxxiv–xxxvii.

Thurloe's hand, but it carries many corrections and additions penned by Cromwell and the document was probably initiated and compiled by the Protector. It was Cromwell, therefore, who suggested that during the intervals of parliament, the Protector should require the Council's consent before making appointments to a number of senior offices of state. Nowhere had the Humble Petition empowered the Council to supervise state finance and the Protector's use of the military budget, and it was Cromwell's paper which first suggested that 'the money directed for supply of the sea and land forces be issued by *the advice of the Council*', a provision duly embodied in the Additional Petition.[52] On 21 April, in a speech to a parliamentary committee outlining his suggested revisions, the Protector had spoken at length about state finance, commenting 'it will be a safety to whomsoever is your supreme Magistrate, as well as security to the public, that the monies might be issued out by the advice of the Council'.[53] Once more, Cromwell appears uneasy, almost fearful, at the prospect of exercising wide and potentially corrupting political power.

Neither of Cromwell's Protectoral parliaments seems to have viewed conciliar restraints on the Single Person as a worthless sham. The 1654 parliament was mildly purged, but it remained strongly critical of the Instrument and M.P.s devoted much of the session to devising a written constitution of their own. The Government Bill retained the concept of an advisory and restraining Council, though, in line with the general aim of advancing parliamentary controls, Councillors were now to be appointed, reappointed or dismissed by each succeeding parliament. The Council would continue to supervise the Protector and, at all times or during the intervals of parliament, would possess joint control over finance, appointment to senior offices, foreign policy, diplomacy and the conclusion of peace; while Cromwell lived, it also had joint control over the standing forces.[54] Clearly, nine months' experience of seeing Cromwell and his Council in action had not shaken the M.P.s' faith in conciliar restraints as an effective, necessary and workable constitutional safeguard. Over two years later an admittedly quite heavily purged house felt much the same, and Cromwell's suggestions embodied in the Additional Petition merely strengthened the already extensive supervisory role ascribed to the Council in the final version of the Humble Petition. The Council's powers had already been strengthened considerably during March in the course of debates on the draft constitution, originally titled the

52 Text and notes in Abbott, *Writings and speeches*, IV, pp. 498–500; certain phrases have been underlined in the original manuscript.
53 Ibid. IV, p. 492.
54 S. R. Gardiner, *Constitutional documents of the Puritan revolution, 1625–1660* (Oxford, 1906 edn), pp. 427–47.

Remonstrance.[55] The diaries and other accounts of the two parliaments record no sweeping attacks on the Council, no under-current of hostility or scepticism of its role, no broad condemnation of the conciliar restraints on the Protector as an ineffective and empty façade.[56]

V

A clearer, sharper picture of the Council's role and its relations with the Protector can be built up only by a close study of the manner in which specific items of business were handled by the executive. To examine in detail scores if not hundreds of individual cases is clearly impossible here and instead just three items of business will be followed, though three of the most important issues of the whole Protectorate.

Article xxi of the Instrument authorized the Council to examine newly elected M.P.s and exclude from the house those not qualified under the constitution. This was one of very few powers given to the Councillors alone and, in theory at least, the Protector had no say in the matter. The exclusion of elected members was a sensitive business and was largely omitted from the order books, but a comparative abundance of conciliar and other sources indicate that in practice it was the Council which excluded M.P.s and that Cromwell took little or no part in the process. In 1654 the Councillors used their powers very sparingly, excluding less than a dozen clearly unqualified members. Cromwell apparently played no part in the proceedings and, although the results aroused little controversy or comment at the time, he was nonetheless careful to distance himself from the Council's handiwork.[57]

In September 1656 the terms of the constitution were employed to devastating effect to bar around 100 political opponents and undesirables from the house. Although the order books rarely mention exclusions, they do record a Council order of 15 September to exclude Charles Hussey, M.P. for Lincolnshire, and a request of 28 August that all Councillors in and around London attend Council to dispatch important (but unspecified) business concerning the forthcoming parliament. The frequent and well-attended Council meetings of early to mid September were probably given over to examining the written and oral evidence against M.P.s submitted by the

55   The original or very early draft of the remonstrance is at Worcester College, Clarke MS xxix and Bodl. Lib., Clarendon MS 54. The debate and amendments can be followed in C[ommons] J[ournal] (London, n.d.), vii, pp. 496–535.

56   Diary of Thomas Burton, esquire, ed. J. T. Rutt (4 vols., London, 1828); vols. i and ii contain Goddard's diary of the 1654 parliament and Burton's of the session of 1656–7.

57   For full details of the 1654 exclusions and the sources upon which these statements are based see my 'Cromwell's purge? Exclusions and the first Protectorate parliament', Parliamentary History, 6, part i (1987), pp. 1–22.

major generals and their agents.[58] No-one was better placed than Thurloe to know the truth, and on 16 September he wrote that 'the councell, upon consideration of the elections, have refused to admitt of neare 100 of those, who are chosen'.[59] Once the session opened, M.P.s attacked the Council for the exclusions and called on Councillors to explain their actions. In the course of defending exclusions in the house on 22 September, Councillor Fiennes repeatedly stressed that the action had been taken by the Council – the Council was empowered to do this, the Council had examined and excluded M.P.s, the Council had taken care to exclude no-one unfairly – and made no mention of the Protector being involved in any way. Excluded members were subsequently directed to appeal to the Council for admission and in due course the Councillors did review and reverse several exclusion orders.[60]

In truth, Cromwell seems to have played no part in exclusions and to have been disturbed by their extent. On 9 September Thurloe directed Henry Cromwell to detain and thus exclude an Irish M.P., calmly adding in passing 'I have not had tyme to acquaint his Highness with it'.[61] In his angry outburst to the army officers on 27 February 1657 Cromwell was bitterly scornful of the mass exclusions and stressed that he had had no part in them, though surviving accounts of the speech have him ascribing responsibility to the officers themselves rather than to the Council.[62] Perhaps George Courthope is more accurate when he reports Cromwell's declaration in spring 1657 that exclusion 'was an act of the Council's, and that he did not concern himself in it'.[63] Certainly, Cromwell had been absent from most

---

58   C.S.P.D., x, 1650–7, pp. 90, 109–10; P.R.O., SP25/75, fos. 350–400; A collection of the state papers of John Thurloe, esquire [hereafter T.S.P.], ed. T. Birch (7 vols., London, 1742), v, passim.

59   T.S.P., v, p. 424. See also an undated note, drawn up by Thurloe, confirming that the Councillors had completed the task and fulfilled their constitutional obligations by examining and excluding M.P.s and that they stood 'ready to give an account of their proceedings thereupon, when they shall be required thereunto by his Highness or the parliament', T.S.P., v, p. 426.

60   C.J., vii, pp. 424–6. For the speedy reversal of Salisbury's and Lucy's exclusions see Worcester College, Clarke MS xxviii, fo. 76v.

61   T.S.P., v, p. 398. Thurloe later confirmed in the house that the M.P. in question, John Davies, had been excluded and denounced him as unfit: 'I hope I shall never see him sit within these walls', Diary of Thomas Burton, ii, p. 269.

62   Abbott, Writings and speeches, iv, pp. 417–19. The speech as reported ascribes almost all the important political developments of 1653–7 to the army officers, including many which were undoubtedly discussed and decided by the Protectoral Council. It is not clear whether our reports are at fault or whether Cromwell lost control in what was clearly an angry and impassioned outburst and sought to blame everything on the officers. It was presumably this speech which led Kenyon in The Stuart constitution to ascribe Protectoral policy-making to a 'Council of Officers'.

63   Cromwell directed Courthope to President Lawrence, who gave him a very frosty reception. 'The Memoirs of Sir George Courthop', ed. S. C. Lomas, Camden Miscellany, xi (London, 1907), p. 141.

Council sessions during September 1656, including all those held in the week prior to the opening of parliament at which the exclusion orders had probably been issued.[64] It is tempting to see Cromwell's poor attendance at Council during September – present at just four of the nineteen meetings, compared with seventeen of the twenty-four held in July and August and fourteen of the seventeen held in October and November – as evidence of his distaste for, as well as non-involvement in, the process of mass exclusions pursued by his Council.

C. H. Firth described the meeting of the 1656 parliament as 'the turning-point in the history of the Protectorate'.[65] It was an 'additional' parliament, summoned under article xxiii of the Instrument by 'the Lord Protector, with the advice of the major part of the Council' in order to meet 'the necessities of the State'. The most pressing necessity in 1656 was money. The halving of monthly assessments between September 1654 and February 1655, the continuing decline in customs and excise returns and the escalating costs of the Spanish war had together turned the precarious inheritance of December 1653 into near bankruptcy by spring 1656. The constitution placed control of the state finances jointly in the hands of Protector and Council and throughout the Protectorate the Councillors handled all important financial business, working closely with the Protector to solve the regime's apparently unending financial troubles. They managed and ordered every aspect of central income and expenditure, from drafting and issuing the ordinances, proclamations and other directives under which money was collected to supervising the operation of the Treasury, from setting the level of assessments, customs and excise and other exactions to the desperate attempts to trim the military budget during 1655, involving the greater use of local militias, decimation on royalists and the appointment of a dozen major generals as overall regional administrators. But despite the Council's efforts, the regime plunged ever deeper into deficit and by early May 1656 Cromwell and his Councillors were holding a series of crisis meetings to discuss the looming financial disaster.

Cromwell was present at most of the frequent and well attended Council sessions of the first half of May and he and his Councillors also held a number of informal meetings around this time, including a Sunday session, a previously unheard-of occurrence. Despite the order books' silence, other sources reveal that Protector and Council were deeply divided over the various options available, with one group favouring summoning another parliament and laying the problem before the legislature, another, including Cromwell, fiercely opposed to it and advocating purely financial measures, the doubling of assessments, the extension of decimation or the imposition of forced

64   P.R.O., SP25/77, fos. 360–400.
65   C. H. Firth, *Last years of the Protectorate* (2 vols., London, 1909), I, p. 1.

loans. The arguments raged for over a month and although the Venetian ambassador's colourful tales – of Cromwell crying in Council and at one stage decamping to Hampton Court with his allies on the Council in order to get away from other members with whom relations were 'not quite cordial' – may owe much to imagination, it seems that feelings were running high; Thurloe and Fleetwood both speak of long and hot debates preceding the final decision. Cromwell initially favoured increasing assessments but that argument was lost by 9 May, when direction was given to draft an order continuing assessments at the existing rate. Thereafter Cromwell reportedly supported the extension of decimation and maintained that position for several weeks. Eventually, however, a clear majority on the Council came to support the parliamentary option and on or around 10 June Cromwell was persuaded to issue the writs. The major generals were also meeting in London at the time and doubtless their confidence in controlling the elections helped sway the argument, but Thurloe is quite specific that the decision to call a parliament had been taken by 'His Highness and the Counsell' and that the major generals had merely 'assented' to the decision.[66]

Once again, Cromwell's attendance record at Council may indicate something of his feelings towards the Councillors' decision. His repeated absences during June, missing seven of the ten meetings – in marked contrast to May, when he attended assiduously – may have been a response to the Council's rejection of his proposals for purely financial expedients and its insistence on a parliament.[67] That Cromwell had initially opposed a parliament but been rather unwillingly pushed into it by others certainly comes across in later angry outbursts. 'I gave my vote against it' and 'it was against my judgment, but I could have no quietness till [it] was done', he told the officers during his February 1657 tirade, again apparently laying the blame on the officers themselves.[68] But a year later, on 6 February 1658, he was more accurate in ascribing responsibility: '. . . as also of his calling this Parliament, whereunto, being advised by his Council, he yielded, though he professed it, in his own judgment, no way seasonable'.[69] 'He was against the calling of the late Parliament. But the Councell urged it soe'.[70] Puppet and puppeteer reversed?

66   C.S.P.D. 1655–6, passim; P.R.O., SP25/75; Worcester College, Clarke MS xxviii, fos. 29, 32v; The Clarke papers, iii, p. 67; Bodl. Lib., Carte MS 73, fo. 20; Bodl. Lib., Clarendon MS 51, fo. 309; T.S.P., iv, pp. 764–5; T.S.P., v, pp. 9, 19, 33, 45, 54, 63, 122, 176; C.S.P.Ven., xxx, pp. 221–41; B.L., Lansdowne MS 821, fos. 184–5; Historical manuscript commission: fifth report appendix (London, 1876), pp. 152, 180; see also Gardiner, History of the Commonwealth and Protectorate, iv, pp. 253–5.
67   P.R.O., SP25/77, fos. 92–212. Although Cromwell attended some of the major generals' meetings from late May onwards, it seems unlikely that this alone can fully explain such a dramatic fall in his attendances at Council.
68   Abbott, Writings and speeches, iv, pp. 417–19.
69   Ibid., iv, p. 736.
70   Letter quoted in D. Underdown, 'Cromwell and the officers, February 1658', English Historical Review, lxxxiii (1968), p. 107.

The premature dissolution of the second Protectorate parliament in February 1658 threw the regime into chaos and Cromwell's last months were spent searching for escape from financial disaster and looming constitutional crisis. The government had looked to the second session to cover its spiralling expenses but after barely a fortnight, and before a penny more had been voted, the turbulent session was brought to an ill-tempered close. Over the following weeks ministers reported that the debts were insurmountable and growing, that treasuries and reserves had been searched in vain, that the 'clamours . . . from land and sea' could not be answered and that affairs of state were grinding to a halt for lack of cash. The Secretary of State and several Councillors quickly concluded that the only solution was to summon another parliament; Thurloe hoped that the legislature would also counter threats to the regime at home and abroad. But although the calling of another parliament was under consideration in government circles by late February and although the financial situation continued to deteriorate, the writs were not issued until the end of the year, long after Oliver was dead and buried. A string of distractions – Cromwell's ill-health immediately after the dissolution, another conspiracy and the resulting treason trials, the onset of summer and the approach of the harvest – only partly explains the delay. In practice, the decision did not rest with Cromwell alone and from the outset the whole matter was referred to the Council, where it received long and repeated attention over the spring and summer. It was the failure of the Councillors to reach a clear decision and their bitter divisions on certain matters relating to the proposed parliament which delayed the writs for so long.[71]

Reliable and informed sources reveal the Council's central role in considering the financial problems and possible solutions during 1658. The letters of Thurloe and Fleetwood talk of long and complex debates in Council and of a vocal minority resisting the 'major part' who 'inclyne to a parliament'. Fearing that parliament would revise the constitution once more and suspecting that Cromwell had resolved to accept any renewed offer of the crown, the old opponents of monarchy felt that the only way to prevent its restoration was to avoid summoning another parliament for as long as possible. Where in 1657 the Council had split in half over the issue, by the following year the changes in membership and the altered stance of Fleetwood and possibly of other former opponents tipped the balance. But a strong minority remained bitterly opposed to any move towards kingship and, led by Disbrowe and Sydenham, they conducted an active campaign which delayed the decision for months. Finance and security were discussed

---

71   *T.S.P.*, vi, pp. 779, 786, 817, 820, 839–40, 871–2; *T.S.P.*, vii, pp. 21–2, 38, 99–100, 144. The whole matter is discussed by Firth, *Last years*, ii, pp. 257–80, and by R. C. H. Catterall, 'The failure of the Humble Petition and Advice', *American Historical Review*, ix, (1903–4) pp. 58–65. Catterall argues that by spring 1658 Cromwell had decided to accept any renewed offer of the crown.

time and again in Council and its committees and the minority opinion, that decimation on royalists and other non-parliamentary exactions should be imposed or reimposed, was at last overcome. Even then, a final decision was deferred indefinitely as the Councillors debated 'what to aske that Parliament and what to submitt unto', attempting to agree in advance a united stance and so avoid repetition of the bitter divisions which had racked the Council in 1657. At length Cromwell tried to break the deadlock by referring the question of 'what is fitt to be done in the next Parliament' to an entirely independent committee, but its report of 8 July was anodyne, contradictory and avoided the central issue of kingship. Within a week Cromwell had retired to Hampton Court to nurse his daughter's and then his own ill-health and no decision had been reached by 3 September. For almost six months urgent business of the highest import had been argued in Council, Cromwell remaining undecided, generally inactive and for the most part seemingly outside and irrelevant to the top-level debates. There is the unmistakable impression of the reins of government slipping from his hands as his health deteriorated from early 1658 onwards. Under the Humble Petition, he had not even been obliged to seek the Council's advice or consent on this matter in the first place.[72]

It would, of course, be as foolish to portray Cromwell as a servant of the Council as it would to disregard completely the overwhelming consensus of contemporary opinion. Stripped of embellishment and exaggeration, the seventeenth-century image of a very powerful Chief Magistrate dominating the Council undoubtedly contains a large element of truth. Cromwell clearly towered over the Protectorate and remained firmly in control of government, at least until his health finally broke in spring 1658. With a large standing army at his command, he could almost certainly have overridden the constitution and its paper restrictions at will. Even if he did not, in fact, openly resort to the sword to impose his wishes in central government during the Protectorate,[73] the knowledge that military force was available doubtless encouraged respect and some deference in parliament and Council alike. But the picture of Cromwell as an all-powerful, unfettered autocrat who knew no constitutional restraints, and of his Council as a politically impotent façade, overawed, manipulated or ignored by a tyrannical Protector, is fundamentally inaccurate. Despite the paucity of surviving evidence, there are clear indications that Cromwell usually observed the terms of the written constitutions, that he worked with his Council and

72　T.S.P., VII, pp. 21–2, 38, 56, 84–5, 99–100, 113, 144, 153, 158–9, 176–7, 192–4, 218, 269–70, 282, 294–5, 309, 354–6; The Clarke papers, III, p. 145. Cromwell attended just 19 of the 72 Council meetings recorded during 1658.
73　With the possible exception of his use of soldiers briefly to close the house on 12 Sep. 1654.

respected conciliar independence, even when he disapproved of its actions, that he advised with his Councillors, sought and obtained their consent where required and was occasionally deflected from his preferred path by their persuasion or prohibition, even in the most important matters of state or those over which he strongly disagreed with the conciliar consensus. Ultimately, Cromwell's references to the Council's vigour and independent resolve seem closer to the truth than Hobart's clever and colourful condemnation.

5

Oliver Cromwell and the Localities: The Problem of Consent

Anthony Fletcher

Originally appeared as Anthony Fletcher, 'Oliver Cromwell and the Localities: The Problem of Consent' in Colin Jones, Malyn Newitt and Stephen Roberts (ed.), *Politics and People in Revolutionary England.* Copyright 1986 Blackwell Publishers, Oxford.

Editor's Introduction

Cromwell's ambitions to turn England into a godly nation have been extensively analysed but, as Anthony Fletcher observes at the start of this essay, their impact in the localities, the extent to which they were enforced, and how far they commanded consent, have been much less fully researched. Fletcher addresses this problem by presenting a case study of one particular episode: the creation of the Major-Generals in 1655. He provides a fascinating insight into the many problems they faced and their attempts to overcome them.

Fletcher begins by noting how short-lived the Major-Generals experiment was. They were only fully in operation for about six months from October 1655, and the scheme had in effect collapsed in most parts of England and Wales well before Parliament's abolition of the Decimation Tax in January 1657 finally ended it. The Major-Generals were a diverse group united only by two traits: they were all Cromwell's men, dependent on the Lord Protector, and they were all driven by an intense religious zeal. Their careers rested on military service rather than inherited social status, and they did not come from within the traditional circles of county government.

The Major-Generals were created not only to tighten up security after the abortive Royalist Penruddock's Rising (March 1655), but also to implement a 'reformation of manners'. This goal of moral reform was particularly close to Cromwell's heart, and the instructions to the Major-Generals 'to encourage and promote godliness and virtue' probably owed much to the Lord Protector himself. Later, in September 1656, Cromwell claimed that the Major-Generals had been 'more effectual towards the discountenancing of vice and settling religion than anything done these 50 years'.

Fletcher assesses the validity of this claim, and concludes that the long-term impact of the Major-Generals in reforming local government was probably minimal. Although the assistance of effective commissioners could make a difference, as could personal attendance at local court sessions and good relations with the county bench, more lasting moral reform depended on a firm lead from the county elites. Yet the fact that the godly remained a minority within county society meant that such a lead was not forthcoming. It was not so much that the county gentry were openly hostile to attempts at moral reform as that they generally lacked Cromwell's strong sense of urgency.

Overall, provincial elites retained their hold on local government and justice, and central government failed to erode the authority of traditional offices such as the Justices of the Peace. Possibly the most unpopular aspect of the whole scheme was the Decimation Tax on former Royalists, which was widely regarded as a violation of the Rump Parliament's Act of Oblivion (February 1652). In the end, a combination of inertia, divisiveness and recrimination frustrated Cromwell's attempts to introduce the rule of the godly.

Oliver Cromwell and the Localities: The Problem of Consent

Anthony Fletcher

Historians have long recognized that the regime of Oliver Cromwell involved a particular kind of minority rule. Some have labelled it the rule 'of the saints' or 'of the godly'.[1] What matters in such a case, G. E. Aylmer remarked in his introduction to a set of essays on the Interregnum published in 1972, was 'not the size of the minority, but its morale and coherence and the degree of acceptance accorded it by the rest of the population'.[2] Surprisingly little work has appeared since Aylmer's essays on the nature and impact of the Cromwellian regime. There have been two PhD theses on the army and Cromwellian politics and administration and there is work in progress on the well-documented 1656 elections.[3] But the full studies we need of the enforcement of Cromwellian government and of the acceptability of the Protector's rule in the provinces remain to be written. All that will be attempted in this essay is a brief reassessment, as a pointer to the larger problem of consent, of one aspect of Cromwell's rule: the experiment of sending out the major-generals.[4]

It is worth emphasizing at the start how short-lived the major-generals scheme turned out to be. They went down into the counties in October 1655 and gave sustained attention to their duties for about six months.[5] Thereafter their engagement seems to have been generally more erratic. They were all in London on 21 May 1656 following a summons from the Protector to gather there, ostensibly for a review of their work. The meetings that were held developed into a wrangle over the financial crisis of the regime from which the major-generals emerged triumphant, persuading Cromwell to call a parliament to obtain money. The major-generals returned to their districts to manage the elections in late June or July,[6] but

---

1   For example, A. Woolrych in *The English Civil War and After*, ed. R. Parry (London, 1970), pp. 59–77.
2   G. E. Aylmer (ed.), *The Interregnum: The quest for Settlement, 1646–60* (London, 1972), pp. 27–8.
3   D. P. Massarella, 'The politics of the army, 1647–60', University of York PhD thesis, 1977; H. M. Reece, 'The military presence in England 1649–60', University of Oxford DPhil thesis, 1981.
4   For previous accounts of the scheme see I. Roots, 'Swordsmen and decimators' in Parry, *English Civil War and After*, pp. 78–92, and D. W. Rannie, 'Cromwell's major-generals', *English Historical Review*, X (1895).
5   *Thurloe State Papers*, IV, passim.
6   Massarella, 'Politics of the army', pp. 435–6.

they were back in London for the parliament in September. It is difficult to be certain how far the major-generals were actively concerning themselves in local government during the spring and summer of 1656. It should not be assumed that, because their spate of letters to John Thurloe slackens after a series of reports on the Lent assizes in March, those who no longer wrote were relaxing their efforts. Some at least were still indefatigable. James Berry reported on 26 April that he was 'going his circuit once more'; Charles Worsley told Thurloe, in a letter of 29 April, that he had held meetings at Preston the previous week from Tuesday till Saturday.[7] The Cheshire gentleman, Thomas Mainwaring, noted in his diary that he attended a meeting of the commissioners there, sitting under Worsley's chairmanship, in the second week of every month from November 1655 until June 1656.[8] Unfortunately this kind of specific evidence about meetings is exceptional. But the very real practical difficulties that the major-generals were encountering by the spring of 1656 in keeping their troops in harness must certainly have distracted them from day-to-day matters. William Goffe, forced to dismiss Colonel Busbridge's troop in Sussex in March for lack of funds, found himself involved in angry exchanges with Busbridge and his men.[9] Berry and Worsley were others who were having to deal with reductions in their militia troops around that time.[10] So far as the autumn of 1656 is concerned, the fact that the decimation tax was still then being levied in a number of counties and that major-generals were signing warrants for arrears of pay does not of course mean that their oversight of the provinces remained an effective reality.[11] The scheme had clearly collapsed in most areas several months before the vote on 29 January 1657 which, by rejecting the decimation tax, deprived the major-generals of the financial basis of their administration.[12]

'We have at last settled the major-generals all over England,' wrote Thurloe to Henry Cromwell in Ireland on 16 October 1655, 'the greatest creation of honours his highness hath made since his access to the government'. Listing the appointments, he went on to summarize the long and detailed instructions with which the chosen men had been sent out in a succinct statement: 'these are to command the forces within their several precincts and to see to the good government thereof.'[13] So what advantages and disadvantages did the major-generals take with them as they rode down

---

7   *Thurloe State Papers*, IV, pp. 742, 746.
8   J. S. Morrill, *Cheshire 1630–60* (Oxford, 1974), p. 284.
9   A. J. Fletcher, *A County Community in Peace and War: Sussex 1600–60* (London, 1975), p. 306.
10   *Thurloe State Papers*, IV, p. 742; Morrill, *Cheshire*, p. 278.
11   For example, A. Everitt, *The Community of Kent and the Great Rebellion* (Leicester, 1966), pp. 293–4; Fletcher, *A County Community*, p. 306.
12   C. H. Firth, *The Last Years of the Protectorate* (London, 1909), I, p. 125.
13   *Thurloe State Papers*, IV, p. 88.

into the shires? Their biggest handicap undoubtedly was that they were outsiders, not in the sense of birth, for most of them hailed from the areas to
which they were directed, but in the sense that they did not have a purchase
upon power in the districts it was intended they should rule. How far they
came from mean social backgrounds can be disputed. If Thomas Kelsey is
said to have been a button-maker and James Berry had served as a clerk
in a Shropshire ironworks, William Boteler was educated at Oundle and
Hezekiah Haynes came of an Essex family of minor gentry.[14] What mattered
was that these men's names were not names that counted in the circles of
those who by tradition and prescriptive right saw it as their responsibility to
govern in the counties concerned. Their qualification was service, not
status. They were military careerists who had risen to prominence by their
vigour and commitment to the parliamentarian cause. Only William Boteler
had never commanded a regiment of his own, but he could offer valuable
civilian experience as a JP and government agent during the early 1650s in
Northamptonshire and Bristol. Several others – Thomas Kelsey, William
Goffe, John Barkstead and Charles Worsley – had been active in army
administration. Berry, it was alleged, helped John Lambert draw up the
Instrument of Government.[15] Above all, these men were Cromwell's men.
That is, they identified themselves with him, trusted him, leaned upon him.
'The Lord give me a heart to answer his goodness towards me and make me
able to answer the expectations of his highness and council,' wrote Kelsey
on 20 November 1655. A few days later Berry asked Thurloe to tell the
Protector that though his business was 'toilsome and tedious to me, and
indeed somewhat chargeable', yet he would 'go on with comfort and confidence, hoping for the assistance of God and his highness acceptation'.[16]

The major-generals' sense of urgency, based on the knowledge that they
were serving a demanding and expectant master, was reinforced by their
intense faith. They shared Cromwell's zeal, his belief in God's mission for
England as a protestant nation, his conviction that providence led the godly
on.[17] There is perhaps no better insight into their mentality than Berry's
account of his conciliatory talk with the Welsh Fifth Monarchist Vavasour
Powell:

I told him with what confidence I came forth in this work, as sent of God:
and that my heart had been towards those poor people in Wales, and

14 Parry, *English Civil War and After*, pp. 83, 91; W. L. F. Nuttall, 'Hezekiah Haynes',
Transactions of the Essex Archaeological Society, 1 (1964), p. 196.
15 Massarella, 'Politics of the army', pp. 427–9; P. H. Hardacre, 'William Boteler: a
Cromwellian oligarch', *Huntington Library Quarterly*, 1 (1947), p. 4.
16 *Thurloe State Papers*, IV, pp. 225, 237.
17 A. J. Fletcher, 'The religious motivation of Cromwell's major-generals', in *Religious
Motivation: Biographical and sociological problems for the church historian*, ed. D. Baker, Studies
in Church History, XV (1978).

> particularly I did expect help and encouragement from him and his people
> and did not doubt that we should come to a right understanding of each
> other and I should prove useful to them for the obtaining of much good.[18]

Yet for all this general unanimity of purpose, the major-generals were a het-
erogeneous collection of men, differing in their politics and temperaments.
Ivan Roots has noted how strikingly this appears from the record of their
contributions to the parliamentary debates on the punishment of the
Quaker James Nayler.[19] Out in the provinces, faced with the tangles and
thickets of local politics, some proved of stronger mettle than others.
Nothing daunted Charles Worsley or Edward Whalley, but William Goffe at
times became pathetic. He was too weak for 'this difficult affair'; he was
a 'poor and inconsiderable creature'; he was 'in many respects unworthy
of the employment'. The unnerving aspect of a major-general's task, the
testing of men's reactions with which the work had to begin, comes into
clear focus with Goffe's heartfelt comment from Chichester on 13 November: 'I do not know the hearts of men but I thank God I have not wanted
the civil respects of all sorts of persons with whom yet I have had to do'.[20]

There must have been a good deal of trepidation, both in London and in
the minds of the major-generals themselves, as they arranged their first
meetings to call in royalist or allegedly royalist gentry in order to receive
particulars of their estates as a basis for imposing the decimation tax. This,
after all, was a fiscal expedient of a designedly political nature which was
bound to seem provocative to enemies of the Cromwellian regime. It could
be expected to open old wounds in local society. Several of the major-
generals seem to have found considerable encouragement in the first stage
of their work in the deference and quietness with which cavaliers submitted to their demands. 'Our business goes on very well,' declared Edward
Whalley on 14 November, after a busy session with Lincolnshire royalists.
Goffe was evidently pleasantly surprised that Sir William Morley, who
insisted that he took it very much to heart that he should be still reckoned
malignant 'having long been satisfied of the justness of our cause', had
nevertheless consented to be taxed for an estate of £1,500 per annum.
Haynes was delighted how smoothly things had gone in Norfolk:

> such acceptance had this affair in the hearts of all that it carried its con-
> viction with it, honest men encouraging one another in the action and
> the delinquent not one word to say why ought should be remitted him:
> that every tongue must confess it was of the Lord, who is a righteous God

18   *Thurloe State Papers*, IV, p. 228.
19   Parry (ed.), *English Civil War and After*, p. 83.
20   *Thurloe State Papers*, IV, pp. 151, 190, 752; V, p. 151; Fletcher, *A County Community*,
p. 307.

in the execution of his judgements and when his hand is lifted up he shall not only make them (though most unwilling) to see but also make them ashamed for their envy to his people.[21]

Another constant refrain in the first reports to London was the encouragement the major-generals found in the energy and enthusiasm of their commissioners and militia officers. Worsley was perhaps the most ecstatic, writing as follows from Manchester on 3 November: 'truly I find a spirit extraordinarily bent to the work and plainly discern the finger of God going along with it.' Haynes found the Norfolk commissioners 'exceeding real and forward' about the Protector's policies. William Boteler, arriving at Bedford, was met by 'no less than a jury of them at my alighting from my horse' who at once expressed and quickly showed readiness in getting down to work.[22] Berry found the Worcestershire commissioners equally energetic. Kelsey reported an attendance of almost twenty commissioners at Maidstone, 'all unanimously very hearty and cordial to the work'. Robert Lilborne attained an even larger attendance at York on 14 December, when the commissioners 'put things into as ready a method as could be'.[23] It is evident that almost everywhere there were small groups of militant Puritans ready to undertake the Cromwellian programme. These, in the major-generals' terminology, were the 'good people', 'the best of the people', the 'people of God'.[24]

When, as in some cases they did, the commissioners themselves wrote to Thurloe or even Cromwell himself about their task they revealed themselves in their full colours. The Norfolk commissioners were happy to:

promote so good and just a work as the making of a discrimination betwixt the innocent and the guilty, thereby also to provide a necessary revenue for the securing, under God, the cause of God and the good people of this commonwealth in the peaceable enjoyment of their dear and dearly bought liberties so much envied at by that generation of men.

Sir Thomas Barnardiston, Haynes related, penned the letter from the Suffolk commissioners which is redolent of the same partisanship. It came well from the son of the great Puritan patriarch of the county, Sir Nathaniel Barnardiston of Kedington. Nothing was more equal, it asserted, than that those 'who by their restless turbulency do create new troubles and disquiet to the commonwealth' should bear the charge themselves: 'we do pray that as the Lord hath been able to make use of your highness as the instrument of our deliverance from that implacable generation of men, so that he will

---

21 *Thurloe State Papers*, IV, pp. 197, 208, 216. For the political career of Sir William Morley see Fletcher, *A County Community*, pp. 240, 258, 266, 278.
22 *Thurloe State Papers*, IV, pp. 149, 171, 207.
23 Ibid., IV, pp. 215, 224, 321.
24 Ibid., IV, pp. 179, 187, 324.

be pleased to use your highness as the instrument of our preservation and further reformation'.[25] The Essex commissioners approved the new measures for 'restraining the power of that irreconcilable interest'. The Gloucestershire ones spoke bitterly of the 'inveterate and implacable malice of the late King's party', who sought 'upon all occasions to involve the nation in a continuous deluge of blood'. They gave their blessing to a work to secure the well-affected, 'whom God hath owned and stood by the day of their distress'.[26] The ideological conflict at the heart of Cromwellian politics is inescapable in these missives.

It seems likely that the instructions with regard to administrative and moral reform owed much to Cromwell himself. The major-generals were to 'inform themselves of all such idle and loose people that are within their counties who have no visible way of livelihood, nor calling or employment' and see them set to work; to ensure that the genuinely needy were provided for; to 'encourage and promote godliness and virtue and discourage and discountenance all profaneness and ungodliness' by seeing to the execution of the laws against 'drunkenness, blaspheming and taking the name of God in vain, by swearing and cursing, plays and interludes and profaning the Lord's Day and such like wickedness and abominations'; and to regulate alehouses, suppressing all of them except those that were 'necessary and convenient to travellers'.[27] Leaving aside the other major topics in the programme – security and decimation – these demands in themselves amounted to a massive task. Suddenly and decisively Cromwell's agents were expected to shake the processes of local government into life, not in one county at a time, which in itself would be difficult enough, but simultaneously in two, three or more shires. They knew what was expected of them. So, from the moment they left London and started writing in to Thurloe, there was the danger that those who read their letters at Cromwell's court would cherish a false view of how much was being achieved. For the major-generals were bound to want to please, to relay their little victories, to leave aside the question of what happened to their new brooms when they left town, as they always did very quickly because they were men constantly on the move. John Thurloe's huge correspondence, now preserved in the Bodleian Library and largely available in print, is a marvellously rich source of information about the major-generals experiment but every sentence in it has to be interpreted with care if it is to be made to yield a balanced assessment of their achievement.

Cromwell's speech to the mayor and corporation of the City of London on 5 March 1656 shows how determined he was about reforming local

25   Ibid., IV, pp. 131, 225, 227; for Sir Nathaniel Barnardiston see P. Collinson, *The Religion of Protestants* (Oxford, 1982), pp. 164, 181, 273.
26   *Thurloe State Papers*, IV, pp. 317, 354.
27   J. P. Kenyon, *The Stuart Constitution* (Cambridge, 1966), pp. 349–50.

government. There were many and good laws, he announced, 'yet we have lived rather under the name and notion of law than under the thing, so that 'tis resolved to regulate the same (God assisting) oppose who will'. He returned to this theme in September 1656 when he opened the new parliament, naming the lax execution and administration of the law as the 'general grievance in the nation'. He did so once more in a speech to a committee of MPs on 20 April 1657, when he urged them to consider how the good laws on the statute books against 'the common country disorders that are everywhere' might be properly implemented. This was the occasion when he revealed the full extent of his scepticism about the vigour of the magistracy: 'really a justice of peace shall from the most be wondered at as an owl if he go but one step out of the ordinary course of his fellow justices in the reformation of these things'. So much did Cromwell care about the 'reformation of manners' that he could not help taking an optimistic view of the progress of the major-generals in this respect. Their betters fed his enthusiasm, leading him into something of a fool's paradise. Hence his dramatized picture, in the March 1656 speech, of the major-generals driving all those who were idle and vagrant from the shires towards London. The City was a place known to give 'shelter to many such idle, loose persons', he reminded the aldermen, but Major-General Skippon and those commissioned with him were ready to deal as severely with them in the capital as his colleagues had done in the localities. Hence also his exaggerated claim in September 1656 that the experiment had been 'more effectual towards the discountenancing of vice and settling religion than anything done these fifty years'.[28]

How exaggerated was that claim? What did the major-generals actually do during their brief interventions in the shires they commanded to reform government, to improve the enforcement of the poor laws and the moral code on the statute book? One way of approaching this question, although we have noted its difficulties, is to consider what they themselves boasted about or harped upon. The overall impression left by the letters to Secretary Thurloe is that much more time was devoted to extracting the decimation tax from royalist gentry and to security in all its aspects than to mundane aspects of government. Yet it quickly becomes obvious, once the record offered by individual major-generals about their performance in particular counties is compared, that will and interest led each man in his own direction. Goffe, preoccupied with attempting to establish working relationships with local gentry and to check disaffection, made no mention at all of administrative matters in more than twenty letters from Sussex.[29] Worsley, by contrast, writing less often, hardly ever omitted them from his Cheshire

28   W. C. Abbott (ed.), *The Writings and Speeches of Oliver Cromwell* (4 vols, Cambridge, Mass., 1937–47), IV, pp. 112, 274, 494.
29   Fletcher, *A County Community*, pp. 302–10.

reports. One of his first actions was to insist upon proclamations in the market towns against drunkenness and profaneness, accompanied by searches of the streets at night by the constables. In January 1656 he was able to announce that alehouse regulation was in hand: within a month nearly 200 alehouses had been closed in the county. He and his commissioners also gave attention to brewers and maltsters, ensuring that they gave sureties not to sell to unlicensed persons. They imprisoned a number of people who had been living together after a church wedding but without having gone through the civil marriage procedure established in 1653. They also sent to the house of correction 'many suspicious idle and loose persons, some whereof to continue till they give very good sureties for their good bearing for the time to come'.[30] This much can be gleaned from *Thurloe State Papers* alone. When we also bring the Quarter Sessions papers into play, as John Morrill has done in his study of Cheshire, the contrast between Worsley's attention to government there and Goffe's total neglect of it in Sussex becomes even more striking. The Cheshire files are full of pitiful appeals from men deprived of their livelihood by the selling of ale. One in particular from Robert Bulkeley, whose neighbours supported his plea that he had kept an alehouse without ever being accused of allowing disorder for twenty years, confirms the harshness of the 1656 purge. More interesting than this, because it received no mention in the letters to Thurloe, are the scraps of information about Worsley's scheme to check vagrancy at the county borders by penalizing townships there which let wanderers enter the shire. The constables of Warburton, for example, found themselves being ordered to pay twelve pence a head for certain vagrants who, it was alleged, had crossed the boundary into their parish.[31]

Something then could be achieved, at least temporarily, as Worsley's performance shows, through the co-operation of a zealous group of commissioners. But what was really critical, in order to impose a general reinvigoration of local government, was personal attendance at sessions and a satisfactory working relationship with the county bench. Patchy survival of sessions records makes it impossible to determine how many of the major-generals ever did attend sessions in at least one of their counties. At Epiphany or Easter 1656 they had the chance to do so, but of course they could not be in several places at the same time. Not that it was easy for any of them to make a sudden impact if and when they did sit. The magistracy was generally slow to be moved: campaigns and policy changes arose from a gradually emerging consensus or from changing contingencies rather than from readiness to respond to the intervention of a government inspector. John Desborough sat regularly on the Devon bench for much of the 1650s but his role in magisterial policy-making there appears to have been

30   *Thurloe State Papers*, IV, pp. 247–8, 473, 522–3.
31   Morrill, *Cheshire*, p. 283.

slight.[32] John Barkstead was one of the most active and conscientious of the Middlesex justices from 1652 until 1658 but his impact at Midsummer 1656 was hardly impressive, although one would suppose this to be the height of a reform campaign if one was initiated by the major-generals. The number of recognizances for moral offences taken for this Middlesex sessions was certainly a good deal higher than at the same sessions in 1652. Barkstead took some of them himself. The sin and vice of the Long Acre and Covent Garden district was under attack: seventy-five persons were ordered to appear for drunkenness, swearing, profanation of the sabbath, prostitution, keeping disorderly alehouses, keeping brothels, unlawful games, bigamy and fornication. But Barkstead's role in all this must be put into perspective. Over nine per cent of recognizances taken at the Midsummer sessions in 1642 had been for moral offences, and eleven per cent had come into this category in 1652. Eleven per cent would do so again in 1661. The struggle against sin in the Middlesex jurisdiction was endemic. It owed little to Major-General Barkstead. Moreover there were other counties, like Staffordshire and Sussex, where full documentation reveals conclusively that there was no reform campaign at all in 1655 or 1656.[33]

There were occasions when a major-general's chivvying had a material effect at sessions or assizes. General orders about alehouse licensing issued in Hertfordshire and Norfolk can be related to the presence of Tobias Bridge and Hezekiah Haynes respectively. In both cases there was an insistence that the man licensed should be 'well affected to the present government' as well as, more conventionally, 'of an honest life'.[34] Edward Whalley was deeply involved in the management of the grand jury presentments of the 1656 Lent assizes in all the counties of his charge. He settled an enclosure dispute in Leicestershire at the assizes there on terms which, he told Thurloe, he hoped meant that 'God will not be provoked, the poor not wronged, depopulation prevented and the state not damnified'.[35]

By and large, though, there was probably a better chance of achieving higher standards of government on a lasting basis through appointments and procedural reforms than through direct personal initiatives with regard to policy. The crucial issues were the quality of justices, juries and constables. Worsley was quick to notice the inadequacy of the Cheshire, Lancashire and Staffordshire magistracies. 'Upon my observation of the condition of these counties', he wrote on 3 December 1655, he was struck by 'the want of good justices of the peace . . . both as to the condition of

32   S. K. Roberts, *Recovery and Restoration in an English County: Devon local administration, 1646–70* (Exeter, 1985), pp. 49–51, 82–7.
33   J. Mather, 'The moral code of the English Civil War and Interregnum', *The Historian*, 64 (1982), pp. 222–5.
34   G. E. Aylmer, *The State's Servants* (London, 1973), pp. 313–14.
35   *Thurloe State Papers*, IV, p. 686.

some already in and also for the number of them which was very small'. He promised to send up nominations but then twice in the following weeks apologized for his failure to do so. It did not prove easy finding suitable men. But Worsley had put his finger on the necessity of doing so in a letter of 14 December. Moral reform depended upon a firm and reliable lead from the top of county society. He found several constables, he explained, 'that are honest who are doubtful of what power they have and how far they may proceed of themselves in punishing sin'. 'The law is very dark in that,' he declared: these constables had informed him how difficult it was to find justices that 'will encourage them in that work'. Whalley faced the same problem in Coventry and Lincoln where, his allies told him, 'wicked magistrates, by reason of their number, overpower the godly magistrates'. Alehouses were no sooner suppressed than a more lenient justice set them up again. Berry was similarly balked in Wales: 'reformation', he sighed in a letter from Wrexham on 21 December 1655, 'hath many enemies and indeed here wants matter.'[36] The situation in the 1650s was no different from what it had been in the 1580s or 1620s: the godly had always been and were still a minority among the country gentry.[37] In this sense, even if they had been given longer to achieve their aims, the major-generals were fighting a losing battle. Those, like Desborough and Goffe, who did make a number of nominations to the bench, were not necessarily reinforcing the campaign for moral reform. Goffe certainly was shamelessly lobbied by men who wanted to sit on the bench for much more traditional reasons than creating the New Jerusalem.[38]

Jury reform was a problem which had received periodic attention from the Council and judges over the previous fifty years.[39] Cromwell took the matter up after an initiative by a group of Devon justices in April 1655. They planned to make jury service the duty of a reduced body of freeholders, chosen and supervised by the JPs rather than the sheriff. The scheme did not get off the ground in Devon until the following summer when the twelve men on the Midsummer sessions trial jury were newcomers who, unusually, came from a wide area rather than from the hundreds nearest to Exeter. The JPs on this occasion had obviously gone to a good deal of trouble to ensure a jury of approved men.[40] But the major-general in the west, John Desborough, had no part in their proceedings. Indeed he was sceptical, in a letter to Thurloe of 4 February 1656, about the practicability of any kind of jury

36 Ibid., IV, pp. 273, 277–8, 315, 334, 473, 485.
37 Collinson, *Religion of Protestants*, pp. 141–88; J. T. Cliffe, *The Puritan Gentry* (London, 1984), pp. 43–62.
38 *Thurloe State Papers*, IV, pp. 353, 520; Fletcher, *A County Community*, p. 308.
39 A. J. Fletcher, *Reform in the Provinces* (London, 1986), pp. 117–20.
40 S. K. Roberts, 'Initiative and control: the Devon Quarter Sessions Grand Jury 1649–70', *Bulletin of the Institute of Historical Research*, 57 (1984), pp. 169–71.

reform.[41] The Protector, pressed to do so it seems from Devon, was at that time attempting to extend the Devon scheme to the nation as a whole. In a letter to all the major-generals of 29 January, he had instructed them to ensure that JPs selected men of 'clearest integrity and prudence, of honest and blameless conversation' from the freeholders books for jury service at the forthcoming assizes.[42] This instruction received a mixed reception. Whalley on the one hand doubted, by the time he had contacted the justices of his counties in early February, whether it was practical to rectify the juries before the sheriffs acted 'in the old way and course'. Worsley, on the other, reported that his commissioners in Cheshire, Lancashire and Staffordshire welcomed the plan and had agreed lists of 'honest judicious freeholders for this year'.[43] The Devon initiative for reform evidently had some impetus because it was pursued on and off until 1664. Elsewhere revision of the freeholders books in the 1650s probably proved as short-lived as it had previously been.

The key officers in the day-to-day conduct of local government were the high constables, who co-ordinated business in each hundred, and the petty constables, who were responsible for reporting village defaults. Their efficiency, or their lack of it, in the last resort determined the tempo of government: they were men who needed to be constantly watched, instructed and chivvied. Several of the major-generals grasped this point but none of them perhaps did so as fully as Charles Worsley who, copying widespread magisterial practice earlier in the century, issued articles to the Cheshire constables.[44] A list of specific questions about their duties which had to be answered one by one was the only effective way to preclude the constable's resort to the customary *omnia bene*.[45] There is evidence that the Cheshire bench was particularly eager to enhance the role of high constables in the 1650s, giving them fresh duties and a new freedom of action.[46] This may explain the readiness that Worsley found there to replace unsuitable constables with 'honest, faithful and judicious men'. It was his sabbatarian zeal which first alerted his interest in the quality of local officers. For he discovered soon after he set to work that in a number of the towns of his district the weekly market was held on Saturday or Monday. The result was that either men spent the sabbath suffering the effects of a long night in the alehouse or they had to travel on Sunday to get to market the next day. In many cases, Worsley found, the parish constables, far from setting an example, were themselves the worst offenders, being 'the meanest sort of men' who served the office by rota from house to house along the village street.[47]

41   *Thurloe State Papers*, IV, p. 501.
42   Abbott, *Writings and Speeches of Oliver Cromwell*, IV, pp. 87–8.
43   *Thurloe State Papers*, IV, pp. 511, 534.
44   Morrill, *Cheshire*, p. 285.
45   Fletcher, *Reform in the Provinces*, pp. 137–42.
46   Morrill, *Cheshire*, pp. 238–9.
47   *Thurloe State Papers*, IV, pp. 278, 473, 522.

Taken as a whole the major-generals' achievement in reforming local government appears to have been minimal. This conclusion is the more convincing when their efforts in any particular sphere are seen in the perspective of the Interregnum decades or of the whole century. Reform in the seventeenth century was always an erratic process, a matter of stabs at problems pursued with varying degrees of energy according to the inclinations of one group of magistrates or another. Cromwell in 1655 and 1656 was no more able than Charles I had been with his *Book of Orders* in 1631 to obviate the independence of the country gentry.[48] Not that he and they were at odds about the basic desiderata for order. It is important to stress that there was a considerable degree of moral consensus among the magistracy and between the magistracy and the central government. Where the Protector differed from many of the provincial JPs was in his sense of urgency. Richard Baxter touched the heart of the problem of enforcement in a letter of advice about the new parliament of 1656 to Sir Edward Harley. 'It will never be well', he wrote, 'till we have either more zealous justices than most are or else there be greater penalties on magistrates and constables for neglect of their duty'.[49]

The hazards of reading more into the major-generals' reports than is warrantable are well illustrated by the case of Robert Beake, the mayor of Coventry in the year that Edward Whalley was active in Warwickshire. Spending a few days in the city in late November 1655, Whalley got to know Beake quite well. After an initial misunderstanding about the mayor's stance, his assessment was that Beake was 'zealous for the present government', the constitutional basis of which, Beake had assured him, he had carefully studied. 'There is none here', he wrote, 'I am confident will be more faithful to his highness, none I am sure so able to serve him in these parts, having a very great interest with the godly'.[50] Beake, as it happens, kept a diary in which he noted his day-to-day activities as mayor of Coventry. This shows that he was indeed a militant reformer and a very conscientious governor of the city. But it is evident that he did not become so at Whalley's prompting nor did his talks with him bring new vigour, for the diary indicates that he was just as busy seeking morality and order during the fortnight before Whalley's visit as during the few months after it. On 14 November, for example, Beake sent two servants to gaol for fornication, on the 17th he walked 'to observe what order the streets were in and gave a special charge to remove muckhills', on the 18th and 19th he had people caught travelling on the sabbath set in the stocks and cage; on the 23rd he summoned some alehouse-keepers before him to give an account of misbe-

48   Fletcher, *Reform in the Provinces*, pp. 56–61.
49   R. Schlatter, *Richard Baxter and Puritan Politics* (New Brunswick, NJ, 1957), pp. 55–6.
50   *Thurloe State Papers*, IV, pp. 272–3.

haviour in their establishments.[51] Here certainly were Cromwell's 'common county disorders' being scrupulously checked and regulated. The reformation of manners could only be achieved in so far as individuals like Beake gave it their sustained and personal attention. In this sense the major-generals scheme, seen as an administrative experiment, did contain a problem of consent. For there were not enough men like Robert Beake.

If what has been said so far in this chapter is accepted, it follows that the administrative work of the major-generals is largely irrelevant to an assessment of the political response of the country gentry to the scheme. What the gentry felt, in their pockets, or in the pockets of friends and neighbours who were unfortunate enough to be tainted with royalism, was the decimation tax. This rankled exceedingly, as did the insistence in many parts of England on men under suspicion giving security for themselves and their servants. The correspondence of the Verney family between the autumn of 1655 and the spring of 1657 is full of discussion and rumour about the decimation and the taking of bonds.[52] H. M. Reece has argued persuasively that it was the tax, not the military nature of the scheme, which caused fierce opposition.[53] The cry 'no soldier, decimator or man that hath salary' which Goffe reported was heard at the Sussex election for parliament in August 1656, can be regarded as an expression of generalized localism rather than of specific anti-militarism. Kelsey found the same mood in Kent, where the people were 'generally bitter against swordsmen, decimators, courtiers etc.'[54] When John Desborough brought in his bill for the continuation of the decimation tax in December 1656, it was debated in its own terms, not simply as the adjunct of a system of military rule. The diarist Thomas Burton records only one instance of the kind of anti-army rhetoric we might expect. This was Sir John Trevor's declaration that the scheme involved 'a new militia raised with a tendency to divide this commonwealth into provinces, a power too great to be bound within any law.' Trevor spelt out the constitutional implications of the experiment in this speech on 7 January with a clarity no one else had yet achieved. The major-generals, given permanence, would 'cantonise the nation and prostitute our laws and civil peace.' But we should note that this rousing passage came at the end of an argument against the bill which concentrated on the injustice of the decimation tax itself. Trevor believed this violated the public faith of the nation set out in the Act of Oblivion. His condemnation of the bill for its divisiveness was probably the point that struck the deepest chord in many of his hearers:

---

51 'Diary of Robert Beake, mayor of Coventry 1655–6', in R. Bearman, *Miscellany*, I, Dugdale Society, XXXI (1977), pp. 114–37.
52 M. M. Verney, *Memoirs of the Verney Family* (4 vols, London, 1970), IV, pp. 254–92.
53 Reece, 'Military presence in England', pp. 203–5.
54 Fletcher, *A County Community*, p. 310; Everitt, *Community of Kent*, p. 295.

> I am not ashamed to plead for my enemies . . . What do we by this but incorporate them against us and put such a character of distinction upon them that they will never be reconciled . . . You provoke and unite your enemies and divide yourselves and necessitate new arms and charges and raise new dangers . . . I like not this middle way of policy neither to oblige nor destroy. It leaves things doubtful and puts men into a constant danger to be undone. To forgive our enemies is God's rule and it is the only way to make them our friends.[55]

From the 1660s until the 1890s there was a current myth about the major-generals: that they were satraps and kill-joy Puritans who successfully imposed some kind of military despotism on rural England. D. W. Rannie's article in the *English Historical Review* and S. R. Gardiner's *History* then showed that this view was untenable. Yet there has still, ninety years later, been no major study made of the scheme as a whole. G. E. Aylmer's suggestion that the major-generals 'represented an infusion of central authority into the localities which was not to be exceeded until the two world wars of this century' deserves to be fully tested.[56] H. M. Reece by contrast has emphasized the continuity of military involvement in local government from 1649 to 1660. He sees the decisions of 1655 as 'a formalisation of the army's existing role in administration, a difference in degree rather than kind.'[57] Certain tentative conclusions can be offered on the basis of this brief reassessment of aspects of the major-generals' work. It is inappropriate to describe the administrative experiment we have been discussing as the 'rule of the major-generals'. They never did rule. There was not, as has been suggested, an 'interruption' of the accustomed authority of the JPs.[58] In fact in many counties there were still numerous active JPs who broadly represented the leading county families. It can be argued that weakness at the centre in the 1650s gave the rural justices an exceptional and fortuitous chance to consolidate their hold on the processes of government. The confirmation of their autonomy that occurred after 1660 was the predictable outcome.[59] The major-generals did not achieve any appreciable degree of centralization. The whole episode instead reveals the limitations of government at this time. The letters to Thurloe are full of pleas for practical and propagandist support that was not forthcoming. The decimation tax was persistently sabotaged by the skilful manoeuvres of royalist gentry who obtained assistance in escaping it from the Protector

---

55   The debates on the tax can be followed in *Diary of Thomas Burton*, ed. J. T. Rutt, reprint edn (London, 1974), I, pp. 228–43, 310–19, 364–6, 368–9.
56   Aylmer, *The State's Servants*, p. 48.
57   Reece, 'Military presence in England', p. 202.
58   D. E. Underdown, 'Settlement in the counties 1653–8', in Aylmer, *The Interregnum*, p. 176.
59   Fletcher, *Reform in the Provinces*, pp. 357–8.

himself. As Stephen Roberts has put it, 'the government was trying to operate on the frontiers of procedural possibility and it is difficult to see how it could have fared better.'[60]

This revisionism of course can be taken too far. Nothing much about the scheme, except possibly the administrative emphasis on the traditional tasks of magistracy, conduced to settlement. The presence of the major-generals in the localities, with their troops of horse and their comings and goings, was bound to reinforce an atmosphere of political insecurity. This is what Sir John Trevor fastened upon so perceptively in his speech at Westminster. The very notion of sending out men with the powers that Cromwell gave to the major-generals ran counter to the gentry's main aims of reconciliation and the reassertion of class solidarity at the apex of county politics and government. A single vignette will illustrate the divisive impact of the scheme. One night early in 1657 John Pellet and Colonel Culpepper shared a room for the night at the Bull Inn at Lewes in Sussex. When the time came to settle the bill the next morning, Culpepper refused to pay his share, bitterly inveighing against the Cromwellian government for decimating him. Pellet was overheard justifying the policies of the Protector and his Council in reply by Henry Woodcock, who happened to be at the inn at the time. Woodcock took Pellet on more ferociously and a furious quarrel developed. He declared that 'if he had as many lives as he had hairs, taking himself by a lock of hair, he would spend them all against such traitors and rebels as were against the cavaliers.' 'We have always beaten you,' mocked Pellet. But who, Woodcock replied, did he mean by saying we? 'He meant the Protector and those that took part with the late parliament . . . who had conquered the cavalier party at Marston Moor, at Naseby, Cheriton, Oxford and all places else, where God had given signal testimonies of his power against the late King's party.'[61] Here is the bedrock of 1650s politics in a country inn. If Oliver Cromwell's rule of the godly was defeated by inertia, it also dissolved into recrimination and rancour.

60 S. K. Roberts, 'Local government reform in England and Wales during the Interregnum: a survey', in '*Into Another Mould*', ed. I. Roots, Exeter Studies in History, 3 (1981), p. 38.
61 *Thurloe State Papers*, V, pp. 779–80.

6

Cromwell's Religion

Colin Davis

Originally appeared as Colin Davis, 'Cromwell's religion' in John Morrill (ed.), *Oliver Cromwell and the English Revolution*. Copyright 1990 Longman, Harlow.

Editor's Introduction

Most recent accounts of Cromwell's life and career have placed his religion at the centre of their discussion. However, as Colin Davis points out, considering its importance, Cromwell's religion has been relatively under-studied. There are good reasons for this: he left no religious journal or self-examination, and the lack of private sources for his religious thinking leaves historians dependent on his public utterances. Furthermore, he cannot be identified with any one church, sect or position, yet Davis argues that this is itself a clue to the essence of his religion.

Davis shows that providentialism saturated Cromwell's view of the world and the events through which he was living. Throughout the Civil Wars, he regarded each new victory as a further sign of God's favour and when, in 1655–6, the Western Design proved a failure he wondered what he and the people of England had done to provoke God's anger. Cromwell's profound belief in providence, and his desire to remain a servant to it, in turn gave Cromwell a mistrust of human agencies and institutions.

That leads us to the heart of Davis's argument. He suggests that Cromwell wished to transcend religious forms and to reunite the godly. In the immediate term, that meant promoting liberty of conscience for any who were within the mainstream of evangelical, Trinitarian Protestantism, and encouraging unity through diversity among the godly. Such liberty was not to be extended to a point where it turned to licence: for example, those who denied the divinity of Christ were not to be tolerated. But Cromwell's sympathies were very broad and transcended the traditional sectarian grid. Outward forms of religious belief and practice were, he insisted, human and worldly: the godly must rise above them and rediscover unity among themselves. Intolerance stemmed from elevating forms above substance, and liberty of conscience was only the first step towards unity.

Just as Cromwell was not 'wedded and glued to forms of government', so he wished to transcend religious forms as well. These attitudes help to explain the diversity of Cromwell's religious contacts during the 1640s and 1650s, which ranged from the Quaker leader George Fox to the Anglican Archbishop of Armagh, James Ussher. Cromwell protested against the execution of the Jesuit John Southworth just as he opposed the death sentence for the Quaker James Nayler and granted a personal pension to the imprisoned Socinian John Biddle. Cromwell's chaplains apparently shared his antiformalism, most notably John Owen and Peter Sterry.

Antiformalism thus emerges from this powerfully argued essay as the foundation of Cromwell's religion. Other characteristic Cromwellian attitudes, such as liberty of conscience, ultimately derived from that basic premise. Davis shows that Cromwell's mistrust of human forms and agencies served to limit his own religious radicalism. It also helps to explain why so many groups came to regard him as a hypocrite or apostate. Yet, in underpinning his commitment to liberty of conscience, his antiformalism was responsible for a genuine Christian achievement: it is better to concentrate on that, Davis argues, than on a search for Cromwell's religious identity.

Cromwell's Religion

J. C. Davis*

'... wherever anything in this world is exalted or exalts itself, God will pull it down, for this is the day wherein He alone will be exalted.'
[*Cromwell to William Lenthall after the battle of Preston, 20 August 1648*]

'Whatsoever our profession were, that is that would do it, namely the power of godliness.'
[*Cromwell speaking to ministers of the French Church, 5 January 1654*]

If we take Oliver Cromwell's words at their face value, it has been suggested, we should then see his religious attitudes and views as the most important thing about him.[1] It is an appraisal of which we can imagine him approving. We are obliged, even when adopting a healthy scepticism, to give full weight to the religious context which shaped and gave force to his religious utterances. As it was not a context of naive, banal or clichéd religious expression, we must allow for a degree of sophistication in Cromwell's religious, if not theological, thought and belief. Considerable importance should be attached to the form and content of what he said in religious terms.

Yet, before the 1980s, surprisingly little, of a serious and direct kind, had been written about Cromwell's religion. A biography which saw religious faith as the crucial dimension of his life[2], two books purporting to be studies of his religion, only one of which lived up to that promise[3], and a handful of articles[4] make up a meagre yield, of specialized reconstructions of his beliefs and their context, from the rich harvest of Cromwell studies. Blair

*   I would like to acknowledge the assistance of the following, all of whom read an early version of this essay and made valuable comments on it: Glenn Burgess, Anthony Fletcher, John Morrill, Jonathan Scott and Blair Worden.

1   George Drake, 'The ideology of Oliver Cromwell', *Church History* XXXV (1966), p. 259.
2   Robert S. Paul, *The Lord Protector* (London, 1955).
3   Robert F. Horton, *Oliver Cromwell: a study in personal religion* (1897) which despite its subtitle remains a conventional biography; H. F. Lovell Cocks, *The Religious Life of Oliver Cromwell* (1960).
4   Winthrop S. Hudson, 'Denominationalism as a basis for ecuminicity: a seventeenth century conception', *Church History*, XXIV (1955), pp. 32–50; John F. H. New, 'Cromwell and the paradoxes of Puritanism', *Journal of British Studies*, V (1965), pp. 53–59; Drake, 'Ideology', pp. 259–72; Sarah Gibbard Cook, 'The congregational independents and the Cromwellian constitutions', *Church History* XLVI (1977), pp. 335–57.

Worden's brilliant and, to a large extent, pioneering work of the 1980s –
on Cromwellian toleration, providentialism and the political/spiritual crisis
of the mid-1650s[5] – has refocused our attention in this direction and offered
an enticing prospect of a freshly envisaged and recovered Oliver.

How are we to explain the previous neglect of a dimension so important
to understanding the man? Partly because of the very confidence with
which his religious identity was asserted, it was assumed that there was virtually nothing to explore. Oliver was a puritan, a Calvinist, an Independent,
the darling – at least in his rise – of the sects. These assurances passed down
the historiographical chain from one historian to the next. Between 1890
and 1914 our view of Cromwell's religion was confirmed and stabilized in
the consensus of a remarkable series of biographies and related works.[6]
When W. C. Abbott's apparently definitive edition of Cromwell's writings
and speeches appeared between 1937 and 1947, his commentary did
nothing to revise the perceived image of Cromwell's piety.[7] For want of disturbing evidence to the contrary, his assumed religious identity could
remain unchallenged. But there are problems facing any historical account
of Cromwell's religion which need to be confronted at the outset.

First, there are problems of evidence. Cromwell left no programmatic
statements, no credos on which we can base a description of his faith and
its personal or social meaning. There are no verbatim records of the discussion by him of matters of spirituality which we may presume occupied
the circles to which he belonged; no confessional records. Unlike many of
his pious contemporaries, Cromwell left no journal, no diary revealing the
nature of his spiritual self-examination. No record of his reading nor of the
contents of his library survives. The only book which he recommended –
apart from the Bible – was Raleigh's *History of the world*.[8] For all the sermons
which he must have heard and their presumed importance to him,
Cromwell never discusses or criticizes one in his extant utterances. What

5   Blair Worden, 'Toleration and the Cromwellian protectorate', in W. J. Sheils (ed.), *Persecution and Toleration: Studies in Church History*, 21 (Oxford, 1984), pp. 199–233; 'Providence and
politics in Cromwellian England', *Past and Present* CIX (1985), pp. 55–99; 'Oliver Cromwell and
the sin of Achan', in Derek Beales and Geoffrey Best (eds), *History, Society and the Churches*
(Cambridge, 1985), pp. 125–45.
6   Frederic Harrison, *Oliver Cromwell* (1890); Samuel Rawson Gardiner, *Oliver Cromwell*
(1899); John Morley, *Oliver Cromwell* (1900); C. H. Firth, *Oliver Cromwell and the Rule of the
Puritans in England* (Oxford, 1901). Also influential were: William A. Shaw, *A History of the
English Church during the Civil Wars and under the Commonwealth 1640–1660* (2 vols, 1900);
G. B. Tatham, *The Puritans in Power: a study in the history of the English church from 1640 to
1660* (Cambridge, 1913).
7   *Writings and Speeches of Oliver Cromwell*, ed. W. C. Abbott (4 vols., Cambridge, MA,
1937–47, repr. Oxford, 1988), for which see John Morrill (ed.), *Oliver Cromwell and the English
Revolution* (Harlow, 1990), pp. 282–3.
8   Abbott, II, p. 236. Cromwell to Richard Cromwell, 2 April 1650. By the 1650s this was a
conventional choice.

form of service did his worship take in the 1630s, the 1640s and the 1650s? Did he lawfully adopt the Directory of Worship when its enforcement might have been thought realistically obligatory? How far was he personally prepared to participate in the services of the Book of Common Prayer by which, we assume, he himself was married, his children were baptized and at least one of his daughters was married?[9] If, and when, neither of these service books was endorsed by him, what form of worship did he observe? Our inability to answer any of these questions with precision exposes an ignorance of the religious practice of so public a figure which can only be regarded as remarkable.[10] It is with due caution then that we should approach the next vexed question of Cromwell's religious identity.

So conventional is his brief, almost cryptic, account of his conversion experience, down to castigating himself 'the chief of sinners' and lamenting his pre-conversion hatred of light, as to tell us almost nothing specific. What was he converted to: a church-puritanism compatible with his business associations with Ely cathedral in the later 1630s, or something closer to a quasi-separatism epitomized by the cause of John Lilburne for which he showed some zeal in 1640 and 1645?[11] Even confident assertions of Cromwell's religious identity have to be qualified. In an untypical piece of confusion, S. R. Gardiner could describe Oliver as 'the foremost Independent of the day', while acknowledging on the previous page that 'in the sectarian sense indeed, Cromwell never attached himself to the Independent or any other religious body.'[12] On the one hand, the evidence is lacking. As Christopher Hill concluded, 'Cromwell can be identified with no sect.'[13] On the other, our confidence in the old religious discriminators – puritan, Independent, Calvinist – is not what it was. 'Puritan' is a term which some historians would discard, others would confine to conformist, protestant zeal.[14] The study of the Independents, who in some sense disintegrated in 1648–49 under the pressure of a coup in which Cromwell played no small

9   Ibid., IV, p. 664. Marriage of Mary Cromwell to Lord Fauconberg at Hampton Court on 18 November 1657.

10   Symbolic of the problem is the fact that, despite lavishly detailed accounts of Cromwell's funeral procession, we know next to nothing about the actual service.

11   Abbott, I, p. 29. For Cromwell's support of Lilburne see ibid., I, pp. 120, 363–4.

12   Gardiner, *Cromwell*, pp. 28–9. See also Paul, *Lord Protector*, p. 66; Geoffrey F. Nuttall, *Visible Saints: the Congregational way 1640–1660* (Oxford, 1957), p. 105.

13   Christopher Hill, 'Oliver Cromwell', in Hill, *Collected Essays*, III (Brighton, 1986), p. 75. This essay was first published as an Historical Association pamphlet in 1958. Cf. Hill, 'History and denominational history', in *Collected Essays*, II (Brighton, 1986), p. 7. 'Who knows what label to attach to Oliver Cromwell, John Milton, Major-General Fleetwood, John [sic] Ireton?. . . .'

14   C. H. George, 'Puritanism as history and historiography', *Past and Present*, XLI (1968), pp. 77–104; R. T. Kendall, *Calvin and English Calvinism to 1649* (Oxford, 1979). Kendall avoids the term 'Puritan' as unhelpful. Patrick Collinson, *The Religion of Protestants: the Church in English society* (Oxford, 1982).

part,[15] is bedevilled by problems associated with the legacy of using the term in divergent political and religious senses, by a denominational hindsight which imposed too rigid a categorization too early, and by uncertainties as to precise membership and identity before some confessional coherence was established in 1658, the year of Cromwell's death.[16] Finally, by the mid-seventeenth century, 'Calvinism' was a category of such elasticity as, without qualification, to explain almost nothing in terms of specific individuals. Cromwell never showed the slightest interest in declaring himself an experimental predestinarian or an orthodox Calvinist predestinarian. His views, if he had any, on the pre-Laudian Church as a Calvinist consensus or otherwise, he wisely kept to himself.[17] Robert Paul has argued that an Independent identity for Cromwell can be based in his experience of a kind of congregational, gathered Church within the army and that this experience partly shaped his spirituality, religious policy and political attitudes.[18] However, while such experience was no doubt influential, it was too diffuse to be given specific denominational identity. In the seventeenth century sense of a covenanted Church, there is little upon which to base conferring congregational cohesion and identity to a diverse and soon to be conflicting cluster of associations which Cromwell enjoyed through his military career. Like a significant number of his contemporaries – Lambert, Ireton, Berry, Milton and many others – Cromwell is impossible to identify with any one Church, sect or 'way'.[19]

A third problem, compounding and illustrating that of his religious identity, arises from the evidence that we have of his relationship with other religious groups, the sects in particular. Richard Baxter saw Cromwell as a patron of the sects, gathering and favouring sectarians in his military commands.[20] There is no evidence that Cromwell ever saw things in these terms. He did seek godly men for his service but, in individuals, sectarian, or other,

15   David Underdown, *Pride's Purge: politics in the Puritan revolution* (Oxford, 1971).
16   George Yule, *The Independents in the English Civil War* (Cambridge and Melbourne, 1958); Tai Liu, *Discord in Zion: the Puritan divines and the Puritan revolution 1640–1660* (The Hague, 1973); Hudson, 'Denominationalism'. The most helpful studies in this field remain the works of Geoffrey F. Nuttall, esp. *Visible Saints*.
17   Kendall, *Calvin and English Calvinism*; Nicholas Tyacke, *Anti-Calvinists: the rise of English Arminianism c. 1590–1640* (Oxford, 1987); Peter White, 'The rise of Arminianism reconsidered', *Past and Present*, CI (1983), pp. 34–54; William Lamont, 'The rise of Arminianism reconsidered', *Past and Present*, CVII (1985), pp. 227–31; Peter Lake, *Moderate Puritans and the Elizabethan Church* (Cambridge, 1982).
18   Paul, *Lord Protector*.
19   See also Geoffrey F. Nuttall, 'The Lord Protector: reflections on Dr. Paul's life of Cromwell', in Nuttall, *The Puritan Spirit: essays and addresses* (1967), ch. XIII. For some suggestive comments on process rather than organization as an approach to religious history in this period see Jonathan Scott, 'Radicalism and Restoration: the shape of the Stuart experience', *H.J.*, XXXI (1988), p. 455.
20   R. Sylvester (ed.), *Reliquiae Baxterianae* (1696), pp. 47–8, 50.

religious identity seems to have been a matter of indifference to him. Given that the heresiographers' trade of identifying and inventing sects flourished from the early 1640s, it is worth noting that the impact of the sectarian phenomenon on Cromwell's consciousness seems to have come relatively late.[21] Even in 1658, speaking to his last parliament, he was hesitant about the usefulness of the category.[22] Furthermore, once the phenomenon was accepted, and despite his willingness to persist in dialogue with the most recalcitrant of his sectarian opponents, Cromwell showed an antipathy to religious parties, sects and sectarianism amounting to aversion. The sects were associated in his mind with the 'scatterings, divisions and confusions' which he came to lament so ruefully. They lacked 'that spirit of kindness' that could encourage mutual toleration, that charity without which the forms of religion were as nothing. They were merciless, ready to 'cut the throats of one another, should not I keep the peace'. They were hypocritical in their demands for liberty, all too ready to deny to others what they insisted on for themselves. In them were 'Christ and the Spirit of God made the cloak of all villany and spurious apprehensions'. Their internecine squabbling prevented the achievement of any consensual basis for a post-monarchical regime. Indeed they were subversive to the point of intriguing with royalists. All Cromwell's efforts to talk them into some compliance with the regime in return for reasonable liberty seemed fruitless. In March 1654, the nation was called upon to fast and pray for an end to 'Faction' in 'Profession', to overcome the absence of 'Brotherly Love' and 'Healing Spirit'. Writing to Major-General Fleetwood a year later, Cromwell struggled with despair:

> The wretched jealousies that are amongst us, and the spirit of calumny, turns all into gall and wormwood. My heart is for the people of God: that the Lord knows, and I trust in due time will manifest; yet thence are my wounds; which though it grieves me, yet through the Grace of God doth not discourage me totally.[23]

So far was he from welcoming the sects and sectarianism that towards the end of his life he could only encourage himself and others with the thought that in the end God would wipe them all away.[24]

21 His first reference to the term 'sect' comes in October 1646 in a letter to his daughter, Bridget: Abbott, I, p. 415.
22 Abbott, IV, pp. 716–17, 718; 'each sort of people, if I may call them sects', 'I speak not of sects in any ill sense, but the nation is hugely made up of them.'
23 Ibid., III, p. 461; III, pp. 89, 92; IV, p. 278; III, p. 615; IV, pp. 716–17; III, p. 459; III, p. 436; IV, pp. 221, 267; III, pp. 225–7, 756. For examples of Cromwell's attempts to conciliate the sects, see ibid., III, pp. 119, 125–6, 176n, 116, 373.
24 Ibid., IV, pp. 776–7: conversation with Mr Wheelwright, pastor of Hampton, Massachusetts. 'Mr. Wheelwright stand fast in the Lord, and you shall see that these notions will vanish into nothing.'

How important to Cromwell was religion and how sincere was he about it? These two related questions have been perennially posed since the post-Restoration vilification of him as a Machiavellian or Faustian figure. There can no longer be any doubt that Cromwell was saturated in the providentialism of his contemporaries. No event or facet of his life was untouched by God's presence and guiding will. That presence was not simply a piece of self-justifying, ego-boosting, self-deception. The news of the failure of the Hispaniola expedition, which arrived in July 1655, threw him into a crisis underlain by the sense that God's favour had come to an end. Perhaps he, like Achan,[25] had turned away from the path of the Lord and he, and his people, were being punished accordingly. The crisis of 1655–56 was a political, diplomatic and foreign policy crisis but it was also, as Blair Worden has shown, a spiritual trauma and a crisis of religious prestige. The notion of a self-deceiving manipulator of the language of religion, imperturbably confident in the 'Divine Right of Oliver' will no longer survive critical examination.[26] The high years of the protectorate – 1654 to 1656 – should be seen as years of profound religious/political crisis. The declaration, on 20 March 1654, of a day of national fasting and humiliation was a graphic indicator of anxiety that the bondage of Egyptian tyranny might only have been escaped for a loss of bearings in the wilderness. Oliver devoted his opening speech to the first protectoral parliament, in September 1654, to what might be called a crisis of spiritual enthusiasm. The nation, he urged, must progress out of the wilderness and not repine there forever. Only in a second speech, eight days later, did he turn to constitutional matters and, even then, the twin problems of sectarian disunity and sin loomed large. Into this context the Hispaniola defeat came like a hammer blow from the Lord. On 17 September 1656, speaking at the opening of his second parliament, Cromwell's theme was again 'the dispensations of God' in a world where His 'most peculiar interest' was beset by external enemies and torn by merciless dissension and a soul-killing lack of charity. Later, 'a great deal of experience of providence' prefigured his rejection of the Crown. 'I would not seek to set up that that providence hath destroyed and laid in the dust, and I would not build Jericho again.' He would not repeat the sin of Achan.[27] The Cromwellian regime has frequently been criticized for an absence of clear policy objectives and of management strategies for their

---

25   Achan was the man who brought the wrath of God down on the Israelites by taking plunder, 'the accursed thing', after their successful capture of Jericho. The Book of Joshua, 7. For a brilliant treatment of this theme see Worden, 'Cromwell and the Sin of Achan'. For a broader colonial context in which the providential rebuke at Hispaniola should be placed see Karen Ordahl Kupperman, 'Errand to the Indies: Puritan colonization from Providence Island through the Western Design', *William and Mary Quarterly*, XLV (1988), pp. 70–99.

26   The phrase in Christopher Hill's. See Hill, 'Oliver Cromwell', pp. 75, 72–3.

27   Abbott, III, pp. 225–8, 434–41, 451–61; IV, pp. 260–78, 473.

realizations. But such criticism overlooks the fact that reliance on providence implied, in one sense, the absence of policy, the foregoing of trust in fleshly reasoning and its instruments and institutions. We will only fully understand if we accept the centrality and seriousness of religious concerns.

Cromwell's private religious thinking and devotion are sparsely documented. We are dealing almost entirely with public utterance; to a surprising degree with public, pastoral utterance. The language is of comfort, exhortation, rebuke, counsel.[28] Personal spirituality, confessional definition, liturgical theory or practice cannot be the concern of an examination of Cromwell's religion which must be primarily an exercise in the uncovering of a public spirituality enunciated for essentially public purposes. At the heart of that public spirituality is an image of God presiding over the national destiny and pursuing it through varying, if chosen, agents. The context which Cromwell occupies here is not that of high theology nor that of popular *mentalité*. On the one hand, it is the landscape of the good constable or the godly magistrate; on the other, it is that of the divinely chosen and providentially endorsed instrument, leader, pastor and virtual prophet of God's peculiar interest at what might very well be an apocalyptic moment in the cosmic drama.

We can divide the record of Cromwell's religious experience into four broad phases or periods. The first two phases – his early religious experience and his commitment to reforming the Reformation in the root and branch campaign of 1640–42 – are dealt with by John Morrill elsewhere in this volume. I deal here only with what, for Cromwell's religious sense, was the enormously formative experience of war and then the more chastening experience of government – phases which can be taken as running from 1642 to 1653, and from 1653 to 1658 respectively.

If it was religious feeling which mobilized the country outside Westminster for war in 1642–43, Cromwell stands as an archetypal figure of that process. The third phase of his religious experience from 1642 to 1653 is that of a man of action; in war, politics and things of the spirit prepared to follow God's leading in the wilderness, to stake his all on providence and its tutelage. However godly the man, this can have been no easy thing for a forty-three-year-old with no fitting experience, a family to provide for and a measure of material security only recently achieved. By 1646 Cromwell's already astonishing run of military successes left no room for doubt of the hand of the Lord. Time after time, his reports on military activities insisted that God was directly the author of all that parliament's forces had won. Indeed 'God', he complained to the Committee of Both Kingdoms in April

28 For one example, among many, see Cromwell's letter to Blake and Montagu, 28 April 1656 (Abbott, IV, p. 148). The naval commanders are instructed to rely on providence and to follow the counsel of Solomon. See also Paul, *Lord Protector*, pp. 222, 273–80.

1645, 'is not owned enough.' Five months later he informed the Speaker of the House of Commons that the fall of Bristol was the work of God, warning that 'He must be a very Atheist that doth not acknowledge it'. God it was who would bring forth 'a glorious work for the happiness of this poor Kingdom' reconciling 'righteousness and peace'.[29]

The best agents for God's work were 'honest men', 'godly, honest men', 'conscientious men'. Describing his troops to his cousin, Oliver St John, in September 1643, he denied that they were anabaptists, sectarians. They were 'honest, sober Christians' who expected to be used as men. Rather than deliberately recruiting sectarians, he seems to have looked through and beyond the formal religious affiliations of individuals in search of the qualities he prized and respected – earnest godliness and 'honesty'. Against Major-General Crawford's zealous presbyterian arrest of Packer, an anabaptist, Cromwell objected not by insisting on the rights of sectarians but on the wisdom of the State's choosing men who would serve it faithfully regardless of their opinions.[30] In part such pragmatism derived from a sense of the unfathomable nature of providence and its choice of instruments. When, on 13 September 1644, Cromwell argued in the Commons for due provisions for 'tender consciences' it was only on the stipulations that their doctrines were compatible with the 'Word of God', the public peace and, significantly, the advancement of business.[31] It may be more sensible to regard Cromwell in his military decade, not so much as a promoter or defender of the sects, as a man enamoured of godliness but indifferent to its forms, provided they fell within the limits of mainstream, evangelical, Trinitarian protestantism.

We have no record of Cromwell's attitude to the Westminster Assembly or the debates about forms of Church government which it engendered. But his attitude towards the prospect of a presbyterian settlement was relaxed, as we would expect of one to whom forms were secondary. He took the Covenant himself early in 1644 and was known to require it of others. In 1647 not only was he reported to be willing to accept a presbyterian system but on 13 October he acted as a teller for the ayes in the vote on a Commons proposal to establish presbyterianism for three years. As late as April 1649, he was, according to Walker, prepared to move a presbyterian settlement in parliament.[32] Cromwell then does not emerge as the anti-presbyterian champion of Independency. He was no more wedded and glued to forms of Church polity than he was to forms of civil government. The substance of God's will was not found in such forms but in the dynamic interplay of individual and corporate wills with a chain of mercies, a series of providential

29   Abbott, I, pp. 341, 377, 387.
30   Ibid., I, pp. 256, 258, 277; Baxter, *Reliquiae*, pp. 50–1.
31   Abbott, I, p. 294.
32   Ibid., I, pp. 275, 276–7, 460; II, pp. 50, 52.

indicators which could in the end lead men, who had thought of no such things, to regicide and the overthrow of the old order.

At the expulsion of the Rump in April 1653, Cromwell's sympathizers saw him as a Moses who had shaken off the last vestiges of his people's bondage to Egypt. Before him, and the three nations he had united with the armies of the Lord, lay – variously interpreted – a godly mission of purification at home and apocalyptic imperialism abroad.[33] The snares in his path were, on the one hand, that he could stray after 'the accursed thing', into the sin of Achan, pursuing fleshly reward, heeding the carnal reasoning of policy; on the other hand, that, heeding the religious zealots who were all too quick to accuse him of apostasy, Cromwell could reduce the nation to ungovernability and become himself a 'man of blood'. It was a dilemma which was to haunt the last phase of Cromwell's religious experience and the tragic dimensions of it have already been outlined by Blair Worden.[34]

What briefly were Cromwell's religious objectives?[35] First, he wished to remain a servant of providence, guarded against 'unbelief, self-seeking, confidence in an arm of the flesh, and opinion of any instruments that they are other than as dry bones'. Secondly, he belonged to that evangelical, magisterial tradition that sought a 'reformation of manners' in society at large. God would, in fact, chastize any nation which did not purify itself. The English gentry and nobility, prized by Cromwell as by Harrington, could only be preserved by such a self-purification. Thirdly, he saw himself and his followers 'at the edge of the promises and prophecies',[36] obliged to weigh seriously the prospect of a coming millennium, the conversion of the Jews, and Christ returning to rule with his Saints: his own role as Godly Prince to prepare the nation for that happy consummation.[37] His fourth objective was to end the 'penal statutes that force the conscience of honest conscientious men', to create an environment of liberty of conscience for all those whom he bluffly regarded as 'honest', 'godly' or 'conscientious'.[38] They were those who pursued Christianity in substance and not merely for form's sake,

33   For Cromwell's depiction of this as early as 1650 *via* sustained commentary on Psalm 110 see *Ludlow*, I, p. 246.
34   Worden, 'Sin of Achan'.
35   These are discussed more fully by Anthony Fletcher below, pp. 212–15 [in the original publication].
36   Abbott, II, pp. 127, 325, 215; II, pp. 110–11; III, p. 845; IV, p. 273; III, p. 64. See also John F. Wilson, *Pulpit in Parliament: Puritanism during the English Civil Wars* (Princeton, 1969), esp. pp. 212–23.
37   See Bernard Capp, 'The political dimension of apocalyptic thought', in C. A. Patrides and Joseph Wittreich (eds), *The Apocalypse in English Renaissance Thought and Literature* (Manchester, 1984), pp. 113–16; Paul J. Korshin, 'Queueing and waiting: the apocalypse in England, 1660–1750', in ibid., p. 251.
38   Abbott, II, p. 104.

and Cromwell's fifth objective was to promote a Christianity of substance, of the heart and spirit. We shall look at these fourth and fifth objectives more closely shortly, but Cromwell's final religious objective was clearly and understandably his own salvation. In the midst of all his 'mercies', it was his sense of the redeeming Christ within which gave assurance. It was this which he tried to convey to his son, Richard, that, indeed, Christ's kingdom and image came inwardly first.[39] In the light of these objectives, four themes are worth exploring further. They are: liberty of conscience and Cromwell's consistency in regard to it; his desire for religious unity; his providentialism; and what I shall call his antiformalism, his concern to raise the substance – as he saw it – of religion above its forms.

Cromwell and the Cromwellian regime have long been famous for the extent of religious toleration that they were prepared to embrace. We are again indebted to Blair Worden for sharpening our perception of what is at issue here.[40] He draws the distinction between toleration and liberty of conscience. The unacceptable danger of toleration was that, in permitting heresy, it could condemn those who espoused it to eternal damnation. Liberty of conscience, on the other hand, arose out of a concern not to impose human authority between God's grace and the soul. Underlying the Cromwellian attitude on liberty of conscience was the faith that truth lay in the spirit rather than the institution – in spiritual power rather than ecclesiastical, confessional or liturgical form. A religion of conscience, rather than ritual, could not bind pilgrims from their future judgments nor spiritual stewards from their obligations to God in the management of their own consciences. But central to Cromwell's motivation remained the desire for unity in diversity among the conscientious godly. Cromwell's definition of the latter was, in Worden's view, not wide-ranging. His fitful extensions of it owed more to diplomatic and political considerations than to the Lord Protector's own convictions. Cromwell, Worden concludes, 'neither wanted toleration nor provided it' but his entourage contained a group of rational, sceptical erasmians who did favour a 'wider liberty of belief' – Bulstrode Whitelocke, Matthew Hale and Sir Charles Wolseley. It is worth re-examining Cromwell's attitudes on liberty of conscience in the light of Dr Worden's reassessment.

God would work what He willed in the minds of men. In *A declaration of the army of England upon their march into Scotland* (July, 1650), the standard

---

39   Ibid., I, p. 646; II, p. 236; III, pp. 226, 437.
40   Worden, 'Toleration and the Cromwellian protectorate'. Inevitably my synopsis simplifies Worden's argument. Also useful on this issue is Roger Howell, 'Cromwell and English liberty', in R. C. Richardson and G. M. Ridden (eds), *Freedom and the English Revolution: essays in history and literature* (Manchester, 1986), pp. 25–44.

by which his apostasy was later to be judged,[41] Cromwell stated this as his motivation for defending liberty of conscience against a nation bent on defying providence to coerce consciences. No form of Church government should be imposed by force. True Christianity did not inhere in forms but in faith working by love.[42] Undoubtedly godly, Scottish protestantism presented a particularly illuminating case of Cromwell's response to religious coercion. The justification for a war, which Fairfax had blenched at, against erstwhile Scots allies, was that they had succumbed to sacerdotalism and religious violence. As Naseby had been fought for civil freedom, so Dunbar was a crucial contest over religious freedom. Writing to the governor of Edinburgh castle, in the aftermath of his providential victory at Dunbar, Cromwell pointed out that in England ministers had liberty to preach but not to rail, nor to overtop and debase the civil power. No man was molested for preaching the gospel, since neither force nor compulsion but the Word of God alone would accomplish what was necessary.[43]

In Ireland the lines were more sharply, but not simplistically, drawn. After the brutalities of Drogheda and Wexford, Cromwell called upon the defeated Irish to build on faith, not on the practice of 'mumbling over Matins'. 'Keeping ourselves in the love of God, not destroying men because they will not be of our Faith.' The majority of poor, lay people in Ireland were, he claimed, ignorant of the grounds of the Roman Catholic religion. Whereas the Scots were portrayed as enlightened but wrong-headed, the Irish were either papist barbarians or the poor deluded. Of the Irish, the former 'must expect what the Providence of God . . . will cast upon them'. The latter, as long as they behaved peaceably and honestly, would receive equal justice with the English.[44] Active, proselytizing papists – anti-Christians in Cromwell's terms – were beyond the limit of liberty of conscience. The rest would be afforded such liberty as the law – English law – allowed.

The liberty of the godly was the irreducible cause. To Cromwell's mind, in the Second Civil War, it appears to have become the dominant one. 'I rejoice much to hear of the blessing of God upon your Excellency's endeavours,' he wrote to Fairfax on 28 June 1648,

> I pray God to teach this nation, and those that are over us, and your Excellency and all us that are under you, what the mind of God may be in all this, and what our duty is. Surely it is not that the poor godly people of

---

41   See, for example, 'A word for God' reprinted in *T. S. P.*, IV, pp. 380–4 (also reprinted in [William Sedgewick] *Animadversions upon a letter and paper* (1656); report on a sermon by Christopher Feake on 5 January 1657, *T. S. P.*, V, p. 758.
42   Abbott, II, pp. 285–6. See also Nuttall, *The Holy Spirit*, pp. 125–33.
43   Abbott, II, pp. 335–6.
44   Ibid., II, pp. 199–205.

this Kingdom should still be made the object of wrath and anger, nor that our God would have our necks under a yoke of bondage; for these things that have lately come to pass have been the wonderful works of God; breaking the rod of the oppressor, as in the day of Midian, not with garments much rolled in blood, but by the terror of the Lord; who will yet save His people and confound His enemies as in that day.[45]

To Lenthall, after the battle of Preston, he urged that parliament exalt God 'and not hate His people who are the apple of His eye, and for whom even Kings shall be reproved'. Two weeks later, writing to his friend Lord Wharton, Cromwell identified himself with 'the poor godly people' and their weakness.

When we think of our God, what are we. Oh, His mercy to the whole society of saints, despised, jeered saints! Let them mock on. Would we were all saints. The best of us are (God knows) poor weak saints, yet saints; if not sheep, yet lambs and must be fed. We have daily bread, and shall have it, in despite of all enemies.[46]

There were, however, two problems which came to haunt Cromwell and which were already implicit in his vision of unity in diversity amongst 'the poor godly people'. One was that the godly adamantly refused to recognize a mutuality of rights among themselves. The other was the problem of distinguishing between the liberty of 'the poor godly' and the licence of the impious.

At times Cromwell seemed genuinely bewildered by the propensity of those who had been granted a newly-won liberty of conscience, to deny the same right to others.[47] 'Every sect saith, Oh! Give me liberty. But give him it, and to his power he will not yield it to anybody else. Where is our ingenuity? Truly that's a thing ought to be very reciprocal.' The ideal could readily be stated:

. . . a free and uninterrupted Passage of the Gospel running through the midst of us, and Liberty for all to hold forth and profess with sobriety, their Light and Knowledge therein, according as the Lord in his rich Grace and Wisdom hath dispensed to every man, and with the same freedom to practice and exercise the Faith of the Gospel, and to lead quiet and peaceable Lives in all Godliness and Honesty, without any Interruption from the Powers God hath set over this Commonwealth . . .

45   Ibid., I, p. 619. For God's dealings with the Midianites see Numbers 21.
46   Abbott, I, pp. 638, 646.
47   Cf. his comment at the Putney debates, Abbott, I, p. 534. For George Fox's insistence to Cromwell that his followers had a monopoly of godliness and providential favour see Wilson Armistead, Daniel Pickard and Norman Penny (eds), *The Journal of George Fox* (2 vols, 1901), I, p. 363.

But this statement is itself drawn from a proclamation announcing policies designed to prevent the godly from disturbing one another in the professions of godliness.[48] The Protector came increasingly to see his task as that of keeping all the godly of several judgments in peace, striving for some reciprocity, mutuality. To restrain those who railed against others was immediately to be charged with persecuting the godly. 'I tell you there wants brotherly love, and the several sorts of forms would cut the throats of one another, should not I keep the peace.[49]

While Cromwell could bemoan the hypocrisy of those, freed from episcopal oppression, who could not resist putting 'their finger upon their brethren's consciences, to pinch them there', at the same time he pointed out that profanity, blasphemy, sedition, evil-speaking and loose conversation should be being disciplined by the magistrate but were not. The problem was to distinguish those 'who are sound in the Faith, only may perhaps be different in judgment in some lesser matters' from those who had run out of godliness into blasphemy and impiety.[50] What were the distinguishing characteristics of soundness in the faith? Various official attempts were made under the Protectorate to tackle this problem. The Instrument of Government offered toleration to all but Roman Catholics and the amorphous category of the 'licentious'. In the oath taken by the Protector, council and MPs under the Humble Petition and Advice it was 'the True, Reformed, Protestant, Christian, Religion' based in the scriptures of the Old and New Testaments which was to be maintained.[51] The Triers, appointed in 1654 to approve candidates for benefices or lectureships, were given slight criteria to operate with: evidence of grace, 'holy and unblameable conversation', 'knowledge and utterance fit to preach the Gospel'. No doctrinal tests were recommended. When it came to the complementary activity of removing scandalous incumbents the guidelines were explicit on moral failings, offering only blasphemous or atheistical opinions, and frequent use of the Prayer Book as doctrinal grounds for dismissal.[52] The debate on a statement of fundamental doctrine, adequate to the identification and disciplining of blasphemy and impiety, rumbled through the 1650s flaring up in the face of apparent provocations.[53]

48   Abbott, III, pp. 459, 626.
49   Ibid., III, pp. 607–16.
50   Ibid., III, p. 586.
51   Ibid., III, p. 149; IV, pp. 565–6.
52   *An ordinance appointing commissioners for approbation of public preachers: Monday March 20 1653* (i.e. 1654); *An ordinance for the ejecting of scandalous, ignorant and insufficient ministers and schoolmasters: Tuesday August 29 1654* (1654). Presumably infrequent use of the Prayer Book was acceptable.
53   For the 'fundamentals' exercises see Abbott, II, pp. 520–37; III, pp. 284, 834; 'Guibon Goddard's journal of a parliament 1654–5', in Burton, I, pp. xvii–cxxx. For the attempt of a voluntary association to confront the same problem see H. W. P. Stevens, 'An ecclesiastical

Cromwell was clear that liberty of conscience was not to be stretched to the denial of the divinity of Christ, the socinian blasphemy, as he saw it, of the 'unitarian', John Biddle. But getting beyond the self-evident truths of a reformed protestant godliness was not an enterprise that appealed to his antiformalistic pragmatism. 'Whoever hath this faith, let his form be what it will.' The magistrate had, in Christian charity, a duty to punish outward abuses. He must react when there was a danger of disorderly confusion. But ideas could surely be let alone. 'Notions will hurt none but them that have them.' He could sympathize with one 'that having consulted everything' could hold to nothing – not 'Fifth Monarchy nor Presbytery, nor [Independency], nothing but at length concludes he was for nothing but an orderly confusion'.[54] The rub, of course, was in the chasm between order and disorder; a distinction which Oliver related to that between diversity within a framework of a common, Christian (preferably reformed, protestant) charity, and an internecine conflict in which brotherly love had withered and domination was all. The tragic side of this he brought out to parliament in January 1658, employing one of his most vivid metaphors. Not content with variety, he said, every sect sought to be uppermost, 'to be not only making wounds, but as if we should see one making wounds in a man's side and would desire nothing more than to be groping and grovelling with his fingers in those wounds'.[55]

The sincerity of Cromwell's religious faith was seldom questioned by his contemporaries but many regarded his profession of concern for liberty of conscience as specious. Edmund Ludlow saw it as 'an engine by which Cromwell did most of his work', a device to gull those who would otherwise have opposed him or opposed him earlier.[56] Dr Worden rejects such cynical motivation. Cromwell was sincere but his puritan theological conservatism endowed him with a narrower concept of religious freedom than has often been allowed. His concern was unity, not toleration. God's peculiar interest was to be found almost exclusively among presbyterians, independents and baptists. Oliver remained unsympathetic to quakers, socinians, anglicans and Roman catholics. Such extensions of religious liberty as there were to these groups came under political/diplomatic pressures or the influence of the Christian stoics – Whitelocke, Hale and Wolseley. First, however, it is by no means clear that the last group exercised anything like the influence which Worden claims for them. Secondly, it is doubtful whether Cromwell's

experiment in Cambridgeshire', E. H. R., X, (1895), pp. 744–53. Incidents like the publication of the Racovian catechism in 1652, parliament's censure of John Biddle in 1654, and outrage over James Nayler's activities in 1656, revived the quest for defining fundamentals.

54   Abbott, III, p. 834; IV, p. 272; III, pp. 436–8; IV, p. 719.
55   Ibid., IV, p. 717.
56   Ludlow, I, pp. 378–9.

religious views can be traced to any one source of influence but others seem to have as good a claim, if not better, to having been taken seriously by the Lord Protector in religious policy formation. It is always difficult to disentangle public and private attitudes in the occupant of a quasi-monarchical position and the attempt may be suspected of anachronism. It is clear, nevertheless, that Cromwell's legal position under the protectorate constrained him, as it was intended to do. Allowing for this, his operation both within and outside those constraints remains strikingly untypical of his age and may suggest a broader tolerance of attitude than Dr Worden concedes.

Although John Biddle was, in Cromwell's eyes, rightly condemned for an intolerable heresy, Oliver provided, apparently out of his own pocket, a weekly allowance of ten shillings for the condemned man who was safely confined to the Scilly Isles.[57] Quakers were released by the personal intervention of Cromwell. Many of them had sufficient faith in 'that of God' remaining in the Protector to assume that he could be influenced on their behalf.[58] Anglicans likewise could see some hope of toleration in Cromwell. Archbishop Ussher, John Gauden, Nicholas Bernard all had sufficient faith in Cromwell's sincerity to sustain the hope that he would deliver liberty of conscience and practice to them.[59] The Lord Protector's nominations of parochial incumbents included many who conformed to the Restoration and it was not unknown for royalist anglicans to be admitted by the Triers.[60] As John Morrill has argued, there may have been a good deal more continuity at the parish level than has been supposed[61] and given the apparatus at his disposal it is hard to imagine that Cromwell would have been unaware of this. His own admiration for James Ussher, archbishop of Armagh – payment for his funeral in Westminster Abbey and generosity towards his

---

57   *T. S. P.*, VIII, p. 288.
58   Cf. Geoffrey F. Nuttall, *Studies in Christian Enthusiasm: illustrated from early Quakerism* (Wallingford, Pennsylvania, 1948), pp. 29, 33. Worden seems to me to be right about Cromwell's lack of personal sympathy for Nayler. Cf. Abbott, IV, p. 350.
59   *T. S. P.*, V, pp. 597–600; J[ohn] G[auden], *A Petitionary Remonstrance* (1659); Abbott, III, p. 714; IV, pp. 69, 102. Nicholas Bernard, chaplain to Cromwell in the 1650s, was chaplain to Ussher in 1627.
60   Much more work needs to be done on Cromwell's ecclesiastical patronage as Lord Protector but in Sussex, for example, of 33 nominations by him, five of those for whose fate at the restoration we have evidence conformed in 1660–61. E. H. W. Dunkin, 'Admissions to Sussex benefices . . . by the commissioners for the approbation of public preachers', *Sussex Archaeological Collections*, XXXIII (1883), pp. 213–24; R. W. Blencowe, 'Extracts from the journal and account book of the Rev. Giles Moore rector of Horstead Keynes from 1655–1679', *Sussex Archaeological Collections*, I (1848), pp. 65–127.
61   John Morrill, 'The Church of England 1642–9', in J. S. Morrill (ed.), *Reactions to the English Civil War* (1982), pp. 89–114. For a regional example see Bryan Dale, 'Ministers of the parish church of Bradford and its three chapels during the puritan revolution', *The Bradford Antiquary*, n.s., II (1905), pp. 124–34, 360–84.

dependents – is well known.[62] In July 1649 Ireton and Cromwell had acted as tellers against a Commons ordinance to curb preaching against the new regime. Consistent with this, in December 1656, Cromwell was writing encouragingly to presbyterian ministers in north-eastern England.[63]

It may well be that some of Cromwell's discreet consideration towards Roman catholics had more to do with political prudence than with his own personal preferences. His assurances to cardinal Mazarin and his refusal to restrict admission to catholic services at the Venetian ambassador's residence may fall into that category. But, unless we make some allowance for a personal disposition towards a broader tolerance, other actions of his are not so easy to accommodate. His protest against the execution of a jesuit, John Southworth (or Southwell) appears genuinely disinterested.[64] Friendships within the Cromwell family circle could extend to catholic ex-royalists.[65] Most extraordinary of all, the catholic Lord Baltimore was restored to his full proprietorial rights in the colony of Maryland. There was toleration for all trinitarians in the colony but governmental control remained firmly in catholic hands. The vindication of Baltimore's rights came after the second protectoral parliament attempted to tighten up the prosecution of papistry by the Act of 26 June 1657.[66]

Cromwell's tolerance may not have been quite so narrow nor so *politique* as Worden would have it. Religious unity was a priority *not* to be achieved by the coercion of the conscientious spirit. But the problem of interpretation is engendered at a deeper level. Onto the question of Cromwell's tolerance we impose a sectarian grid. Did Cromwell, we ask, extend liberty of conscience to anglicans, presbyterians, independents, baptists, roman catholics and the sects alike? The question is badly put, I would suggest, because the sectarian grid is inappropriate and I shall want to argue shortly that it is Cromwell's antiformalism which makes it so. It was only when unity had been abandoned as an unrealizeable goal that a sectarian or denominational response became appropriate, and this was not to be for Cromwell and others in the 1650s. Where Worden is absolutely correct is in linking the twin Cromwellian aspirations of unity and liberty of con-

62   *T. S. P.*, IV, pp. 121–2; Nicholas Bernard, *The Life and Death of . . . Dr James Ussher* (1656); R. Buick Knox, *James Ussher, Archbishop of Armagh* (Cardiff, 1967); James Caulfield (ed.), *Cromwelliana* (Westminster, 1810), p. 156; *Mercurius Politicus*, 27 March–3 April 1658.

63   Abbott, II, p. 90; IV, pp. 361–2.

64   Ibid., IV, p. 69; III, p. 321; *Cal. St. Pap. Ven. 1653–4*, pp. 253–4.

65   For the friendship of Elizabeth Claypole with Sir John Southcote see John Morris (ed.), *The Troubles of our Catholic Forefathers related by themselves* (1872), 1st ser., vol. 1, ch. VIII, esp. pp. 393–6.

66   James W. Vardaman, 'Lord Baltimore, parliament and Cromwell: a problem of church and state in seventeenth century England', *A Journal of Church and State*, IV (1962), pp. 31–46. See also Dom Hugh Bower (ed.), *London Session Records 1605–85*, Publications of the Catholic Record Society, XXXV (1934), p. xlvi.

science. Paralleling Cromwell's fear of disintegration, wounding ourselves and others, is a deep desire for unity as not only healthy but God's will for us, a hatred of 'carnal divisions and contentions among Christians'. Liberty of conscience is in a sense the response of charity and faith in God's providence to a situation where unity is not yet possible. In this regard, Cromwell's aspiration, if not his optimism, remained constant.[67] In the autumn of 1644 Cromwell, Vane and St John initiated moves for an accommodation between presbyterians and independents with the proviso that, if this were not possible, there should be liberty for tender consciences.[68] Liberty was a second best to unity. A year later Cromwell could rejoice in the unity of the godly in the army: 'Presbyterians, Independents, all had here the same spirit of faith and prayer; the same pretence and answer; they agree here, know no names of difference: pity is it should be otherwise anywhere'. 'I have waited', he wrote to Hammond in November 1648, 'for the day to see union and right understanding between the godly people (Scots, English, Jews, Gentiles, Presbyterians, Independents, Anabaptists and all).' It was, of course, not to come. '. . . how hard and difficult a thing it was to get anything carried without making parties. . . .' Still it might be that, at least temporarily, God had a providential purpose in this diversity. So Oliver could pray: 'God help England to answer His minds.' Unity would come in the end out of diversity, out of the plurality of God's minds.

> . . . sure I am, when the Lord shall set up the glory of the Gospel Church, it shall be a gathering [of] people as out of deep waters, out of the multitude of waters: such are his people, drawn out of the multitudes of the nations and people of this world.[69]

Like William Erbery, Cromwell waited for the Spirit to make us one and take us out of Babylon.[70] Apparently, the waiting could not be endured without anxiety and nowhere is this better illustrated than in the tormented questions, about division, lack of brotherly love, and pride, accompanying the announcement in March 1654 of a day of national fasting and humiliation.[71] Given the perdurability of sin, providence, not human effort, seemed still to offer the best hope and it is to this theme that we now turn.

In what remains one of the better biographies of Cromwell, John Morley suggested that his religion was one, not so much of dogma, as of providen-

---

67   Abbott, III, p. 437. Cf. William Lamont, 'Pamphleteering, the protestant consensus and the English Revolution', in Richardson and Ridden (eds), *Freedom and the English Revolution*, pp. 72–92.
68   John Willcock, *Life of Sir Henry Vane the Younger: statesman and mystic 1613–1662* (1913), p. 145; Shaw, *English Church*, II, pp. 35–48.
69   Abbott, I, pp. 377, 677; III, p. 57; I, p. 639; III, p. 65.
70   *Clarke Papers*, IV, p. 239. Cf. Abbott, IV, pp. 776–7.
71   Abbott, III, pp. 225–7.

tial experience. The context of that providentialism and its importance has been magisterially laid out by Blair Worden and there is little to add to what he has said.[72] In the mid-seventeenth-century heyday of providentialism, God's constant intervention in human affairs, to admonish or encourage, reward or scourge, was assumed. Providences were not isolated, disconnected interventions but linked sequences expressive of God's will for men and nations. Defiance of providence, neglect of providential signals, failure to respond, could themselves provoke providential reaction. Cromwell was not only seen by many of his contemporaries as an agent or instrument of providence, he was almost archetypal in his immersion in providential ways of thinking. He affectionately compared himself to Vane, who made not enough of providences, while he himself perhaps made too much. In this scheme of things there was no room for blind fate, chance, *fortuna* perceived as a pagan concept. Ultimate unity was in the hands of providence but disunity would persist until:

> we admire God and give Him glory, for what He has done. For all the rest of the world, ministers and profane persons, all rob God of all the glory and reckon that to be a thing of chance that has befallen them.[73]

Two things are worth emphasizing about Cromwell's providentialism. One is a marked distrust of the human agencies and institutions through which God mediately operates. Often, in fact, God's appearances were to be seen 'crossing and thwarting the purposes of men' even on the winning side. Only God's 'counsel shall stand, whatever the designs of men, and the fury of the people shall be'. Had human design engineered the death of the king it would have been an outrageous crime but providence had cast them on it. To the sceptical Wharton, Cromwell conceded that it was easy to condemn the 'glorious actings of God' if we only regarded his human instruments. Wharton paradoxically, as Oliver pointed out of him, ran the risk of setting his own human judgment up against providence. Success came not from human attributes – brains, courage, strength, which were as dry bones – but through following God and gathering 'what he scattereth'. We cannot, he admonished Blake and Montagu, turn away evil or attain good through our own efforts. Human endeavours and abilities were to be distrusted; all reliance placed in divine providence. Writing in 1652, Cromwell warned his daughter to beware of fear. Love casts itself on prov-

---

72   Morley, *Cromwell*, p. 55; Worden, 'Providence and politics'.
73   Abbott, I, pp. 621, 687; II, p. 287; III, p. 572; I, p. 644; II, p. 38. In this context Worden's contention that Cromwell's quest for unity was at war with his providential zeal is too simplistic. Worden, 'Providence and politics', pp. 95–6. For a dismissal of the notion of the chance of war see Abbott, II, p. 205. Cf. C. H. Firth (ed.), *Memoirs of the Life of Colonel Hutchinson by his Widow Lucy* (2 vols, 1885), I, pp. 1–2.

idence.[74] Cromwell himself was constantly reminded by others not to put faith in human institutions, resources, knowledge or policy.[75] As Hugh Peter had said, 'Outward strength & human policies are no sufficient Bulwark against Batteries from heaven. . . .'[76]

The corollary of distrust in the human was, accordingly, total trust, whatever human prudence might suggest, in the divine. Nothing illustrates this better than Cromwell's attitude to the Irish expedition: 'It matters not who is our Commander-in-Chief if God be so; and if God be amongst us, and His presence with us, it matters not who is our Commander-in-Chief'. He repeatedly presented the Irish mission as one conducted under God's direct command.[77] Cromwell was by no means alone in these general attitudes. At the Whitehall debates in late 1648 much of the discussion was about the extent to which any constitutional provision usurped God's providential freedom of action and the necessity for faith. The only true agreement, or constitution, was from God and not from men.[78] Similarly pervasive was suspicion 'of men's inventions in God's worship'.[79] For many of his critics, the essence of Cromwell's apostasy lay in his reliance on men's inventions rather than on divine providence.[80] Such reliance was an invitation to divine chastisement. Vavasor Powell replied to an invitation to attend the Savoy conference in 1658 with the dour warning, 'if you go upon political or worldly accounts, or by a humane spirit, to work, you may expect God to blast the work'.[81] Even a 'cool rationalist' like Cromwell's neo-platonist chaplain, Peter Sterry, warned against trust in reason and human prudence.[82]

Distrust of human prudence, policy and invention and the injunction to total faith in God's sustaining and guiding providence led to one of the most important aspects of Cromwell's religious disposition, his antiformalism. Forms divided the godly. They were man's work, fleshly, not God's, divine. Led by their Lord, godly people would transcend forms and rediscover unity. Writing to Hammond on the eve of the regicide, Cromwell argued that, while authority is of God, its forms are of human institution and therefore

74   Abbott, III, pp. 53–4; I, pp. 421, 719; II, p. 189; II, pp. 328, 453; II, pp. 215, 235; IV, p. 148; II, p. 602.
75   For example: T. M., *Veni, vidi, vici* (1652); Arise Evans, *The Voice of Michael the Archangel* (1653); Colonel Edward Lane, *An Image of our Reforming Times* (1654).
76   Hugh Peter, *Digitus Dei* (1631) – quoted in Raymond Phineas Stearns, *The Strenuous Puritan: Hugh Peter 1598–1660* (Urbana, Illinois, 1954), p. 63.
77   Abbott, II, pp. 37, 39. For the general point about the Irish expedition see ibid., II, pp. 107, 110, 127, 128, 142, 165, 205.
78   *Clarke Papers*, II, pp. 76–100, 184–6.
79   Firth (ed.), *Memoirs of Hutchinson*, I, p. 3.
80   'A word for God' in *T. S. P.*, IV, p. 381.
81   Geoffrey F. Nuttall, *The Welsh Saints 1640–1660* (Cardiff, 1957), pp. 50–1.
82   Peter Sterry, *The Spirits Conviction of Sinne* (1645), pp. 16–17; *The Clouds in which Christ Comes* (1648), pp. 40–2.

may be lawfully resisted.[83] John Owen, preaching at the opening of parliament in September 1656, warned against attaching any importance to debates over forms of Church worship and discipline. God would achieve what he willed with these things in his good time. Our wills and judgments must not be allowed to run before his. As part of our preparation, Owen recommended, we should eliminate 'formality'.[84] A more extreme version of the same message is William Erbery's reported assertion that Christ 'would confound all forms'.[85]

Cromwell, in this regard, is best seen as a 'meere Catholic', putting substance above form, the spirit above the letter. It is this which leads him to regard the clerical/lay distinction as anti-Christian. The only ministry of true descent, he informed the Nominated Assembly, was through the spirit.[86] Distrust of forms helps to explain Cromwell's lack of interest in a Church establishment alternative to the abortive presbyterianism of the Westminster Assembly. His faith, as an actor of rich, providential experience, was that God would provide and that His custom was not to work through forms, institutions and rituals but inwardly through the hearts of men. According to Mr Bacon at Whitehall, magisterial power was one of outward forms and coercion but 'all matters relating to the Kingdome of God and purely and altogether spiritual'.[87] God moved spiritually through the world, His providential substance subverting the shells of form that were irrelevant to it.[88]

While both the Irish and Scots wars could be seen as providential exercises, the Scots campaign was specifically against formalism, its divisive violence, against Scots faith in coercion which, in turn, betokened a lack of trust in providence and its spiritual efficacy. Providence had been slighted by the Scots in 1650 when they chose to follow human instruments, platforms, 'your form's sake', rather than the will of God. They had preferred forms to love and accordingly had found that God would not do their will.[89] Peter Sterry, in a dramatic sermon which argued that England's delivery from Scots presbyterianism was a greater mercy than its delivery from the Roman papacy – a sermon published in both Scotland and England – acknowledged that presbyterianism might be one of the purest forms. 'Yet there is a more excellent way which is that of Love'. Outward forms should not divide. The marriage between the saviour and the soul was spiritual. 'No union with any form makes this marriage. . . .' The endeavour of both

83   Abbott, I, p. 377; II, p. 173; III, pp. 51–65; I, p. 697.
84   John Owen, *Gods Work in Founding Zion* (Oxford, 1656), pp. 30–1, 36–8, 41, 43.
85   *Clarke Papers*, II, pp. 234, 236–7.
86   Abbott, II, p. 197; III, p. 63.
87   *Clarke Papers*, II, p. 108.
88   Abbott, II, pp. 199, 285.
89   Ibid., II, p. 340; II, pp. 286, 325, 340.

papistry and Scots presbyterianism was the 'Annexing the Spirit to outward Formalities', 'Legall Dispensation' and 'Carnall Administration'.[90]

Cromwell's antiformalism may have strengthened as his assurance of providence grew. At Putney in 1647 he insisted on the obligation to honour prior engagements or covenants. Three years later, in the wake of the Scots campaign, covenants could be regarded as formalistic contrivances, inessential to the progress of providence and therefore disposable. In his post-Dunbar letter to the governor of Edinburgh castle, Oliver asked, 'Whether the Lord's controversy be not both against the ministers in Scotland and in England, for their wresting, straining, and improving the Covenant against the Godly and Saints in England (of the same faith with them in every fundamental) even to a bitter persecution.' Ministers, the engineers of formalism, had brought men of a faith united in substance to a conflict over forms. In the process providence had been slighted, forms preferred to brotherly love.[91] The watchwords of the two armies at Dunbar –'The Covenant' for the Scots; 'The Lord of Hosts' for the English – were held to symbolize this struggle between forms and substance. The Lord of battle had decided accordingly.[92]

However dramatic God's demonstrations in the field, men perversely reinsinuated preoccupation with form rather than spirit into public life. Opening the Nominated Assembly, Cromwell complained, 'How God hath been compassed about by fastings and thanksgivings and other exercises and transactions I think we have all cause to lament.' In the aftermath of that assembly's failure, both he and John Rogers could argue against each other that they represented the claims of substance over form. To the ministers of the French congregations in London, Cromwell stressed the importance of 'the power of godliness' over the formalities of profession. Toleration should be extended to all who live in the love which is in Jesus Christ.[93] Conversely, intolerance of spirit betokened a raising of forms above substance, an unwarranted trust in fleshly instruments and a lack of faith in divine providence. The declaration of a day of national fasting and humiliation in March 1654 was also an invitation to consider whether preoccupation with forms was shattering unity, undermining brotherly love and engendering a many-sided conflict of reciprocal intolerance. A series of questions directed attention to these points.

> iv. Is Brotherly Love, and a Healing Spirit of that force and value amongst us that it ought? v. Do we own one another more for the grace of God and

90   Peter Sterry, *England's Deliverance from the Northern Presbytery compared with its deliverance from the Roman Papacy* (Leith, 1652), pp. 6, 7, 18, 43.
91   Abbott, II, p. 340.
92   See, for example, John Canne, *Emanuel, or, God with us* (1650), p. 19 and *passim*.
93   Abbott, III, pp. 61, 157. For the exchanges between Cromwell and John Rogers see Hur Horton &c., *The Faithful Narrative* (1654), p. 37.

for the Spiritual Regeneration, and for the Image of Christ in each other, or for our agreement with each other in this or that form, or opinion? . . . viii. Are there not too many amongst us that cry up the Spirit, with a neglect of Love, Joy, Peace, Meekness, Patience, Goodness, Temperance, Longsuffering, Forbearance, Brotherly Kindness, Charity, which are the fruits of the Spirit . . . x. Do not some of us affirm ourselves to be the only true Ministry and true Churches of Christ, and only to have the Ordinances in purity, excluding our Brethren, though of equal gifts and having as large a seal of their Ministry, and desiring with as much fervour and zeal to enjoy the ordinances in their utmost purity?

Beyond these causes of 'Faction' in 'Profession' the godly were asked to consider whether they remembered primitive simplicity – self-denial, mercy to the poor, uprightness and justice – and whether in these aspects of practical christianity they were not put to shame by the anti-christian and the carnal.[94]

It was this yearning to get beyond forms, and the ugly strife which preoccupation with them engendered, to the unity which he believed lay in the substance of faith, that enabled Cromwell to maintain an extraordinary range of religious contacts and counsellors through the 1640s and 1650s.

Whosoever hath this faith, let his form be what it will . . . Give me leave to tell you, those that are called to this work, it will not depend upon formalities, nor notions, nor speeches [but upon] . . . men of honest hearts engaged to God, strengthened by providence, enlightened in his works to know his word, to which he hath set his seal, sealed with the blood of his Son in the blood of his servants.[95]

Such people were found by Cromwell in a surprising diversity of situations. From Sir Henry Vane with his 'withdrawing from all forms'[96]; to Archbishop Ussher's combination of deep hostility to Roman catholicism with temperate pragmatism about protestant forms and great personal piety[97]; to Walter Cradock, of the Welsh saints, with his insistence on the simplicity of the gospel, the priority of the spirit to the form, Cromwell found 'fellowe citizens of the commonwealth of Israell' whatever the formal barriers.[98] As early as 1643, Charles Herle had warned against taking differences over presbyterian and independent church politics too seriously. 'Our difference 'tis such as doth at most but ruffle a little the fringe, not any way rend the garment

---

94   Abbott, III, pp. 225–7. The significant texts of Jude 4 and 2 Peter 2:1, warning against false prophets and a general apostasy, were invoked.
95   Abbott, IV, pp. 272, 277–8, 965.
96   Willcock, *Vane*, p. 254. The comment is Burnet's. See also Vane's final advice to his children, ibid., pp. 336–7.
97   Knox, *Ussher*.
98   Nuttall, *Welsh Saints*, pp. 25, 28. The phrase is Cradock's, see ibid., p. 3.

of Christ'.[99] Jeremiah Burroughes in *Irenicum* (1646) had explained that differences between saints arose because of human weakness. No faith therefore should be placed in them but rather in God's unifying providence. In the same year, in an atmosphere of rising disillusion with religious fragmentation, John Goodwin urged faith in this providence and less confidence in human formalities and institutions:

> . . . reformation according to the Word of God must give leave to the wind to blow where it listeth and give liberty to the Spirit of God to do with his own what he pleaseth; to make what discovery of truth he pleaseth and to what persons and when and where he pleaseth; and must not confine him to his market or compel him to traffic only with councils and synods for his heavenly commodities.[100]

Mention of Goodwin, the republican critic of the Cromwellian church settlement brings us to Cromwell's own spiritual spokesmen and defenders, his chaplains, a subject worth further investigation for, amongst other things, the degree of antiformalism amongst them. John Owen, one of the most famous of them, was clear that to place form before substance in religion was to enter 'the confines of self-righteousness, if not hypocrisy'. No form of church government was immune to degeneration. His own recommendation for church reform was to be relaxed about institutional issues and to give priority to pastoral care.[101] Peter Sterry insisted that 'to be subject to . . . the Church in the outward forme for the outward forme's sake is a bondage'. In an important sermon delivered to the House of Commons in October 1647, Sterry likened reliance on human prudence to the Israelites' worship of the golden calf. Glossing Colossians 2:20, he asked,

> If Christ be Risen from the dead, why do you subject him to Ordinances?
> . . . Formes are sweet Helps, but too severe Lords over our Faith . . . When we Consecrate, or converse with any Ordinance or Peculiar way of Worship; let us then remember, that our Object is the Person of Jesus Christ, that Wisdome of God, whose way is more untrac'd than the Eagle, whose extent is wider than the Earth. The Heaven of Heavens cannot take in All of Him, to containe or Confine Him, much lesse any One Ordinance in this World, or Fleshly Fashion . . . Tis in vain to attempt to shut up Christ in any Thing.[102]

---

99   Charles Herle, *The Independency on Scriptures of the Independency of the Churches* (1643). Cradock also used the ruffling of the fringe metaphor.
100   John Goodwin, *Twelve Considerable Serious Cautions* (1646). See also Hudson, 'Denominationalism', pp. 36–42.
101   John Owen, *Complete Collection of Sermons* (1721), pp. 73, 221–2, 562–5.
102   Tai Liu, *Discord*, p. 49; Sterry, *The Clouds*, pp. 40–1, 46, 47–8.

Sixteen months later, in February 1649, Sterry was appointed preacher to the republican Council of State as he was Cromwell's personal chaplain throughout the Protectorate. Such men formed what might be called the hard core of Cromwell's spiritual entourage when he was at the height of his power. At a superficial level they may be seen as denominationally diverse.[103] At a deeper level they shared a common antiformalism. These are the men with whom and through whom Cromwell worked for religious harmony without uniformity, for unity in diversity.[104] Their greatest achievement, which now has to be seen as an intentional one borne out by Oliver's personal interest, was the Cromwellian Church settlement which avoided liturgical and ecclesiological formalism while trying to guarantee substantial and decent Christian provision throughout the nation.[105]

In his own day, Cromwell's antiformalism fed the charges of hypocrisy and apostasy against him. In his search for the substance which united, he frequently appeared willing to agree with his last interviewee, if not every-one. To those – Levellers, Fifth Monarchists or others – committed to forms of government he seemed to have a slippery way with forms, civil or eccle-siastical, apparently holding that 'it is lawful to pass through any Forms of Government for the accomplishing his Ends'.[106] Perhaps especially to radi-cals, liberating themselves from established forms, Cromwell's antiformal-ism gave the appearance of freedom to act and to transform. The faith of radicals in Oliver is certainly remarkable. Fifth Monarchists, Republicans, Levellers, Winstanley, Harrington, even anglican, royalist, millennialists like Arise Evans, Elinor Chanel, Walter Gostelow and John Saunders, were prepared, temporarily perhaps but in many cases with surprising persis-tence, to put their faith in him. Once we look at his religion out of the strap-ping of a denominational grid, the connections and shared contexts can be surprising. Aspects of his emphasis on the sovereignty of conscience look like William Walwyn; his providential warrants for action combined with his belief in Christian liberty remind one of the Christian republicanism of Milton, Vane or Ludlow; his hints of an imminent millennium and the urgency of moral reformation recall fifth monarchism; his emphasis on the second coming of Christ as an inward, spiritual process bring to mind Winstanley; and it may be more than fanciful to suggest that there are

103   Examples of 'presbyterians' in the group are John Howe and Thomas Manton.
104   See, for example, the preaching of William Strong in June 1653 and the initiative of Cromwell and the ministers reported in the autumn of that year. *Several proceedings of state affaires, 27 October–5 November 1653*, p. 3391.
105   A much fuller treatment of this theme is to be found in Chapter 8 [original publication]. See also, Claire Cross, 'The church in England 1646–1660', in G. E. Aylmer (ed.), *The Inter-regnum: the quest for settlement 1646–1660* (1972), pp. 99–120.
106   Abbott, I, p. 627.

parallels between Cromwell's antiformalism and Abiezer Coppe's.[107] The desire to get beyond forms to substance, to get beyond words to things,[108] to cast aside fleshly considerations, to hold fast to the spirit and ride the roller-coaster of providence are all common radical dispositions of the period and Cromwell, too, is imbued with them.

What, it has been asked, held Cromwell back, from the full revolutionary potential of the providentialist,[109] from being the Robespierre of the English Revolution, a role which he almost seemed to envisage when contemplating the *tabula rasa* of post-conquest Ireland?[110] A first answer must be found within his religious attitudes. He is caught and restrained within a cycle. While his antiformalism liberates him for radical potential, it is intimately connected with a providentialism which inculcates distrust of human agency and total reliance on the divine, and so pushes him back to an antiformalist quest for the substance of a simple reliance on the spirit, a primitive piety and a practical Christianity. The qualifiers, or modifiers, of Cromwell's antiformalist providentialism are the word of scripture, the spirit of charitable meekness, and reason.[111] We might perhaps trace a growing insistence on their cautions in the face of an anarchy of formal providentialisms and a mutual harrowing of the saints, but, in a fundamental sense, Cromwell retained an antiformalist faith in providence to the end. It is his distrust of the human which holds Cromwell back from an incipient religious radicalism and allows other, more socially conservative elements in his temperament to dominate. Man, the agent of the divine will operating mediately, must be tolerated but is not to be trusted.

It may be better to drop the search for Oliver Cromwell's religious identity, at least in the traditional terms, not simply because good evidence is hard to find but because it is a counterproductive quest whose terms of reference obscure – even invert – the true situation. The denominational grid – of independent, presbyterian, anabaptist and the rest – is indeed a perverse instrument by which to measure the religious faith and sincerity of a man who struggled to free himself and the godly in his society from formalistic declensions and paradigms. Cromwell's success was as an arm of providence, a servant of the God who made him strong in battles. He did not see himself called upon to formalize the flow of providence in new Church ordinances, politics and confessions. To do so in the civil sphere was

107 For Coppe's antiformalism see J. C. Davis, *Fear, Myth and History: the Ranters and the historians* (Cambridge, 1986), pp. 48–57. See also Abbott, II, p. 325 for Cromwell's view that the exploitation of the poor by the rich did not suit a commonwealth.
108 For Cromwell on words and things see Abbott, III, p. 609; IV, pp. 260, 716–17.
109 Cf. Worden's discussion of this in 'Providence and politics', pp. 88–97.
110 For Cromwell on Ireland: Abbott, II, pp. 93, 110, 186–7, 273, 327; T. S. P., III, p. 715; *Ludlow*, I, pp. 246, 254.
111 Abbott, I, pp. 542–6; III, p. 373; IV, pp. 309, 471–3.

apostasy enough for those among the Saints who became his enemies. Liberty of conscience – also anathema to the formalists – flowered briefly while Cromwell's antiformalism held the stage. Of its very nature it was hard to conceive of its institutionalization and time was denied for its consolidation. Nevertheless, it might be held to represent a greater and more sincere Christian achievement than any for which he has hitherto been credited.

7

Oliver Cromwell, the First Protectorate Parliament and Religious Reform

David L. Smith

Originally appeared as David L. Smith, 'Oliver Cromwell, the first Protectorate Parliament and Religious Reform' in *Parliamentary History* 19. Copyright 2000 Edinburgh University Press, Edinburgh.

Editor's Introduction

One of the many ironies of Cromwell's career was that a figure so prominent in Parliament's resistance to Charles I should himself have found it impossible to achieve an effective working relationship with any Parliament. That failure was in turn an important reason why the Interregnum was unable to generate lasting political stability. This essay offers a case study of Cromwell's inability to work with a particular Parliament, the relatively neglected first Protectorate Parliament, in the cause of religious reform. In a broader context, this highlights not only the fact that many members of Parliament did not share his commitment to liberty of conscience, but also the underlying tension within Cromwell's own hopes that the interests of the godly could ultimately be reconciled with those of the whole nation.

The religious attitudes of many members of the first Protectorate Parliament are difficult to reconstruct, but a significant number of the English members, as well as some of the Irish and Scottish ones, clearly had Presbyterian sympathies. Such members were particularly concerned to stamp out religious errors, heresies and blasphemies, and to maintain public order and conformity to a national ministry. They deeply mistrusted Cromwell's desire to extend liberty of conscience more widely. Cromwell and many of the army officers found this intensely frustrating, and towards the end of 1654 the army submitted a petition calling for greater liberty of conscience. Equally, the Presbyterian members were able to draw on the support of extensive Presbyterian networks, especially within London. This conflict of views came to a head in the case of the Socinian John Biddle, who was imprisoned by Parliament for blasphemy but granted a personal pension by Cromwell.

These tensions demonstrated the fundamental incompatibility of two principles that Cromwell defined, in his speech of 12 September 1654, as 'fundamentals': 'liberty of conscience' and government 'by a single person and a Parliament'. Unfortunately, the single person (Cromwell) and the Parliament could not agree over how far to extend liberty of conscience. This was closely related to a deeper tension within Cromwell's vision of Parliament's role in fostering a godly republic. He hoped that Parliament would be an agent for reconciling the interests of the godly with those of the nation: he wanted the godly to expand until they became coterminous with the wider nation. Parliament, as the 'representative of the whole realm', had a duty to further this process, and the promotion of liberty of conscience and peaceful co-existence among the godly were crucial steps towards it.

Yet for many members of the first Protectorate Parliament, not least some who had been excluded at Pride's Purge and harboured a long-standing hostility towards the religious radicalism of the Army, Cromwell's agenda threatened to unleash widespread heresies and blasphemies. So they stoutly resisted him, and such opposition is crucial in explaining not only his angry dissolution of this particular Parliament on 22 January 1655, but also why his high hopes of every Parliament he met with during the Interregnum were ultimately disappointed.

Oliver Cromwell, the First Protectorate Parliament and Religious Reform*

David L. Smith

The first Protectorate parliament is one of the more obscure of seventeenth-century English parliaments. Apart from Peter Gaunt's important research, the parliament has been relatively neglected and it remains less familiar than the apparently more colourful Rump, or Barebone's, or second Protectorate parliaments.[1] Yet, despite the brevity of its existence, the first Protectorate parliament nevertheless repays careful study. Its proceedings reveal much about the contrasting religious priorities of Cromwell and many members of parliament, and that divergence in turn throws a great deal of light on why Cromwell was never able to establish a stable working relationship with any of the interregnum parliaments. In this paper, I shall argue that the key to the collapse of the first Protectorate parliament lay in Cromwell's attempt to use a body designed as 'the representative of the whole realm' to advance what remained a minority agenda, 'liberty of conscience'. He believed that parliament had a crucial role to play in reconciling the interests of the godly with those of the whole nation. Yet in the end, the first Protectorate parliament was a profound disappointment to him, for his wish to liberate the godly proved incompatible with the determination of many members to prevent heresies and blasphemies. At the heart of this

* I am very grateful to John Morrill and Graham Seel for reading and commenting on a draft of this article, and to Elliot Vernon and Patrick Little for drawing my attention to several sources and for helpful advice on specific points.

1 Whereas the Rump and Barebone's parliaments have both been the subject of outstanding monographs published during the last 25 years (Blair Worden, *The Rump Parliament, 1648–53* [Cambridge, 1974], and Austin Woolrych, *Commonwealth to Protectorate* [Oxford, 1982]), the first two Protectorate parliaments have been much less studied. Of the two, the second is the more fully researched: see, especially, Ivan Roots, 'Lawmaking in the Second Protectorate Parliament', in *British Government and Administration. Essays presented to S. B. Chrimes*, ed. H. Hearder and H. R. Loyn (Cardiff, 1974), pp. 132–43; and Carol S. Egloff, 'The Search for a Settlement: Exclusion from the Second Protectorate Parliament. Part I: The Process and its Architects', *Parliamentary History*, XVII (1998), pp. 178–97. On the first Protectorate parliament there is little apart from two excellent articles by Peter Gaunt: Peter Gaunt, 'Law-Making in the First Protectorate Parliament', in *Politics and People in Revolutionary England. Essays in Honour of Ivan Roots*, ed. Colin Jones, Malyn Newitt and Stephen Roberts (Oxford, 1986), pp. 163–86; and 'Cromwell's Purge? Exclusions and the First Protectorate Parliament', *Parliamentary History*, VI (1987), pp. 1–22. See also Peter Gaunt, 'The Councils of the Protectorate, from December 1653 to September 1658', University of Exeter Ph.D., 1983, ch. 5; and Sarah E. Jones, 'The Composition and Activity of the Protectorate Parliaments', University of Exeter Ph.D., 1988.

parliament's failure, there thus lay fundamentally contrasted visions of the kind of religious reform that parliament should promote.

Much of the received picture of the first Protectorate parliament still derives in some measure from Cromwell's celebrated denunciation of the parliament when he dissolved it, at the earliest possible constitutional opportunity, on 22 January 1655:

> I do not know whether you have been alive or dead. I have not heard from you all this time; I have not . . . Instead of peace and settlement, instead of mercy and truth being brought together, righteousness and peace kissing each other . . . weeds and nettles, briers and thorns, have thriven under your shadow![2]

To Cromwell, the parliament had simply missed the point of its calling by concentrating on revising the Instrument of Government rather than liberating the godly. This view was echoed in Thomas Carlyle's withering condemnation of this 'most poor hide-bound pedant Parliament; which reckoned itself careful of the liberties of England; and was careful only of the sheepskin formulas of these'.[3] S. R. Gardiner argued that the parliament witnessed a power struggle between the civilian politicians and the army leaders, resulting almost inevitably in an impasse.[4] Hugh Trevor-Roper suggested instead that the main problem lay in Cromwell's failure to manage this and other parliaments at all effectively.[5] Most recently, Carol Egloff has written that 'the disastrous session, which produced no legislation but instead witnessed a concerted attempt to dismantle the Instrument and replace it with a parliamentary constitution, made it abundantly clear to the military Cromwellians that the members of future parliaments must be more carefully controlled'.[6] Although there is much in these interpretations that is persuasive, an exploration of the theme of religious reform in this parliament suggests that it is necessary not so much to refute them as to extend and nuance them.

First of all, it is worth stressing, as Peter Gaunt has done, that the parliament's business record demonstrates that its members were very active during the 20-week session.[7] In all, over 40 bills were considered,[8] several of which addressed issues of religious reform, including a bill 'for setling Tenths, and all Impropriacons, belonging to the State, for the maintenance

2   *The Letters and Speeches of Oliver Cromwell, with Elucidations by Thomas Carlyle*, ed. S. C. Lomas (3 vols., 1904), II, pp. 407, 409.
3   *Ibid.*, p. 431.
4   S. R. Gardiner, *History of the Commonwealth and Protectorate, 1649–1656* (4 vols., 1903; repr. 1989), III, pp. 178–255.
5   Hugh Trevor-Roper, 'Oliver Cromwell and his Parliaments', in *Religion, the Reformation and Social Change* (3rd edn., 1984), pp. 345–91.
6   Egloff, 'Search for a Settlement', p. 183.
7   Gaunt, 'Law-Making in the First Protectorate Parliament', esp. pp. 169–76.
8   *Ibid.*, p. 174; Jones, 'Composition and Activity of the Protectorate Parliaments', p. 128.

of ministers', a bill 'against the Quakers, Heresies, and Blasphemyes', and another 'for the restoreinge [of] Cathedralls'.[9] The principal source of disagreement between Cromwell and a majority of members seems not to have been over whether religious reform was necessary, but over what sort of religious reform was desirable. Religion was undoubtedly a priority, and the French ambassador recorded that during Cromwell's opening speech of 4 September 1654, 'as often as he spoke . . . of liberty and religion, . . . the members did seem to rejoice with acclamations of joy'.[10] But the more specific the debates became, the more divergences opened up over what kind of church parliament should promote and construct.

It is virtually impossible to reconstruct the religious attitudes of most members of the Protectorate parliaments. Sarah Jones has argued that only a minority were 'active' or 'expressed opinions' that reveal their religious sympathies, and that the religious affiliations of nearly 70 per cent of members of the first Protectorate parliament remain unknown. Jones argues that of the remainder, presbyterians constituted 18 per cent, independents four per cent, 'radicals' (quakers, baptists etc.) three per cent, and anglicans two per cent.[11] However, these figures are necessarily approximate and it is often difficult to make distinctions with any degree of precision: in particular, presbyterians and independents were even more problematic terms by 1654 than in the later 1640s. It is nevertheless worth noting that various contemporary observers reported the prominence of what they termed presbyterians: Sir Edward Nicholas wrote that 'there are many that now perswade the King to some extraordinary complyaunce with the Presbiterian party, for that soe many of that faccon are chosen to sit in the approaching mock Parliament',[12] while the Venetian secretary in England, Lorenzo Paulucci, observed that 'the members returned for the new Parliament are not quite to the Protector's satisfaction. He wanted a majority of his own creatures, whereas a great part of those already chosen prove to be Presbyterians, the enemies of the dominant military party on which the government depends.'[13]

---

9   See the draft list of bills intended for the first Protectorate parliament in B.L., Stowe MS 322 (Revenue papers), f. 74r–v.

10   *A Collection of the State Papers of John Thurloe*, ed. Thomas Birch (7 vols., 1742), II, p. 588: Bordeaux to the Count de Brienne, 14 Sept. 1654 [n.s.].

11   Jones, 'Composition and Activity of the Protectorate Parliaments', p. 74.

12   P.R.O., SP 18/74/115: [Sir Edward Nicholas] to Mr Jane, 22 Aug./1 Sept. 1654.

13   *C[alendar] [of] S[tate] P[apers] V[enetian]*, XXIX (1653–4), pp. 235–6: Lorenzo Paulucci to Giovanni Sagredo, 17 July 1654. This situation was not significantly altered by the fact that before the parliament assembled the council 'purged' less than a dozen members, only two of whom apparently had presbyterian sympathies. Nor was it decisively changed when over 100 members withdrew on 12 September rather than sign a recognition promising to accept 'the [Instrument of] Government, as it is settled in a single person and a Parliament'. See Gaunt, 'Cromwell's Purge?'; and Gardiner, *History of the Commonwealth and Protectorate*, III, pp. 173–8, 193–7.

The influence of such people among the parliament's most active members can be discerned in the religious reforms that were adopted for inclusion in the draft 'constitutional bill' to which the parliament devoted so much of its time.[14] Initially, the parliament had envisaged creating an assembly of divines which would advise members on religious reform.[15] However, on 5 October, a grand committee for religion was appointed to meet on two afternoons a week, to discuss 'matters of religion' with the advice of between 12 and 20 ministers.[16] The religious measures that the House subsequently adopted fell into two main categories: the provision and maintenance of the ministry, and the prevention of what were deemed religious errors, heresies and blasphemies. On both issues, the principal concern was to create structures that would regulate the nation's religious life. As the French ambassador observed in late October: 'The Parliament is still taken up about religion: I am afraid they are not good enough to be fathers of the Church, to form a true canonical one. In all likelihood, they will set the Presbytery uppermost, and give toleration to the others.'[17]

Within a month of its assembling, the parliament turned to the issue of the ministry. Before it had met, Cromwell had issued two protectoral ordinances specifically designed to improve the quality of the ministry: that of March 1654 established a national body of 'triers' to vet all new clergy, while the following August county commissioners known as 'ejectors' were set up to expel 'scandalous, ignorant and insufficient ministers and school-masters'.[18] The parliament referred both these ordinances to a large committee of 94 members.[19] This committee initially suggested suspending the ordinance for the 'ejectors' while they drafted a new bill, but that proposal was narrowly defeated.[20] I have not found any hints in the surviving sources as to the contents of this new bill. We do know, however, that it was read twice during the course of November and after the second reading was referred back to the committee, 'upon some exceptions', never to resurface during the parliament's lifetime.[21] Pending further progress on that bill, the parliament resolved on 7 December that,

---

14   The text of this 'constitutional bill' is printed in *Constitutional Documents of the Puritan Revolution, 1625–1660*, ed. S. R. Gardiner (3rd edn., Oxford, 1906), pp. 427–47.

15   *Commons Journals* (hereafter *C.J.*), VII, 367. See also *Diary of Thomas Burton, Esq.*, ed. J. T. Rutt (4 vols., 1828), I, p. xxvii (this and subsequent references are to the journal of Guibon Goddard, printed as an introduction to Burton's diary).

16   *C.J.*, VII, p. 373; *Diary of Thomas Burton*, ed. Rutt, I, p. xlvi.

17   *Thurloe State Papers*, ed. Birch, II, p. 697: Bordeaux to the Count de Chavost, 6 Nov. 1654 [n.s.].

18   *Acts and Ordinances of the Interregnum, 1642–1660*, ed. C. H. Firth and R. S. Rait (3 vols., 1911), II, pp. 855–8, 968–90.

19   *C.J.*, VII, pp. 370, 371. See also *Diary of Thomas Burton*, ed. Rutt, I, p. xli.

20   *C.J.*, VII, pp. 377, 381, 382. See also *Diary of Thomas Burton*, ed. Rutt, I, p. lxii.

21   *C.J.*, VII, pp. 377, 381, 382, 384, 385–7. See also *Diary of Thomas Burton*, ed. Rutt, I, pp. lxii, lxxv, lxxix, lxxxix.

until some better provision be made by the Parliament, for the encouragement and maintenance of able, godly, and painful ministers, and public preachers of the Gospel, for instructing the people, and for discovery and confutation of errors, heresy and whatsoever is contrary to sound doctrine, the present public maintenance shall not be taken away, nor impeached.[22]

This was accompanied by a resolution that 'the true reformed Protestant Christian religion as it is contained in the Holy Scriptures of the Old and New Testament, and no other, shall be asserted and maintained as the public profession of these nations'.[23] The next day (8 December), after 'a long debate',[24] the parliament resolved that any subsequent bills that required,

from such ministers and preachers of the Gospel as shall receive public maintenance for instructing the people, a submission and conformity to the public profession aforesaid, or enjoining attendance unto the preaching of the word and other religious duties on the Lord's day . . . shall pass into and become laws within twenty days after the presentation to the Lord Protector, although he shall not give his consent thereunto.[25]

This represented a firm rebuff to Cromwell and a clear indication of the importance that the majority of members attached to public conformity by a national ministry.

These steps to maintain the ministry and the 'public profession' of religion were complemented by measures to suppress 'damnable heresies' and blasphemies. Throughout the deliberations on this subject, liberty of conscience remained a much lower priority, to be denied whenever it conflicted with the prevention of errors, heresies and blasphemies, or the maintenance of public order. Thus, on 15 December, after two days of 'long debates',[26] the House resolved that,

without the consent of the Lord Protector and Parliament, no law or statute be made for the restraining of such tender consciences as shall

22   C.J., VII, p. 397. See also *Diary of Thomas Burton*, ed. Rutt, I, p. cxii. This clause was adopted as chapter 44 of the draft 'constitutional bill'. *Constitutional Documents*, ed. Gardiner, p. 443.
23   C.J., VII, p. 397. See also *Diary of Thomas Burton*, ed. Rutt, I, p. cxii. This clause was adopted as chapter 41 of the 'constitutional bill'. *Constitutional Documents*, ed. Gardiner, p. 442.
24   Bulstrode Whitelocke, *Memorials of the English Affairs* (4 vols., Oxford, 1838), IV, p. 159.
25   C.J., VII, p. 398. See also *Diary of Thomas Burton*, ed. Rutt, I, pp. cxii–cxiii. This clause was adopted as chapter 42 of the 'constitutional bill'. *Constitutional Documents*, ed. Gardiner, pp. 442–3.
26   Whitelocke, *Memorials*, IV, p. 161; *Diary of Thomas Burton*, ed. Rutt, I, pp. cxviii–cxix.

differ in doctrine, worship or discipline, from the public profession aforesaid and shall not abuse this liberty to the civil injury of others, or the
disturbance of the public peace.

To this, however, was added the crucial proviso that,

> such bills as shall be agreed upon by the Parliament, for the restraining
> of atheism, blasphemy, damnable heresies, to be particularly enumerated
> by this Parliament, popery, prelacy, licentiousness, or profaneness; or
> such as shall preach, print, or avowedly maintain any thing contrary to
> the fundamental principles of doctrine held forth in the public profession
> . . . shall pass into, and become laws, within twenty days after their pre-
> sentation to the Lord Protector, although he shall not give his consent
> thereunto.[27]

This remarkable final clause constituted further direct defiance of Cromwell
and his promotion of liberty of conscience.

The most specific illustration of the difference between Cromwell and the
parliament over liberty of conscience was the case of the socinian John
Biddle. In his two books, *A Two-Fold Catechism* and *The Apostolical and True
Opinion, concerning the Holy Trinity, revived and asserted,* Biddle had denied
the Trinity and the divinity of Christ, and London presbyterians were quick
to identify him as a target.[28] He was interrogated by a parliamentary committee, and the House subsequently endorsed the committee's verdict that
the *Two-Fold Catechism* expressed 'many blasphemous and heretical opinions', and that *The Apostolical and True Opinion* was 'full of horrid, blasphemous, and execrable opinions, denying the Deity of Christ and of the Holy
Ghost'.[29] Biddle was imprisoned and his books burnt; and his case soon
prompted a broader attack on the quakers, against whom a bill was prepared.[30] Although Cromwell did not prevent Biddle's punishment, it was

27   *C.J.*, VII, p. 401. See also *Diary of Thomas Burton*, ed. Rutt, I, pp. cxviii–cxix. This clause
was adopted as chapter 43 of the 'constitutional bill'. *Constitutional Documents*, ed. Gardiner,
p. 443. Earlier, the parliament had resolved by 85 votes to 84 (11 Dec.) to provide 'a particular enumeration of heresies' after the words 'damnable heresies' (*C.J.*, VII, p. 399), and then
(13 Dec.) to include the specific words 'blasphemy', 'popery', 'prelacy', 'licentiousness' and
'profaneness' (*C.J.*, VII, p. 400). These resolutions were subsequently confirmed on 3, 12 and
15 January (*C.J.*, VII, pp. 412, 414, 416).
28   Blair Worden, 'Toleration and the Cromwellian Protectorate', in *Persecution and Toleration,*
ed. W. J. Sheils (Studies in Church History, XXI, 1984), pp. 199–233, esp. pp. 218–21.
29   *Diary of Thomas Burton*, ed. Rutt, I, pp. cxxix–cxxx. Parliament's handling of Biddle's case
can be reconstructed from *ibid.*, pp. cxiv–cxvii, cxxiii, cxxviii–cxxx; and *C.J.*, VII, pp. 400, 404,
416.
30   *C.J.*, VII, p. 410; *Diary of Thomas Burton*, ed. Rutt, I, p. cxxvii. The attack on quakers was
also prompted by the bizarre protest outside the palace of Westminster of Theauraujohn Tany,
for whom see especially Ariel Hessayon, ' "Gold Tried in the Fire": The Prophet Theauraujohn
Tany and the Puritan Revolution', University of Cambridge Ph.D., 1996.

characteristic that he ensured that Biddle was imprisoned on the Scilly Isles, beyond parliament's reach, and also granted him a weekly allowance of ten shillings.[31]

To the lord protector, who in his opening speech had called 'liberty of conscience and liberty of the subjects' 'two as glorious things to be contended for, as any God hath given us',[32] the attitudes of some of the parliament's most able and active members were profoundly disappointing. In that speech he went on to lament that there was

> too much of an imposing spirit in matter of conscience; a spirit unchristian enough in any times, most unfit for these; denying liberty of conscience to those who have earned it with their blood; who have gained civil liberty, and religious also, for those who would thus impose upon them

(at which point Carlyle interpolated in his edition: 'stifled murmurs from the Presbyterian sect').[33] In his great speech of 12 September, Cromwell declared that 'liberty of conscience in religion' was 'a fundamental' and 'a natural right'.[34] But such 'a thing ought to be very reciprocal', and in his final speech Cromwell denounced the parliament's failure to give 'a just liberty to godly men of different judgments', and to settle 'peace and quietness amongst all professing godliness', adding: 'is there not upon the spirits of men a strange itch? Nothing will satisfy them unless they can put their finger upon their brethren's consciences, to pinch them there.'[35] On this point Cromwell was fundamentally at odds with the prevailing mood of the parliament. Moreover, the specific limitations that the 'constitutional bill' placed on his capacity to promote liberty of conscience must have heightened his resentment of the parliament's systematic curtailing of other protectoral powers established in the Instrument of Government.

Cromwell's anger at the parliament's failure to ensure liberty of conscience was widely shared among the soldiery. Towards the end of 1654, the army presented a petition to Cromwell that included the demands that 'liberty of conscience be allowed, but not to papistry in publicke worshipp', and that 'a law be made for the righting [of] persons wronged for liberty of conscience'.[36] The Venetian ambassador noted wrily that when, 'in spite of

31 Worden, 'Toleration and the Cromwellian Protectorate', pp. 221–2; J. C. Davis, 'Cromwell's Religion', in *Oliver Cromwell and the English Revolution*, ed. John Morrill (Harlow, 1990), pp. 196–7.
32 *Letters and Speeches of Cromwell*, ed. Lomas, II, p. 345.
33 *Ibid.*, p. 346.
34 *Ibid.*, p. 382.
35 *Ibid.*, pp. 416–17.
36 *The Clarke Papers. Selections from the Papers of William Clarke*, ed. C. H. Firth (4 vols., Camden Soc., new ser., XLIX, LIV, LXI, LXII, 1891–1901), III, p. 13. Cf. *A Perfect Account of the Daily Intelligence from the Armies in England, Scotland and Ireland, and the Navy at Sea* (1–8 Nov. 1654), sig. 9Q (B.L., Thomason Tracts, E 816/9).

the article in the paper presented by some of the Army against interference in religion', the parliament 'decided that the religion generally professed here must be the Protestant', this outcome 'possibly dissatisfied the military'.[37] In fact, a number of the most prominent members, including such figures as John FitzJames, John Bulkeley, Sir Richard Onslow, John Birch, John Ashe and Robert Shapcote, had a long history of antipathy towards the independent cause espoused by the army. With the exception of Fitz-James, who had not sat in the Long Parliament, all these members had been imprisoned or secluded at Pride's purge.[38] The tensions that erupted during the first Protectorate parliament between on the one hand Cromwell and the army, and on the other a number of active members of presbyterian sympathies, thus represented in part the continuation of a long-term fissure within the parliamentarian cause that could be traced back to the later 1640s.

Those within parliament who opposed the unqualified grant of liberty of conscience had close links with like-minded laity and divines in the wider world. Blair Worden has shown how they forged in particular 'an effective alliance with the Presbyterian machine of the City of London'.[39] That machine had two principal motors: the Stationers' Company and the London Provincial Assembly. One leading member of the latter, the presbyterian minister Jeremiah Whitaker, wrote to Cromwell in the summer of 1654 begging him to 'consider seriously how religion is not onely weakened by divisione, but almost wasted by the daily growth of Atheisme and the Prophane: the reignes of Government time let lose, and now lost, in the Church totally'. Horrified to see 'sabboths generally prophaned, ordinances despised, the consciences of men growing wanton abusing liberty to all licentuousnes', Whitaker hoped that the lord protector would 'appoint such Justices whose principles and practices lead them to restrain vice, who do account the Sabboth their delight, that so [lesser?] officers may bee by them encouraged [to] repress prophanes'.[40] No evidence survives of any reply from Cromwell to Whitaker, but the letter is indicative of presbyterian hopes within the city of London. These were again plainly apparent in a petition

37 *Calendar of State Papers Venetian*, XXX (1655–6), p. 1 (Lorenzo Paulucci to Giovanni Sagredo, 2 January 1655 [new style]).
38 For Bulkeley, see David Underdown, *Pride's Purge. Politics in the Puritan Revolution* (1971), p. 369. For Onslow, see Mary Frear Keeler, *The Long Parliament, 1640–1641. A Biographical Study of its Members* (Memoirs of the American Philosophical Society, XXXVI, Philadelphia, 1954), p. 290; Underdown, *Pride's Purge*, p. 381; and the *D[ictionary] [of] N[ational] B[iography]*. For Birch, see Underdown, *Pride's Purge*, p. 368; and the *D.N.B.* For Ashe, see Keeler, *Long Parliament*, p. 91; and Underdown, *Pride's Purge*, p. 367. For Shapcote, see Underdown, *Pride's Purge*, p. 385.
39 Worden, 'Toleration and the Cromwellian Protectorate', p. 218.
40 B.L., Add. MS 4159, f. 113r: Jeremiah Whitaker to Oliver Cromwell, [?summer 1654]. I am most grateful to Elliot Vernon for giving me a transcript of this letter, for advice on its date and significance, and for a helpful discussion about Whitaker.

that the common council submitted to Cromwell towards the end of 1654 'to encourage the Parliament about settling Church government'. To this, Cromwell responded plaintively: 'where shall wee have men of a universall spirit? Every one desires to have liberty, but none will give it.'[41]

It is occasionally possible to reconstruct links between certain members of the first Protectorate parliament and ministers or laymen of similar views outside parliament. The letter-book of one member unsympathetic to liberty of conscience, John FitzJames, reveals that he maintained an extensive correspondence with those of a like persuasion including not only other members, such as Robert Shapcote and Robert Beake, but also ministers like Stanley Gower and William Mew as well as gentry such as Andrew Bromhall and Robert Lewen.[42] FitzJames's own scepticism about liberty of conscience was well captured when he wrote to Shapcote: 'whether a religion that pleases *all* interests can please *one* God, there's the question.'[43] As in earlier seventeenth-century parliaments, an elaborate network existed that transmitted news of parliamentary proceedings back to the provinces, and in turn enabled those at Westminster to draw advice and encouragement from friends and relatives outside the capital.[44]

It is also worth remembering that, under the terms of the Instrument of Government, the first Protectorate parliament included representatives from Scotland and Ireland.[45] The Instrument stipulated that there should be 30 Scottish members and 30 Irish, although the actual numbers returned were probably 22 and somewhere between 15 and 25 respectively.[46] The influence of these members within the parliament generally, and on religious issues specifically, is extremely difficult to determine. However, it is likely that at least some of these members were of presbyterian sympathies and that their presence therefore tended to strengthen hostility towards liberty of conscience. The member for County Cork, Lord Broghill, provides a good case-study of this. Broghill was well connected in both Ireland and Scotland: the owner of extensive lands in Ireland, he was

---

41   *The Clarke Papers*, ed. Firth, II, pp. xxxv–xxxvi.

42   Northumberland MS 551, ff. 3v–13v (duke of Northumberland, Alnwick Castle, Northumberland), letter-book of John FitzJames, V, 9 Sept. 1654–2 Sept. 1656. I am most grateful to Patrick Little for drawing this source to my attention, and to his grace the duke of Northumberland for granting me permission to consult the microfilm of it in the British Library (B.L., Microfilm M 331).

43   Alnwick Castle, Northumberland MS 551, f. 8v: John FitzJames to Robert Shapcote, 8/18 Nov. 1654. Original emphasis.

44   Cf. Richard Cust, 'News and Politics in Early Seventeenth-Century England', *Past and Present*, No. 112 (1986), pp. 60–90.

45   *Constitutional Documents*, ed. Gardiner, p. 407 (Instrument of Government, IX).

46   For the Scottish elections, and the 22 members returned (of whom nine were English), see F. D. Dow, *Cromwellian Scotland, 1651–1660* (Edinburgh, 1979), pp. 148–54. For information about the Irish members, and this estimate of their numbers, I am indebted to Patrick Little.

appointed lord president of the Scottish council in 1655, and in the second Protectorate parliament he sat for both County Cork and Edinburgh.[47] In the first Protectorate parliament he was appointed to the committee to review the ordinance 'for ejecting scandalous, ignorant and insufficient ministers and schoolmasters', and acted as a teller for the noes who opposed its suspension.[48] On 12 December 1654, he was appointed to a committee 'to consider of the particular enumeration of damnable heresies'.[49] Later, on 3 January 1655, he acted as a teller for the yeas in favour of retaining the words 'to be particularly enumerated by the Parliament' after 'damnable heresies' in the House's resolution of 15 December.[50] Broghill's friends included the presbyterian minister Richard Baxter, and Broghill nominated Baxter to the group of divines chosen to confer with parliament's sub-committee on religion.[51] Baxter subsequently wrote of his hostility to 'an universall toleration for all that shall seeke the subversion of the faith of Christ'. Although keen to 'distinguish betweene tolerable and intollerable errours, and restraine only the latter', he was vehemently opposed to 'licentious toleration of Church destroyers'.[52] Broghill's role on committees and as a teller during the first Protectorate parliament suggests that his own stance on religious issues was consistent with Baxter's position.

The lack of sympathy within parliament towards liberty of conscience was crucial in explaining why Cromwell did not find the assembly, in Bulstrode Whitelocke's phrase, 'pliable to his purposes'.[53] The chances of achieving such pliability were not enhanced by the fact that those councillors of state who sat in the parliament do not appear to have formed a coherent group; there is little sign that they attempted to co-ordinate their activities or to set a lead in the House. The government did not introduce any clear legislative programme, and parliamentary business proceeded on an *ad hoc* basis.[54] In part this reflected Cromwell's conviction that he should not interfere directly in the parliament's deliberations.[55] However, the

47   I am very grateful to Patrick Little for this information, and for a helpful discussion about Broghill. For useful outlines of Broghill's career, see the article on him in the *D.N.B.*, and also Dow, *Cromwellian Scotland*, pp. 162–210.

48   *C.J.*, VII, pp. 370, 382. The noes carried the day by 77 votes to 67.

49   *Ibid.*, p. 399.

50   *Ibid.*, p. 412. The yeas carried the day by 81 votes to 75. The resolution is quoted above, pp. 173–4.

51   *Calendar of the Correspondence of Richard Baxter*, ed. N. H. Keeble and Geoffrey F. Nuttall (2 vols., Oxford, 1991), I, pp. 160, 162, 189. I am very grateful to Patrick Little for these references.

52   *Ibid.*, pp. 222–6: Baxter to Edward Harley, 15 Sept. 1656 (quotations at pp. 223, 226). I owe this reference to Patrick Little.

53   *The Diary of Bulstrode Whitelocke, 1605–1675*, ed. Ruth Spalding (British Academy, Records of Social and Economic History, new ser., XIII, Oxford, 1990), p. 400: 3 Feb. 1655. The same phrase also appears in Whitelocke, *Memorials*, IV p. 182: 1 Feb. 1655.

54   Gaunt, 'Councils of the Protectorate', pp. 129–42.

55   See, e.g., *Letters and Speeches of Cromwell*, ed. Lomas, II, pp. 359, 407.

problem went much deeper than that, and it ultimately revealed a basic tension within Cromwell's own concept of the role of parliament which prevented him from achieving a stable working relationship with any of the interregnum parliaments. Throughout his career, he believed that parliament had a constitutional role of central importance: as he put it on 12 September, 'the government by a single person and a Parliament is a fundamental. It is the *esse*, it is constitutive.'[56] Yet how did this relate to that other 'fundamental', liberty of conscience? Cromwell wished to use parliament to unify the interests of the nation with those of the people of God. He was attracted to the Instrument of Government because he felt that within it 'a just liberty to the people of God, and the just rights of the people in these nations [were] provided for'.[57] He believed that if parliament, the 'representative of the whole realm', promoted liberty of conscience, then the interests of the nation and of the godly would eventually be reconciled. This was what a 'pliable' parliament would have done. Unfortunately, this parliament, from which only a few of the most obviously hostile individuals had been purged before the session opened,[58] contained a core of members who were vehemently opposed to any agenda that might lift the lid off a seething mass of sectarian errors and blasphemies.

The story of the first Protectorate parliament was thus part of a wider pattern that characterized Cromwell's relations with successive parliaments throughout the interregnum. His fundamental conviction that parliament had a crucial role to play in reconciling the interests of the godly with those of the nation as a whole helps to explain why he remained committed to working with parliaments. There was not a single calendar year throughout the Commonwealth and Protectorate when a parliament did not meet at some stage. Yet always they disappointed him, for the 'representative of the whole realm' never produced an assembly in which a majority of members shared his and the army's commitment to liberty of conscience. Much of the problem lay in the way that Cromwell viewed the relationship between parliament, the nation and the people of God. Committed to the belief that England was an elect nation, he wanted the godly people to become ever more numerous until they ultimately comprised the whole nation. In that way, the visible and invisible churches would eventually become coterminous. He hoped that parliament, by promulgating liberty of conscience and fostering peaceful co-existence amongst 'God's children', would play a central part in this process. Yet, as Cromwell complained to his confidant Lieutenant-Colonel Wilks in January 1655, 'whosoever labours to walk with an even foot between the several interests of the people of God for healing and accommodating their differences is sure to have reproaches

56   *Ibid.*, p. 381.
57   *Ibid.*, p. 419.
58   Gaunt, 'Cromwell's Purge?'.

and anger from some of all sorts.'[59] The first Protectorate parliament, like those before and after, continued to reflect the widespread civilian unease about liberating the sects. The parliament had been elected on a revised franchise, with a major redistribution of seats towards the counties and a £200 property qualification.[60] As a result, it manifested many of the attitudes that were apparently mainstream within the political and social *élite*, and was deeply reluctant to espouse what remained a minority agenda.

Cromwell's commitment to liberty of conscience thus generated profound tensions between the 'single person and a parliament' which dogged the entire history of the interregnum. By struggling to create an identity between the interests of the nation and those of the godly, he doomed himself to a relationship with parliaments characterized by constant frustration and mutual bafflement. His dealings with parliament in 1654–5 set the pattern for the rest of the Protectorate. Just as he saw the Instrument of Government as a way of reconciling 'a just liberty to the people of God' with 'the just rights of the people in these nations',[61] so, in April 1657, he praised the framers of the Humble Petition and Advice on the grounds that,

> I think you have provided for the liberty of the people of God, and for the liberty of the nation. And I say he sings sweetly that sings a song of reconciliation betwixt these two interests! And it is a pitiful fancy, and wild and ignorant to think they are inconsistent. Certainly they may consist![62]

Yet, like the other interregnum parliaments, the deliberations of the first Protectorate parliament repeatedly demonstrated their essential inconsistency.

When members assembled at Westminster in the autumn of 1654, neither they, nor the lord protector, nor the army leaders doubted that parliament had a crucial role to play in settling the church and the religious life of the nation. In that sense, the relationship between parliament and the church was taken as a given. But what sort of settlement was to be constructed? How rigid should the national structures be, and what measure of liberty of conscience was acceptable? Perhaps more than any other single issue, the differences of opinion between Cromwell and a significant core of members were responsible for destabilizing the parliament and frustrating

59   *Letters and Speeches of Cromwell*, ed. Lomas, III, p. 460: Cromwell to Lieutenant-Colonel Wilks [? 14–18 Jan. 1655].
60   Vernon F. Snow, 'Parliamentary Reapportionment Proposals in the Puritan Revolution', *English Historical Review*, LXXIV (1959), pp. 409–42. The revised distribution of seats is set out in the Instrument of Government, printed in *Constitutional Documents*, ed. Gardiner, pp. 407–9.
61   *Letters and Speeches of Cromwell*, ed. Lomas, II, p. 419.
62   *Ibid.*, III, p. 101.

the lord protector's high hopes of it. In many ways it was a tension within Cromwell's own vision, between his commitment to parliament and his pursuit of liberty of conscience, that doomed both to failure. He was trying to embrace as 'fundamentals' two objectives that were ultimately incompatible. It is uncertain how far he ever perceived this. But we can occasionally hear him, so to speak whistling in the dark, hoping against hope that the two might be reconciled, as for example when he told representatives of the second Protectorate parliament on 3 April 1657:

> If anyone whatsoever think the interest of Christians and the interest of the nation inconsistent, or two different things, I wish my soul may never enter into their secrets ... And upon these two interests, if God shall account me worthy, I shall live and die. And ... if I were to give an account before a greater tribunal than any earthly one; and if I were asked why I have engaged all along in the late war, I could give no answer but it would be a wicked one if it did not comprehend these two ends.[63]

Ironically, it was precisely the attempt to tie those two ends together that had earlier brought the first Protectorate parliament to deadlock; and behind Cromwell's brave words in April 1657, there must surely have lurked, at least in part, the memory of that previous parliamentary disaster.

63   *Ibid.*, p. 31.

8

Cromwell, Scotland and Ireland

David Stevenson

Originally appeared as David Stevenson, 'Cromwell, Scotland and Ireland' in John Morrill (ed.), *Oliver Cromwell and the English Revolution*. Copyright 1990 Longman, Harlow.

Editor's Introduction

In recent years, historians of this period have paid much greater attention to what has been called the 'British Problem': the interaction of, and unstable relationship between, the three kingdoms of England, Scotland and Ireland. In this essay, David Stevenson explores how Cromwell perceived Scotland and Ireland and the development of his policies towards them during the Interregnum. He argues that the common denominator of Cromwell's strategy was to ensure security for the English republic, and that there were significant differences in his handling of the other two kingdoms within the archipelago.

In 1649, Cromwell regarded Ireland as the more immediate threat to English security. His view of the Irish as Catholic barbarians was typical of English prejudices of the period, and it lay behind the savage massacres at Drogheda and Wexford as well as the subsequent destruction of traditional Catholic society in Ireland. The Catholic population was deported to Connaught or Clare, and the proportion of Irish land in Catholic hands fell from 59 per cent in 1641 to 20 per cent by the 1660s. Cromwell apparently believed that Ireland presented almost unlimited opportunities for establishing a new godly society and English legal models. Yet in practice the regime gradually acknowledged the futility of attempts to convert the majority of the Irish population to Protestantism and concentrated instead on making the minority Protestant community as secure as possible.

If Cromwell's deep religious convictions explain the harshness of his conquest of Ireland, they also account for the relative leniency of his treatment of the Scots. He regarded the Scots as fellow Protestants, even though he disliked the inflexibility and intolerance of Presbyterianism, and lamented that many Scots had been seduced by Royalism in 1648–51. His treatment of them was more akin to his handling of his political opponents in England, and he seems to have genuinely believed that he was offering the Scots the legal and social benefits of being treated as honorary Englishmen. The fact that the Scots understandably did not appreciate these benefits, and only accepted the proffered union with England because military defeat left them no alternative, saddened and frustrated him.

In both Ireland and Scotland, Cromwellian government kept coming up against the same fundamental problems: a constant shortage of money; difficulties in finding administrators who would be both reliable and acceptable to the native populations; and uncertainty over whether the authority to take decisions lay in Edinburgh and Dublin or in London. Above all, in neither Ireland nor Scotland did Cromwell win the enthusiastic support for which he yearned. He wanted to make them 'little Englands': he remained sceptical about the concept of 'Britain', and only conquered the periphery in order to protect England. Yet, by a sad irony, that same lack of widespread positive endorsement for his regime was equally evident in England as well.

Cromwell, Scotland and Ireland

David Stevenson*

When Britain collapsed into civil wars in the years around 1640 the crisis began in the periphery, first in Scotland and then in Ireland, and then spread to England as failure to crush revolts in these outlying kingdoms discredited Charles I's regime. A decade later the process was reversed, the power of government centralized in London being first asserted in England, then applied to Ireland, and finally to Scotland where the breakdown of power had begun. And just as failure in the periphery had discredited Charles I, so the assertion of English power in it was central to the prestige of Oliver Cromwell.

In one respect Cromwell's basic attitude to the two outlying kingdoms was the same. They posed threats to England, not just in that they had overthrown control from London, but more actively in that they sought to impose their wills on the central kingdom. The security of England thus necessitated their conquest. Yet in other ways his attitudes to the two differed fundamentally. Whereas from 1641 onwards he can have had no doubt that Ireland would have to be reconquered, until late in the day he hoped it would not be necessary to conquer Scotland.

Where the Irish were concerned, doubtless Cromwell's starting point was the simple view of the Irish as barbarous papists who, through their religion, were potentially disloyal as well as being a standing reproach to the protestant Crown of England. In the later 1630s, however, Cromwell's perceptions of Ireland would have begun to change. The 'thorough' policies of Lord Wentworth as Lord Deputy suggested that in the short term a threat from Ireland might not be presented by native Irish, but through Ireland being deliberately made into a bastion of arbitrary royal power, a test-bed for policies later to be introduced in England. Then, after the Scottish revolt of 1637 broke out, Ireland assumed a new threatening role, when a largely catholic army was raised for use against protestant Scots, a worrying precedent that might later have an application in England.

Yet of course when Ireland did suddenly become a major threat to English interest, it was in a traditional way – by the revolt of the native Irish in October 1641. This revolt, the real suffering inflicted on protestant settlers, and the vastly exaggerated rumours of catholic atrocities hardened and fixed attitudes to the Irish for most Englishmen, Cromwell among them. He took an active part in planning to restore English control of Ireland, and

* I am grateful to John Morrill and Sarah Barber for their comments on a draft of this paper.

was a substantial subscriber under the 1642 Adventurers' Act, by which parliament raised money for a campaign there by promising repayment in land confiscated from the Irish.[1] But with the approach of civil war in England later in 1642 Cromwell's attention, like that of parliament as a whole, was diverted to problems closer to home: Ireland would have to wait until England's destiny had been decided.[2]

After the First Civil War was over parliament had resources free to devote to Ireland, and Cromwell's commitment to reconquest was emphasized by his offer in March 1647 to invest arrears of pay due to him plus up to £5,000 in the Irish venture.[3] In the event a major campaign in Ireland was delayed by the need to deal with the Scottish invasion and English royalist rebellions of 1648. But in 1649 attention swung back to Ireland. With rebellions defeated, Charles I executed and monarchy abolished, the new commonwealth regime was at last free to deal with the threats to its authority presented by Ireland. In all we know of Cromwell's attitude to Ireland and the Irish up to this point, there is no sign of any distinctive outlook, any special insights into the Irish problem. He simply shared the attitudes of most Englishmen. Ireland had to be reconquered, as historically subordinate to England, as a potential strategic threat, and as the home of barbarous papists whose crimes must be punished, whose religion must be suppressed.

By contrast, Cromwell's attitude to the Scots was – or became – more subtle, and he showed a readiness to modify stereotyped attitudes based on prevailing English prejudices. From an English viewpoint the Scots shared some of the characteristics of the Irish: they were poor and backward, even barbarous, and not to be trusted. On the other hand, they were protestants, and by the 1630s traditional perceptions of the Scots were being modified in the eyes of those who, like Cromwell, were worried by Charles I's policies in England, by sympathy for the Scots as a people suffering from the same misguided religious and other policies as Englishmen. Such an attitude would have been strengthened, in Cromwell as in so many other Englishmen, into positive respect and support for the Scots when their open resistance to royal policies demonstrated the brittleness of the king's power in and after 1637. It is said that Cromwell told some officers of the army the king was gathering against the Scots that he disliked the war.[4]

Yet once the Scottish covenanters had defeated the king, their ambitions for a peace settlement protecting their interests seemed to many English-

---

1   See K. S. Bottigheimer, *English Money and Irish Land. The 'adventurers' in the Cromwellian settlement of Ireland* (Oxford, 1971).

2   See *Writings and Speeches of Oliver Cromwell*, ed. W. C. Abbott (4 vols, Cambridge, MA, 1937–47, repr. Oxford, 1988), I, pp. 147–8, 160, 162, 172, 182.

3   Ibid., I, p. 588.

4   Ibid., I, pp. 107–8.

men to amount to interference in English affairs. There is, however, no direct evidence of Cromwell's changing attitude to the Scots until after parliament negotiated the Solemn League and Covenant and a military treaty with the covenanters in the autumn of 1643. Like most parliamentarians Cromwell accepted the necessity for gaining Scottish military help against the king; but he also resented and feared the price the Scots demanded in return. Cromwell's attitude was indicated by his long delay in signing the new covenant,[5] and he quickly emerged as the leader of those parliamentarians opposed to Scottish pretensions on all fronts: in religion he opposed their demands for a religious monopoly for presbyterianism; in the conduct of the war he opposed their demands for a compromise, negotiated peace with the king; and in constitutional affairs he was opposed to what he saw as their attempt to determine England's future.

The hostility of Cromwell to Scottish pretensions came into the open after the battle of Marston Moor in July 1644. The Scots, who had fought alongside parliamentary armies in the battle, claimed the victory as largely a Scottish one, but they found that in London it was widely presented as a victory won above all by Cromwell. As the independents and other opponents of the Scots tried to exploit the victory for propaganda purposes, the embittered Scots found that 'their' victory had greatly increased the prestige of Cromwell and others determined to limit their influence.[6]

The Scots fought back, winning considerable English backing. They seized on evidence that Cromwell had 'spoken contumeliouslie of the Scots intention in coming to England to establish their Church-government, in which Cromwell said he would draw his sword against them' – as readily, indeed, as against any in the king's army.[7] The Scots therefore proposed in December 1644 that he should be impeached under the terms of the Solemn League and Covenant as 'an *incendiary*' who was kindling 'coals of contention and raises differences in the state to the public damage'. The attempt failed, but that it was made at all showed how Cromwell was by this time clearly recognized as the leader of opposition to their ambitions in England.[8]

As anti-Scots attitudes spread among parliamentarians, so Cromwell's prestige grew, he being regarded as 'the first to incense the people against the Scots' nation'.[9] The frustration of the Scots, betrayed (as they saw it) by

5 Gardiner, *Great Civil War*, I, pp. 262, 310–11.
6 D. Stevenson, *Revolution and Counter-Revolution in Scotland, 1644–51* (1977), p. 12; R. Baillie, *Letters and Journals* (3 vols, Bannatyne Club, Edinburgh, 1841–2), II, pp. 203, 209.
7 Baillie, *Letters*, II, p. 245; Gardiner, *Civil War*, II, p. 23.
8 Baillie, *Letters*, II, p. 245; Stevenson, *Revolution and Counter-Revolution*, p. 15; Gardiner, *Civil War*, II, pp. 87–8.
9 E. Hyde, earl of Clarendon, *The History of the rebellion and Civil Wars in England*, ed. W. D. Macray (6 vols, Oxford, 1888), IV, p. 307.

their English parliamentarian allies, led them to sign the secret Engagement treaty with the imprisoned Charles I in December 1647. But the co-venanters were now deeply divided. The dominant faction, the Engagers, was an alliance of moderate covenanters, with royalists, determined to help the king, while the more extreme covenanters, supported by most of the parish ministers, felt there was no justification for a war between the kingdoms.

The split among the Scots into Engagers and their opponents, soon to be known as the Kirk Party, was seen by Cromwell as corresponding to the dichotomy present in his own attitude to the Scots, and this dictated his conduct in the 1648 campaign against the Scots and its aftermath. He accepted that in the past decade the Scots had been essentially agents of God's work, and that in their theology, worship, Church organization at the local level, and generally sober and 'puritan' outlook they had much in common with him and his English allies. Yet in their insistence on a strongly centralized system of Church government and in its complete separation from the state, and in their political ambitions, the Scots were enemies of both God and England. Now the Scots had split. The Engagers were clearly enemies of God and England, while the Kirk Party was revealing the essen-tially godly nature of its supporters by opposing the Engagement. Thus at this point there was no question of a war to conquer Scotland. The war was to defeat the Engagers and help godly Scots gain power in their own country. A new Kirk Party regime, once established in Scotland, would be bound in firm friendship to whatever godly regime emerged in England, tied to it by gratitude (as English intervention had brought it to power), by political expediency (as it had shown that it had the power to make or break a regime in Scotland), and by common godliness. The Scots would recognize that Cromwell's victory was a demonstration that he was indeed an agent through whom God was revealing His intentions.

The Engagers' invasion of England was routed by Cromwell at the battle of Preston in August 1648, and he then advanced north, confident that the Scots would see his victory as overwhelming proof of whose side God was on, as 'The witness that God hath borne against your army'.[10] The Kirk Party now staged a *coup d'état*, and Cromwell believed that it was God's will that he treat the new Scottish regime not as representing an enemy nation, but as an ally with which he should cooperate. One of God's motives in allowing the Engagers and English royalists to rise in arms was to show the necessity for friendship between the kingdoms.[11] Enthusiastically he reported that 'I do think the affairs of Scotland are in a thriving posture, as to the interest of honest men.'[12] The godly now ruled the land, and he was

10   Abbott, I, p. 650.
11   Ibid., I, p. 653.
12   Ibid., I, p. 669.

eager to discuss the future with both politicians and ministers. One account survives of him trying to persuade godly Scots of his sincerity. At a meeting with some ministers he 'had a long discourse to them, with a fair flourish of words, and sometimes tears, taking God to be a witness of their sincerity and good intentions'. On leaving one minister was impressed: 'I am very glad to hear this man speak as he does'; but a harder-headed colleague retorted

> And do you believe him. If you knew him as well as I do, you would not believe one word he says. He is an egregious dissembler and a great liar. Away with him, he is a greeting [crying] devil.[13]

As this indicates, the success of Cromwell's 'hearts and minds' campaign in Edinburgh was in reality very limited. Godly though it might be in many respects, the Kirk Party remained implacably opposed to him on matters of Church government and toleration.

Nor was Cromwell's conduct popular in London. Instead of teaching the Scots a harsh lesson by following up victory at Preston with further military action, Cromwell had offered them friendship. Thus the man notorious for years as a hater of the Scots now came to be suspected of undue leniency to them. This provoked Cromwell into defending his attitude to the Scots. He had prayed and

> waited for the day to see union and right understanding between the godly people (Scots, English, Jews, Gentiles, Presbyterians, Independents, Anabaptists, and all). Our brothers of Scotland (really Presbyterians) were our greatest enemies. God hath justified us in their sight; caused us to requite good for evil, causing them to acknowledge it publicly by acts of state, and privately, and the thing is true in the sight of the sun. It is an high conviction upon them. Was it not fit to be civil, to profess love, to deal with clearness with them for removing of prejudice, to ask them what they had against us, and to give them an honest answer? This we have done, and not more. And herein is a more glorious work in our eyes than if we had gotten the sacking and plunder of Edinburgh, the strong castles into our hands, and made conquest from the Tweed to the Orcades; and we can say, through God we have left by the grace of God such a witness amongst them, as if it work not yet there is that conviction upon them that will undoubtedly bear its fruit in due time.

Conquest 'was not very unfeasible, but I think not Christian' – and anyway parliament had not ordered a conquest. By requiting evil with good

13   T. M'Crie (ed.), *The Life of Mr Robert Blair, Minister of St Andrews, containing his autobiography* (Wodrow Society, Edinburgh, 1848), p. 210; Abbott, I, pp. 665–60.

Cromwell hoped he had put the Scots under an unbreakable moral obligation to live in friendship with England.[14]

Just as the Scots were, Cromwell hoped, ready to learn from him, he was ready to learn from them. The Kirk Party (which only formed a minority in the Scottish parliament of 1648), had, after seizing power, disqualified the Engager majority from sitting in the 1649 and later sessions of parliaments. Cromwell was deeply impressed:

> . . . a lesser party of a Parliament hath made it lawful to declare the greater part a faction, and made the Parliament null, and call a new one, and do this by force. . . . Think of the example and of the consequences, and let others think of it too.[15]

A month later 'Pride's Purge' saw the army expel most of the members of the House of Commons. Cromwell claimed not to have known of the planned purge, but it is hard to believe he did not have a part in inspiring it, through drawing the attention of 'others' to a useful Scottish precedent.

Cromwell was soon disappointed by the Scots. The trial and execution of the king turned uneasy alliance between the revolutionary regimes of the two kingdoms into hostility. Again Cromwell argued with them, seeing their attitudes as tragically misguided rather than totally ungodly. He even, in an argument the irony of which must have been evident to all, cited the very article of the Solemn League and Covenant under which the Scots had once tried to impeach him as justification for acting against the king: Charles was an incendiary![16]

It was all to no avail. When Charles was executed the Scots immediately proclaimed his son Charles II as king – and king of England and Ireland as well as Scotland. Cromwell at last admitted that his policy of leniency towards the Scots had failed. In the new Council of State on 23 March 1649 he explained his understanding of the situation:

> In the kingdom of Scotland, you cannot too well take notice of what is done nor of this; that there is a very angry, hateful spirit there against your army, as an army of sectaries, which you see all their papers do declare their quarrel to be against. And although God hath used us as instruments for their good, yet hitherto they are not sensible of it, but they are angry that God brought them His mercy at such an hand.

The ungrateful Scots had spurned England's proffered friendship, and the godly Kirk Party, like the ungodly Engagers before them, were seeking,

---

14   Abbott, I, pp. 677–8.
15   Ibid., I, p. 678.
16   Ibid., I, p. 746.

through links with royalists, 'the ruin and destruction of those that God hath ordained to be instrumental for their good'.[17]

England having been lost to Charles II, it was obvious that any attempt to restore monarchy would come through Scotland or Ireland. He at first favoured Ireland as the base for an attempt to regain his thrones, and Cromwell told the Council that the Irish might soon be able to land their forces in England. Given the deep divisions in Ireland he probably exaggerated, but his statement showed where he believed England's priorities lay. An informal aside confirmed this:

> I confess I have had these thoughts with myself, that perhaps many be carnal and foolish. I had rather be overrun with a Cavalierish interest than a Scotch interest; I had rather be overrun with a Scotch interest, than an Irish interest; and I think of all this is most dangerous.[18]

Ireland presented the most immediate threat, so action against Ireland was the first priority. Moreover the adventurers, with their claims to land in Ireland in return for their investments, were clamouring for action.

The political situation in Ireland was chaotic. Most of the Irish who had originally rebelled in 1641 had, by 1649, joined themselves to protestant royalists under the marquis of Ormonde, uniting in an uneasy alliance as this seemed to offer the only hope of resisting the attack which would clearly come from the armies of the English parliament – which indeed already held Dublin. But minorities of both protestants and catholics rejected such an alliance based on political expediency, so there also existed forces of Irish catholics which refused to work with royalists, and disaffected protestant royalist forces which were moving towards acceptance of the authority of the English parliament rather than ally with catholics. In Ulster the situation was further complicated by the presence of many thousands of Scots presbyterians whose political sympathies lay with Scotland rather than England.

Cromwell landed in Dublin on 15 August 1649. Just two weeks before parliament's commander there, Michael Jones, had won a remarkable victory at Rathmines over Ormonde's combined Irish and royalist army, a disaster to the Irish which was so complete and demoralizing that they never again dared face the English army in the field. Instead they concentrated on garrisoning towns and castles. Cromwell's campaign was therefore one in which the only large-scale fighting took place at the storming of such strongholds, though there was a good deal of mopping up of small bands of Irish to be done as their armies disintegrated.

17   Ibid., II, p. 37.
18   Ibid., II, p. 38.

Cromwell hailed Rathmines as 'an astonishing mercy; so great and sea-sonable as indeed we are like them that dreamed. What can we say! The Lord fill our souls with thankfulness.'[19] He told Dublin's inhabitants – mainly protestant – that he intended with divine aid to restore them to their just liberty and property.[20] Thus some in Ireland were to be able to win the favour of the commonwealth: but the vast majority of the country's inhabitants were not offered such hopes. It was not just the catholic Irish (who were now taken to include the 'Old English' – catholics of English descent – as well as native Irish) who could expect no mercy. Protestant royalists who were now allied to the Irish were regarded as sharing in their crimes. Even among protestants who had not joined the Irish there were few who had not at some point in the chaotic events since 1641 collaborated with Irish or royalists, and the Scots in the north were suspect as collabo-rators with their misguided countrymen in Scotland. There was, therefore, no possibility of military action in Ireland giving way to a compromise set-tlement negotiated with some existing faction in the country, as had hap-pened in Scotland the year before.

The Cromwellian conquest of Ireland is associated above all else with the names of Drogheda and Wexford. Brutal though the massacres in these towns are in the British context, in a wider context of European warfare they are not outstanding. Indeed they can be taken as examples of the two most common types of massacre after the fall of a stronghold. At Drogheda Cromwell summoned the governor to surrender, adding that 'If this be refused you will have no cause to blame me' for the consequences.[21] Accord-ing to the accepted conventions of warfare, if a garrison inflicted casualties on a besieging army after refusing a summons to surrender, and it was then taken by storm, the victors were justified in exacting retribution for the unnecessary losses they incurred. Cromwell applied this convention: it was his bitterness at the losses of his army in the storm of Drogheda that pro-voked him into sanctioning indiscriminate massacre. But though this pro-vides an explanation, it does not provide an excuse: and undoubtedly the fact that his enemy was 'Irish', representing a people whose blood guilt was regarded as putting them almost beyond the bounds of humanity, con-tributed to his readiness to sanction the deed. In reality, most of the garri-son was composed of English royalists, under an English commander, but in Cromwell's eyes as they had allied themselves to the Irish they shared the blood guilt of the latter.

Cromwell felt no need to excuse his conduct at Drogheda, but he did feel it needed explaining: 'And truely I believe this bitterness will save much effu-sion of blood, through the goodness of God', as it would frighten other gar-

19   Ibid., II, p. 103.
20   Ibid., II, p. 107.
21   Ibid., II, p. 118.

risons into surrendering without a fight. Thus it was 'a marvellous great mercy',[22] a 'righteous judgment of God on these barbarous wretches, who have imbrued their hands in so much innocent blood', and this and the hope of preventing later bloodshed 'are the satisfactory grounds to such actions, which otherwise cannot but work remorse and regret'.[23]

At Wexford Cromwell again summoned the town, but he agreed to negotiate terms for a surrender. The massacre took place in confused circumstances when the captain of Wexford castle suddenly surrendered while negotiations about the town's fate were still in progress, and parliamentary troops broke into the town from the castle and began killing and looting indiscriminately. Drogheda was an officially sanctioned massacre: Wexford was one which took place when a sudden and unexpected development led to soldiers acting outside the direct control of senior officers. Cromwell was probably being honest when he said he had wished to avoid the sack of the town. Yet his conduct at Drogheda had given his men a terrible example to follow, and Cromwell believed that at Wexford his intention to be merciful had been overruled by God's determination to impose justice instead. Cromwell had

> intended better to this place than so great a ruin, hoping the town might be of more use to you and your army, yet God would not have it so; but, by an unexpected providence, in His righteous justice, brought a just judgment upon them.[24]

Cromwell's belief that the bloodbath at Drogheda would limit later bloodshed was probably correct; news of the massacre, and of that at Wexford, led to the rapid collapse of resistance, and town after town surrendered as Cromwell approached.

Not until May 1650, when the back of Irish resistance was clearly broken, did Cromwell return to England and turn his attention to the Scots, who were now replacing the Irish as the main threat to the Commonwealth. Ironically, the very fact that he had been successful in Ireland increased the threat from Scotland, for it had led Charles II to despair of help from Ireland, and this had driven him back to negotiations with the Kirk Party. By the end of April 1650 he had reached agreement with the Scots, and they invited him to Scotland. There could be little doubt that this would mean war with England, and by June 1650 the Council of State had resolved that a preemptive invasion of Scotland should be launched. Cromwell had no doubts as to the justice of this: the Scots had invaded in 1648 and were preparing to do so again. This being the case, it was obviously best from England's

22   Ibid., II, p. 124.
23   Ibid., II, p. 127.
24   Ibid., II, p. 142.

point of view that the war should be fought on Scottish rather than English soil, and that England should seek to strike before the Scots were fully pre-pared.[25] Yet Cromwell regretted having to fight the Scots. Once again godly – or potentially godly – Scots had been deluded into fighting for an ungodly cause. A declaration issued by his army on its march to Scotland in July spelled out his attitude. England hoped bloodshed could be avoided. She was willing to discuss religious and other differences, in attempting to reach agreement on the interpretation of the Word of God. The English had dis-played Christian love to Scotland in 1648, and were willing to do so again.[26]

After the army had crossed into Scotland Cromwell maintained the pres-sure, though with increasing frustration at the lack of response. He wrote to the Church of Scotland expressing sadness at its attempts to prejudice those 'who do too much (in matters of conscience, wherein every soul is to answer for itself to God) depend upon you' against the English. He accused the Church's leaders of suppressing the English declarations offering love to the Scots, and invited them to send as many of their papers to his army as they liked: 'I fear them not.' Were they really sure they spoke infallibly for God? 'I beseech you, in the bowels of Christ, think it possible you may be mistaken.' To their repeated appeals to the covenants he replied 'there may be a Covenant made with death and hell. I will not say yours was so . . .'.[27] But the bald reply of the Church showed a confidence of right-eousness equal to his own: 'would yow have ws to be scepticks in our reli-gion?'[28] Cromwell reported to parliament that 'Since we came in Scotland, it hath been our desire and longing to have avoided blood in this business, by reason that God hath a people fearing His name, though deceived':

> We have been engaged on a service the fullest of trial ever poor creatures were upon. We made great professions of love, knowing we were to deal with many who were Godly, and pretended to be stumbled at our inva-sion; indeed, our bowels were pierced again and again; the Lord helped us to sweet words, and in sincerity to mean them. We were rejected again and again, yet still we begged to be believed that we loved them as our own souls; they often returned evil for good.[29]

These expositions of Cromwell's attitude to the Scots were contained in dispatches announcing the turning point of the Scottish war. A decisive battle had been fought near Dunbar on 3 September. God had arisen and his enemies had been scattered. But even among those who had fought for the enemies of God there were many godly people, and it was his duty to try

25   Ibid., II, pp. 265–70.
26   Ibid., II, pp. 283–8.
27   Ibid., II, pp. 302–3.
28   Ibid., II, p. 305.
29   Ibid., II, pp. 325, 327–8.

to reclaim them for the Lord. Thus when Edinburgh was occupied after the victory Cromwell redoubled his propaganda assault on the Scots.[30] Surely, now that God had shown His will so openly, they could not continue to shut their eyes to the truth?

The propaganda was indeed having an effect on the morale of the more 'godly' Scots, and this worked to Cromwell's advantage – but not quite in the way he had hoped, for only a tiny handful of Scots gave up the fight against him. Many of the more extreme supporters of the Kirk Party, however, concluded that they were suffering defeat because they were offending God: their offence lay not in fighting Cromwell, but in fighting him in the king's name. Remedying this became a matter of urgency after Dunbar, for defeat destroyed the already tottering Kirk Party regime, as worldly arguments convinced most Scots that all men, including royalists or Engagers, should be recruited to face the enemy. Even more clearly than in the past Scotland was fighting for an ungodly king. The godly extremists, concentrated in the western Lowlands, reacted by establishing what amounted to a separate administration and godly army under the name of the Western Association (its very name reflecting grudging admiration for Cromwell and his Eastern Association). In the event, however, God's mysterious failure to bring godly Scots victory continued, and the Remonstrants (so called from the Western Remonstrance in which they set out their attitudes to the war) devoted much of their energy to agonizing over precisely what they were fighting for. It became clear that some of them at least found it increasingly hard to justify fighting Cromwell, whose repeated appeals to them helped to sow dissention in their ranks. Thus though he was disappointed that he could not persuade the Remonstrants to submit peacefully, the speed with which their resistance collapsed after their defeat at the battle of Hamilton (1 December 1650) indicated the extent to which he had undermined their resolve. Yet Cromwell was sad they had had to be defeated in battle: 'Those religious people of Scotland that fall in this cause, we cannot but pity and mourn for them, and we pray that all good men may do so too.'[31]

Cromwell's efforts to conquer Scotland with words rather than bloodshed continued. Since the occupation of Edinburgh he had debated with ministers there. He visited Glasgow to persuade the godly of the west of his sincerity, hoping to win them over by his conduct and arguments.[32] But the majority of those he believed godly remained stubborn in adhering to their errors, and the main enemy, Charles II's army north of the Forth, would not succumb to his rhetoric. It took hard fighting to out-manoeuvre it, push it

30 Ibid., II, pp. 335–41.
31 Ibid., II, p. 365; D. Stevenson, *The Covenanters and the Western Association* (Ayrshire Archaeological and Natural History Society: Ayrshire Collections, 11, no. 1, 1982).
32 Abbott, II, pp. 352–7, 360–72, 408; Stevenson, *Western Association*, pp. 160–3.

into a despairing invasion of England, and finally rout it at the battle of Worcester on 3 September 1651. Thereafter Scots resistance collapsed – and Cromwell could relax and admit something that he had not hinted at while the war was still to be won: of all the regime's actions, justifying the Scots war had caused him 'greatest difficulty', 'by reason we have had to do with some who were (I verily think) godly, but, through weakness and the subtlety of Satan involved in interests against the Lord and His people'. He had therefore proceeded carefully, making sure that his every action was fully justified: and as a result of this care, 'The Lord hath marvellously appeared even against them.'[33]

In 1649–51 Cromwell had conquered two kingdoms for the English commonwealth. But what was to be done with these prizes? How were they to be governed? Ireland presented few problems as to her status once conquered: she was an English dependency in which a great rebellion had been crushed. When the English parliament had abolished monarchy in England and established the republic, it had done the same in Ireland: the new commonwealth was that of England and Ireland. When Cromwell landed there in 1649 he held the traditional office of Lord Lieutenant as well as that of commander-in-chief. But his ambitions for Ireland's future were far from traditional, for he brought ideals as well as an army with him, and he believed that Ireland offered an unrivalled opportunity for implementing these ideals. It had long been an irritation that in England even though power had been seized, introducing radical reform in such matters as law and religion was proving unexpectedly slow and difficult. The dead weight of tradition, of existing legal and administrative frameworks and of strongly entrenched vested interests was almost impossible to overcome. But in Ireland nearly a decade of chaos had virtually destroyed all previous frameworks. The structure of society and authority had collapsed. The opportunity to build a new godly society, and a legal system and government guaranteeing liberty and equality before the law, should not be missed. Thus the Cromwellians, like Wentworth back in the 1630s, saw Ireland as a test site for policies ultimately to be introduced in England.

Cromwell's vision of unlimited possibilities is explained in a letter written at the end of 1649. When his army had landed in Ireland

> there was a dissolution of the whole frame of Government; there being no visible authority residing in persons entrusted to act according to the forms of law, except in two corporations [Dublin and Londonderry] under the Parliament's power, in this whole Land.

This vacuum provided immense opportunities. It would be possible to establish

33   Abbott, II, p. 483.

a way of doing justice amongst these poor people, which, for the uprightness and cheapness of it, may exceedingly gain upon them, who have
been accustomed to as much injustice, tyranny and oppression from their
landlords, the great men, and those that should have done them right, as,
I believe, any people in that which we call Christendom. . . . they having
been inured thereto. Sir, if justice were freely and impartially administred
here, the foregoing darkness and corruption would make it look so much
the more glorious and beautiful; and draw more hearts after it.[34]

A few months later he talked of the exciting possibilities of Ireland to
Edmund Ludlow. In England the law encouraged the rich to oppress the
poor, but the strength of lawyers' vested interests and fears for social
stability prevented reform. Ireland, by contrast was 'as a clean paper',

capable of being governed by such laws as should be found most agree-
able to justice; which may be so impartially administered, as to be a good
precedent even to England itself; where when they once perceive propriety preserved at an easy and cheap rate in Ireland, they will never permit
themselves to be so cheated and abused as now they are.[35]

That parliament shared at least some of this vision is indicated by the abolition of the office of Lord Lieutenant (and the subordinate office of Lord
Deputy) in May 1652: Ireland was to be governed instead by parliamentary
commissioners.[36] The old offices, associated with monarchy and the old
relationship between Ireland and England disappeared now that they
formed a single commonwealth. But many questions remained unanswered. It was evidently intended from the first that the Irish parliament
would be abolished, Ireland instead sending representatives to parliament
at Westminster, but public confirmation of this did not come until March
1653, when the number of such representatives was fixed at thirty. Not
until 1656 was a bill introduced in parliament for the union of England and
Ireland – and though it was revived in 1656–57 it never completed its
passage through parliament.[37]

In Scotland's case explicit definition of the country's place in the political system was required more urgently than Ireland, for here England had
conquered an independent State, not re-asserted control over a dependency.
But whereas in Ireland's case England had sought complete conquest and

34   Ibid., II, pp. 186–7.
35   Ibid., II, p. 273.
36   Ibid., II, pp. 556–7; T. C. Barnard, *Cromwellian Ireland. English government and reform in
Ireland, 1649–60* (Oxford, 1975), pp. 13–15, 18.
37   *Commons Journals* (hereafter *C.J.*) VII, pp. 263, 415, 452–60 *passim*, p. 519; P. J. Corish,
'The Cromwellian regime, 1650–60', in T. W. Moody, F. X. Martin and F. J. Byrne (eds), *A New
History of Ireland*, III, *Early Modern Ireland, 1534–1691* (Oxford, 1976), p. 354.

union into one commonwealth from the start of Cromwell's campaign, this was not so in Scotland. The aim of the Scottish war was to remove the threat the alliance of the covenanters with Charles II presented to the commonwealth: quite how this would be achieved was secondary, dependent on how the situation developed. Thus when Cromwell wrote to the Scots on 9 October 1650, all he said was needed to end the war was for the Scots to give the English 'satisfaction and security for their peaceable and quiet living by you'.[38] Only when it became clear that such satisfaction would not be forthcoming did conquest become the goal.

Not having planned to conquer Scotland, the English had no ready-made plans for what to do with their prize. At first the areas under English control were treated as conquered territory, and many felt that Scotland as a whole deserved no better. But more moderate counsels prevailed. England should offer Scotland union with England and Ireland to form one commonwealth.[39] Expediency suggested that generosity to the defeated would help to reconcile them to the new order. Moreover, how could a regime which claimed to stand for liberty and justice justify ruling its neighbour by brute strength alone? In Cromwell's mind the Scots were already basically godly: treating them justly and removing the forces which had led them astray (king, feudal landlords and bigoted ministers) would convert them into active supporters of the commonwealth.

This policy was fully expounded in a declaration 'concerning the Settlement of Scotland' compiled in October 1651 though not published until February 1652. Parliamentary commissioners for the administration of Scotland were appointed (as they soon were to be for Ireland). Their first priority was to be the advancing of the word of God, protection being given to all who worshipped according to His revealed word. Such toleration would not only allow the spread of Independency in Scotland but would undermine the power over the people of the ministers of the kirk, whom Cromwell believed had misled them. Concerning the 'freedome to be established to the people there', and for future security, Scotland was to be incorporated into one commonwealth with England. To help pay for the wars of 1648 and 1650–51 the estates of all those involved in resistance to the English were to be confiscated (with exceptions for those who had submitted after Dunbar or who had served the commonwealth). Those not liable to punishment who, having at last discovered their true interests, agreed to cooperate with the commonwealth would be taken into parliament's protection and enjoy the liberties of the free people of the commonwealth of England. Vassals and tenants of the nobles and gentry 'the chief Actors in these invasions and wars against England', drawn into participation in the wars by their

38   Abbott, II, p. 350.
39   F. D. Dow, *Cromwellian Scotland, 1651–60* (Edinburgh, 1979), pp. 30–1.

superiors, would be pardoned if they put themselves under parliament's protection, and would be freed from their former feudal dependences, becoming instead tenants of the State on such easy terms that they could live 'like a free People, delivered (through Gods goodnesse) from their former slaveries, vassalage, and oppressions'.[40]

Thus the English would bring to Scotland not just the sword, but godliness, liberty and prosperity. Apart from the upper classes virtually all stood to gain. Further, not only was Scotland offered all these benefits: she was to be allowed to choose whether she wanted them. A forcible union would be an unjust union, based on conquest. Thus after the commissioners for the administration of Scotland had issued the declaration of England's intentions, delegates of the shires and burghs were summoned to receive a 'tender' or offer of union. In reality, of course, the English were making an offer that could not be refused. It was made clear that the alternative to accepting the union was to be treated as a conquered people, and under English threats most of the delegates reluctantly declared their acceptance of the offer.[41] To maintain this stage-managed picture of two countries freely entering into union some of the delegates were then sent to London to negotiate details with parliament, but their presence was merely cosmetic. The process of consultation was a solemn farce, but it revealed the English ideal of what the union should be, insisted on in the face of almost universal hostility in Scotland. That the Scots remained stubbornly suspicious of Englishmen bearing gifts was ignored.[42]

The English sincerely saw themselves as acting generously: they were pressing on the Scots the inestimable gift of being treated as Englishmen. As Ludlow remarked, 'How great a condescension it was in the Parliament of England to permit a people they had conquered to have a part in the legislative power.'[43] Cromwell himself had taken no direct part in the moves towards a peace settlement in Scotland, but his approval of it may be assumed: it was entirely consistent with his attitude to the country in previous years. However, as a result of his quarrels with successive parliaments, it was a long time before the new union was formalized: in April 1654 Cromwell (by now Lord Protector) and his Council of State issued an Ordinance of Union, but a parliamentary act did not come until 1657. As in the case of Ireland, however, it was assumed from the first that union was in operation. Scots and Irish representatives were summoned to 'Barebone's Parliament' in 1653 and the Instrument of Government in December

40   C. S. Terry (ed.), *The Cromwellian Union* (Scottish History Society, Edinburgh, 1902), pp. xix, xxi–xxiii; Dow, *Cromwellian Scotland*, pp. 31–2; L. M. Smith, 'Scotland and Cromwell. A study in early modern government' (unpublished D.Phil. dissertation, Univ. of Oxford, 1979), pp. 55–6.
41   Terry, *Cromwellian Union*, pp. xxvii–xxix; Dow, *Cromwellian Scotland*, pp. 38–41.
42   Dow, *Cromwellian Scotland*, pp. 46–51; Smith, 'Scotland and Cromwell', pp. 57–60.
43   Quoted in Terry, *Cromwellian Union*, p. xv.

which created the Protectorate referred to the Commonwealth as being that of England, Scotland and Ireland, with Scotland (like Ireland) being represented by thirty members of parliament.[44]

Cromwell dreamed of an ideal new society in Ireland, but in reality there were major constraints on the freedom of action of the new regime there. What was the place of the catholic Irish in the new Ireland? Cromwell wrote as if 'the people' of Ireland would benefit from equality before law and good justice, but policies to which the commonwealth was already committed made it almost inevitable that the Irish themselves would be brushed aside as an irrelevance, if not indeed an impediment, to the new just society. Harsh punishment was what was planned for the Irish, and that this would include massive confiscations of land had been made clear by the 1642 Adventurers' Act and further legislation in 1643 and 1649 which provided for payment of the arrears due to soldiers in land in Ireland.[45]

Scotland at least was given a pretence of choice about joining the Commonwealth; Ireland was not consulted. The sorts of benefit and privilege that were offered to most Scots, were only promised in Ireland in vague and general terms, and restrictions and exceptions meant that few if any native Irish would benefit from commonwealth idealism. The October 1651 declaration concerning the settlement of Scotland had been mainly concerned with offering advantages; the 1652 Act for the settlement of Ireland was almost exclusively concerned with punishment. In Scotland the upper classes were to be swept aside to adapt existing society to new ideals; in Ireland almost an entire society was to be destroyed to build a new one, for the guilt of shedding innocent blood was believed to be almost universal. The act was a blueprint for the destruction of the nation – though the preamble of the act denied any design to extirpate 'the entire nation'. All those of rank and quality would be treated according to their 'respective demerits', a phrase which at once indicated that it was assumed that none had merits. Among these classes in society many individuals and categories were singled out for execution. Other landowners, somewhat less guilty, would forfeit their estates, but would receive land elsewhere worth one-third of their value, or in some cases two-thirds. Those whose only crime was that they had not been actively loyal would have one-third of their existing estates confiscated, but would retain the rest. To most of the 'inferior sort' pardon would be granted, sparing their lives and property.[46]

One estimate suggested that if the act had been fully implemented up to half the adult male population of Ireland would have been executed. In the event no more than a few hundred were killed, and while this seeming

---

44   Ibid., pp. xlvii, xlix–l, lxxiv; C. H. Firth and R. S. Rait (eds), *Acts and Ordinances of the Interregnum, 1642–60* (3 vols, 1911), II, pp. 814, 818–19, 871–5.

45   Corish, 'The Cromwellian regime', p. 360.

46   *Acts and Ordinances*, II, pp. 598–603; Corish, 'The Cromwellian Regime', pp. 357–9.

'leniency' can partly be explained by the fact that many of those liable to execution went into exile – there was an exodus of about 34,300 Irish soldiers and a further 10,000 or so Irish were transported to the West Indies – it also reflects both inefficiency and a gradual moderation of desire for revenge.[47]

The place of the former Irish landowners was to be taken by godly protestants, adventurers whose investments in 1642 had at last matured, and former soldiers. These, and other protestant colonists, would form the basis for the new Irish society. Quite what the fate of the Irish landowners was to be in practice was at first uncertain, with many differences of opinion as to how harshly they should be treated and whether any deserved a degree of mercy through only having been marginally or passively involved in the rebellion or through having shown signs of repentance. Eventually, in 1653, the views of those favouring indiscriminate punishment prevailed: catholic Irish landowners in general would have their estates confiscated, the partial compensation due to them being land in Connaught and County Clare.

The site for this vast Irish penal settlement was not chosen because of its lack of resources (Connaught was regarded as a richer province than Ulster) but for strategic reasons. Penned in between the sea and the River Shannon, with a belt several miles wide of protestant soldier-settlers along the coast and the line of the river surrounding them, in an area remote from the centres of commerce and government in the east, it could be ensured that never again would the Irish present a threat to protestant and English interests.[48]

The scheme to transplant the Irish was vastly ambitious. In addition, it was planned to break up the predominantly Scottish population of parts of Ulster, resettling landowners in other parts of Ireland intermingled with English proprietors, so they would no longer be a political threat.[49] Once Scotland was conquered the schemes for moving the Ulster Scots were shelved: but the transplantation of the Irish went ahead. It proved a major millstone round the neck of the regime, for processing the claims of thousands of adventurers and soldiers to land, moving Irish landowners to Connaught, and allocating them land there, represented a huge and complicated administrative burden. Moreover, fundamental flaws and ambiguities in the transplantation and resettlement scheme soon emerged. First, there simply was not enough land available for all the adventurers and

47   Corish, 'The Cromwellian regime', pp. 359–60, 362, 364; R. C. Simington (ed.), *The Transplantation to Connacht, 1654–8* (Irish Manuscripts Commission, Dublin, 1970), p. xxiv.
48   Corish, 'The Cromwellian regime', p. 364; Simington, *Transplantation*, pp. vii, x; N. Canny, *From Reformation to Restoration: Ireland, 1534–1660* (Dublin, 1987), p. 220; Barnard, *Cromwellian Ireland*, pp. 10–11.
49   D. Stevenson, *Scottish Covenanters and Irish Confederates* (Belfast, 1981), pp. 285–90.

soldiers who had valid claims. As a result, much of the land originally assigned to transplanted Irish, including whole counties, was withdrawn from the scheme, while simultaneously the decision not to execute many held to deserve death swelled the numbers of Irish claimants, for those spared were regarded as entitled to land in Connaught. The basic sums for the resettlement of Ireland simply did not add up. As for the ambiguity of the scheme, were all Irish to be transplanted? Or only landlords and their families? The intention at first was probably that virtually all should go: when landlords left, the assumption was that their tenants, dependants and followers would go with them. But in practice in the great majority of cases this did not happen. In time this was tacitly accepted. As the difficulties of resettling even landlords became clear, limiting the numbers transplanted became expedient. Another argument was even stronger: if the common people were transplanted to Connaught, who would work the land for the new protestant landlords? Hopes for large-scale immigration from England of farmers, farm workers and tradesmen soon faded, so the removal of the Irish labour force would have been a recipe for economic disaster. They were too useful to be uprooted. By the time of the 1657 Act for the attainder of rebels in Ireland it was accepted – though still only tacitly – that only land-lords would be forcibly transplanted. But at least where Irish landlords were concerned the transplantation policy was (on its own terms) ultimately fairly successful. Before the troubles catholics had owned about 59 per cent of Irish land: by the 1660s they only owned 20 per cent largely in Con-naught. But if concentrating and limiting Irish landownership was accom-plished, the attempt to build a new protestant society in the rest of the country failed. Some 12,000 soldiers settled, but most of those entitled to land grants in Ireland, whether soldiers or adventurers, preferred to sell their rights rather than settle in Ireland.[50]

The contrast with Scotland is striking. There too it had originally been planned to disinherit many native landowners, though there had been no thought of uprooting whole populations. Virtually all the larger landlords had been involved in making war on England, and it was intended to destroy them – even more thoroughly, indeed, than their Irish counterparts, since there was no provision for compensation in some Scottish Connaught. And what was to happen to confiscated lands in Scotland? Talk of lands being leased on easy terms to those supporting the regime indicated an intention of keeping land in the hands of the State, but in 1651 parliament ordered land grants in Scotland to be made as rewards to senior army officers,[51] and the duke of Hamilton's estates passed into the hands of such officers for

---

50   Corish, 'The Cromwellian regime', pp. 360–2, 365, 368–70, 373; Simington, *Transplantation*, pp. xx–xxv; Barnard, *Cromwellian Ireland*, p. 11.
51   *C.J.* VII, p. 14.

some years.[52] In 1654 trustees for confiscated estates were appointed,[53] but their significance was limited as most estates were either returned to their former owners (on payment of fines) or handed over to their creditors.

Confiscating the lands of most great landowners was supposed to secure the stability of the new regime in Scotland, by removing the powerful elements in society hostile to it. In practice the policy had the opposite effect, for it left such men nothing to lose. The result was the incoherent rebellion of 1653–55 known as Glencairn's rising, based on the Highlands and reducing much of northern and central Scotland to chaos.[54]

The rebellion was crushed, but it forced a rethink of policy, and this was reflected in the 1654 Act of Grace and Pardon. Instead of blanket disinheritance of all tainted with war guilt, it listed twenty-four individuals (mainly nobles) who were to lose their estates, and seventy-three other landlords who were only to retain their lands on payment of heavy fines. Other landlords (except any found to have supported the rebellion) were to retain their estates. Further, in the event those excepted from pardon were shown leniency. In the years that followed fines were often substituted for confiscation, and most of the fines were eventually reduced or cancelled altogether. Thus though at first virtual extinction of Scotland's greater landlords had been threatened, in the end they escaped with lighter punishment than English royalists.[55]

Clearly the commonwealth had watered down its plans in Scotland. It had accepted that seeking to destroy the great landlords was more trouble than it was worth: it was expedient to try to reconcile them to the regime. This was all the more necessary as by the mid-1650s the regime had to admit that it had not won the support it had hoped for among the common people of Scotland. As the people had failed to respond with loyalty to offers of liberty, it made sense to attempt to recruit their former social superiors to influence and control them. There was no question of restoring the feudal powers and jurisdictions of the mighty, but there was an admission that the exercise of their traditional influence would help stabilize the regime.[56]

This change of emphasis was not, of course, an isolated phenomenon. In other aspects of policy in Scotland, and in England and Ireland as well, Cromwell was turning away from ambitions of radical change to concentrate on more immediate problems of maintaining stability and winning

52   R. K. Marshall, *The Days of Duchess Anne* (1973), p. 26; *Register of the Great Seal of Scotland, 1652–9* (1904), nos 188, 453, 568; *Register of the Privy Council of Scotland, 1665–9* (1909), pp. 27–8.
53   *Acts and Ordinances*, II, pp. 885–8.
54   Dow, *Cromwellian Scotland*, pp. 42, 53, 57–8.
55   C. H. Firth (ed.), *Scotland and the Protectorate* (Scottish History Society, Edinburgh, 1899), pp. xxvii–xxxi; *Acts and Ordinances*, II, pp. 875–83; Dow, *Cromwellian Scotland*, pp. 77, 112, 117, 122–3, 157.
56   Dow, *Cromwellian Scotland*, pp. 159–60; Smith, 'Scotland and Cromwell', pp. 209–10.

support for a regime which was deeply unpopular throughout Britain, back-peddling on some of the policies which alienated powerful interests. The acceptance of the title of Lord Protector by Cromwell at the end of 1653 was symptomatic of this change, and the change in form of government at the centre was soon reflected in Ireland and Scotland. In 1654 the office of Lord Deputy was revived, and a Council of State was established in Dublin.[57] Scotland did not receive a deputy – such an appointment would have been regarded in Scotland as implying subordination to England. But she received a Council of State, with a president who was Lord Deputy of Scotland in all but name, in 1655.[58] The establishment of two outlying councils, replacing former parliamentary commissioners in both cases, seemed to imply a degree both of decentralization and of recognition that more permanent and formal arrangements than in the past should be made for governing Ireland and Scotland separately from England. Further, just as executive power had been to some extent concentrated in the hands of one man at the centre, the Lord Protector, so such individuals, subordinate to him, should be established in the peripheral capitals.

With changes in policies and in machinery of government went changes in personnel. The majority of the parliamentary commissioners in Ireland, and after them the Lord Deputy (Charles Fleetwood) and his council, had been radical in their religious and political outlooks. Like Cromwell in 1649–50, they saw Ireland as a land where a new godly society could be built. So far as the future was concerned, the native Irish were brushed aside. Even Ireland's 'Old Protestants' – those there before the Cromwellian influx – were excluded from the new design, being suspect through their political actions in the past and for their episcopalian religious inclinations. Thus the 'Old Protestants' found their advice was not needed. The presbyterian Scots in the north were equally anathema to the sectaries who now prevailed in Dublin. But by the mid-1650s the excessive zeal of the Protectorate's representatives in Ireland was becoming an embarrassment to Cromwell in London, for it alienated many unnecessarily. As in Scotland, one of parliament's first priorities in Ireland was to cut costs so the massive subsidies provided by English tax-payers could be reduced. This meant that reconciling as many as possible to the regime so that the expensive armies of occupation could be reduced and encouraging the recovery of the economy so local tax revenue would increase were now given priority.

The anabaptists and other sectaries in power in Dublin in 1652–55, with their exclusive policies and insistence on pushing ahead with harsh transportation policies, seemed almost to be going out of their way to minimize support and maximize disruption. A lead in attacking such policies was

---

57 Barnard, *Cromwellian Ireland*, pp. 19–20; Corish, 'The Cromwellian regime', p. 354.
58 Dow, *Cromwellian Scotland*, p. 160; Smith, 'Scotland and Cromwell', pp. 77, 83.

taken by Cromwell's son Henry, who was appointed a member of the Irish Council of State in December 1654.[59] Fleetwood remained Lord Deputy in name until late 1657, when Henry replaced him, but Henry was in practice acting deputy from September 1655 as Fleetwood was then recalled to England, leaving Henry as the dominant force on the Irish council. With Henry's rise came more moderate policies. The still powerful Old Protestant interests increasingly found their advice listened to, their support sought. It was in part their arguments about the economic consequences of wholesale transportation of the common Irish to Connaught that led to the policy being tacitly abandoned. Willingness to show favour to presbyterian ministers in the north reconciled many to the regime.[60] Even catholics benefited: while there could be no question of official acceptance of the presence of priests in Ireland, the lessening of repression allowed their numbers to increase significantly in the later 1650s.[61]

In Scotland the same general process can be observed. The replacement of Robert Lilburne as commander-in-chief in Scotland by George Monck in 1654 substituted a presbyterian and former royalist for an independent, a gesture that was conciliatory – though in fact Lilburne had already begun to urge moderation. It went hand-in-hand with the move away from attempting to destroy the greater landlords and instead making it worth their while to accept the regime. The part played by Henry Cromwell in Ireland was shared in Scotland by Monck and Lord Broghill. The son of the earl of Cork, Broghill had played a prominent part in Irish affairs, helping win over his fellow Old Protestants to support the Commonwealth and seeking to persuade Cromwell that they should be treated better. His views finally prevailed in the mid-1650s, but though Old Protestants were increasingly favoured by the regime it was politically inexpedient to promote one of them to high office in Ireland, so reward for Broghill's services and abilities came through his appointment in 1656 to be president of the Council of State in Scotland. Experience gained in dealing with one outlying territory was thus applied in the other. Under the clear-headed and amiable Broghill, progress was made on two fronts: winning the acceptance, if not the active support, for the regime of the landowning classes; and at least partly solving the religious problems which plagued the regime. Broghill left Scotland in August 1656, but he had set the regime on the course it was to follow until after Cromwell's death.[62]

The number of Scots converted to sectarianism under English-imposed toleration was very limited, though handfuls of Anabaptists, Independents

59 Abbott, III, p. 558; Barnard, *Cromwellian Ireland*, pp. 20–1, 98, 102–5, 300, 302.
60 Barnard, *Cromwellian Ireland*, pp. 14, 22, 52, 58.
61 Corish, 'The Cromwellian regime', p. 355.
62 Dow, *Cromwellian Scotland*, pp. 162, 210.

and Quakers can be traced.[63] But this was not seen as necessarily disastrous, for the Church of Scotland was regarded as providing a godly alternative. The problem, as before, was that though Cromwell would tolerate the Presbyterian Church, it would not tolerate him. In any case, the Church was deeply divided. The split which had emerged when the Remonstrants virtually disowned Charles II had spread and solidified. The Protester minority, successors to the Remonstrants, squabbled endlessly with the Resolutioner majority, which supported the exiled king. The split meant that the Church could not unite against the English, and this obviously was to their advantage in some respects, but continued disruption in the church was seen as interfering with the general settlement of the country. At first the English favoured the Protesters: they had refused to fight for the king, so at least they were not tainted by royalist malignancy. The English hoped to win the Protesters' support by giving them control of the Church and helping them against the Resolutioners. In fact there was no real possibility of this: the Protesters would not accept the legitimacy of a regime which insisted on State supervision of the Church and on toleration.[64]

Broghill swiftly broke the religious deadlock. Seeing that the Resolutioners' hostility was partly a reaction to the regime's support for the Protesters, he decided to see what could be done by offering a share of favour to the Resolutioners. In return he did not ask for promises of loyalty to the Protectorate, but simply that ministers should live quietly under the regime and give up their public prayers for Charles II. It is a mark of Broghill's charm and skill as a negotiator that most Resolutioners accepted this tacit bargain in 1656.[65] But further hopes, of reconciling the two factions in the Kirk and winning their positive support for the regime, failed. Representatives of both parties debated the matter with Cromwell in London in 1657, but he found Scots ministers as reluctant as ever to accept his ideas, and threatened that if they could not reform themselves 'an extraordinary remedy' should be employed.[66] But in reality he knew that any attempt to impose unity on the Kirk would cause massive resentment which would be politically dangerous. He could defeat the Scots in war, but not in debate.

Nonetheless, at least a settled parish ministry preached godly doctrine throughout most of Scotland, and in this the country was in a much more satisfactory condition than Ireland. The organization and ministry of the Church of Ireland had been destroyed by the wars since 1641. The commonwealth sought to build a new Church, but there was never any official

---

63   G. D. Henderson, 'Some early Scottish Independents', in *Religious life in Seventeenth-Century Scotland* (Cambridge, 1937), pp. 100–16.
64   Abbott, IV, pp. 399–400.
65   Dow, *Cromwellian Scotland*, pp. 195–8, 206; J. Buckroyd, 'Lord Broghill and the Scottish church, 1655–6', *Journal of Ecclesiastical History*, XXVII (1976), pp. 359–68.
66   Abbott, IV, pp. 399–404, 618–19.

decision as to precisely what form it should take. At first the anabaptists prevailed, but the efforts of their officially sponsored sectarian preachers were concentrated on newcomers – English soldiers and administrators – with little attempt to cater even for other protestants. The best organized Protestant ministry in the country, that of presbyterian ministers in Ulster, was regarded as an alien Scots intrusion to be repressed. Many had expected that propagation of the Gospel in Ireland would mean primarily an attempt to persuade the catholic Irish of the error of their ways, but this was neglected: at heart, it seems, the country's rulers believed trying to convert them was a waste of time. That many wanted transplantation to Connaught to involve Irish commons as well as landowners seemed to reflect such despairing attitudes to the redemption of the Irish, for such a policy would have created an entirely catholic population in much of the province. Those who came to argue against transplanting the commons added to economic arguments a religious one taking a more optimistic view of the potential of the Irish: if the commons were allowed to remain scattered through the country, where most would have protestant landlords and (hopefully) preachers and neighbours, there might be a real chance of converting them.[67]

However, though in the later 1650s a few gestures were made towards concern for the spiritual welfare of the Irish,[68] the emphasis remained on providing a ministry for existing protestants. Henry Cromwell, alarmed by the divisive and exclusive policies of the anabaptists, switched official favour to the independents instead. But they proved just as intolerant of rivals, trying to impose their own monopoly of influence, and eventually Henry swung round to supporting the presbyterians. In 1655 he reached an agreement with the dominant (as in Scotland) Resolutioner party among the presbyterian ministers, whereby they would receive government salaries without having to make any political commitment which would interfere with their loyalty to Charles II. The policy was unpopular both in England and with new protestants in Ireland, but it worked – and formed a precedent for the similar 1656 agreement with the Resolutioners in Scotland. The numbers of State-sponsored ministers rose from about 110 in 1655 to about 250 in 1658, but this was still a remarkably low total – and it was achieved largely by the inclusion of existing presbyterian ministers rather than by provision of new preachers. Overall the efforts of the regime to spread the Gospel in Ireland were a humiliating failure.[69] There was little more success in education. Many had hoped that encouragement of education would convert Irish children. But by 1659 there were only thirty-five State-supported parish schoolmasters – and they mainly served English

67 Barnard, *Cromwellian Ireland*, pp. 12–13, 91–6, 102–21.
68 Ibid., pp. 135, 171–82, 297–8.
69 Ibid., pp. 122–9, 143, 146–7, 155–7, 168.

garrisons.[70] If things were better in Scotland it was, again, because the existing established Church there had not been destroyed by war and continued
to support schools and universities. As in Ireland, Cromwellian attempts to
increase the resources devoted to education were welcome, but very
limited.[71]

Propagation of the Gospel was almost invariably the first priority in commonwealth declarations and instructions to officials in both Scotland and
Ireland. Good intentions were frustrated in Ireland by lack of money, indecision about what sort of religious settlement should be made, and despair
about the unregenerate Irish. In Scotland they were frustrated by failure to
establish a relationship based on mutual trust with either faction in the
Church. Another high priority repeatedly stated by the commonwealth was
the spread of justice and liberty. People must be treated equally by the law,
whatever their social status. Justice should be impartial, cheap, and rea-
sonably swift. But as in so many other spheres, early reforming zeal soon
gave way to expediency. The judicial system had collapsed in Ireland, so
there was an opportunity for a new start. But though the building of a
largely new system of courts began, it was soon abandoned. In 1655 the
traditional Four Courts were revived, and soon the legal system became
almost indistinguishable from that which had existed in 1641. Not only was
reverting to old ways convenient, especially when there was much disagreement about what should replace them, but the speedy justice of those
zealous for new ways had often turned out to be summary justice, making
reverting to old procedures welcome.[72] In any case, as far as the great majority of the population was concerned, talk of liberty was a mockery, for
justice as applied to them was a euphemism for punishment.

Scotland differed from Ireland in that instead of largely conforming to
English law she had her own law and procedures.[73] The general assumption among Scotland's conquerors was that in law (as in many other
matters) things English were superior to things Scots. Thus, paradoxically,
while the existing legal system in England was under strong attack for its
many defects, north of the border it was presented as a model for Scotland.
There was, however, no attempt at immediate wholesale introduction of
English law. The old feudal jurisdictions vanished along with the old central
courts (the Court of Session and Court of Justiciary), which were replaced
by commissioners for civil and for criminal justice. But the new courts continued to work, with a few exceptions, in accordance with existing Scots law.
Parliament's instructions in 1652 were that English law was to be intro-

70   Ibid., pp. 97, 183, 186–8, 194, 206.
71   Dow, *Cromwellian Scotland*, pp. 58–60; Abbott, III, pp. 395, 874; IV, pp. 794–5, 582–3,
825, 852–3.
72   Barnard, *Cromwellian Ireland*, pp. 249–61, 267–8, 274–7.
73   Ibid., p. 250.

duced only 'as to matters of government', and even then only as far as 'the constitution and use of the people there' and circumstances permitted.[74]

The quality of justice provided by the Cromwellian regime in Scotland is often cited as a major achievement,[75] but the praise heaped on it appears to be exaggerated. Glowing tributes by Englishmen to their achievements among the benighted Scots should not be accepted uncritically, for obviously they are likely to be biased, and the one Scottish source supporting them is no more convincing. In his *Diary* John Nicoll writes enthusiastically of how fast and impartial English-administered justice was, and how delighted litigants were with it in comparison with old Scottish justice.[76] However, Nicoll requires to be used with great care, for he himself explained that what he wrote was not what he believed, but 'the reall wordis, deidis and actiones' of those in power at the time.[77] Thus the views he expressed changed according to what regime was in power, and he is not a reliable witness.

It would, however, be going too far to say English rule brought no benefits in the administration of justice in Scotland. It seems very likely that the English judges were more impartial than their predecessors, less influenced by vested interests and the power of great men. But above all what contributed to making the courts popular was the simple fact that they sat regularly and gave judgments at all. Scotland had experienced nearly fifteen years of turmoil, during which much had happened that tended to increase the amount of litigation, while the meetings of courts had frequently been interrupted. Thus for many, any settled system of justice which resolved cases was welcome. The commonwealth worked hard and honestly to improve justice in Scotland, and the number of cases settled is impressive. But the evidence for this being perceived as a major benefit by Scots is unconvincing.[78]

The other main benefits that the Cromwellian regime sought to bring to the people of Scotland were freedom from feudal and clerical oppression. Again there is virtually no evidence of a positive response to this. The abolition of feudal jurisdictions and superiorities appears to have been greeted

---

74 Firth, *Scotland and the Protectorate*, p. 395. H. R. Trevor-Roper, 'Scotland and the Puritan Revolution', *Religion, the Reformation and Social Change* (1967), p. 420, erroneously cites this as a general attempt to introduce English law into Scotland.
75 Trevor-Roper, 'Scotland and the Puritan Revolution', pp. 418, 421; Dow, *Cromwellian Scotland*, p. 56; A. R. G. McMillan, 'The judicial system of the Commonwealth in Scotland', *Juridical Review* (1937), pp. 232–55; Smith, 'Scotland and Cromwell', pp. 120–1, 244.
76 J. Nicoll, *A diary of public transactions and other occurrences, chiefly in Scotland, from January 1650 to June 1667* (Bannatyne Club, Edinburgh, 1836), pp. 64, 66, 69, 104.
77 Ibid., pp. ix–x; D. Stevenson, 'The covenanters and the court of session, 1637–51', *Judicial Review* (1972), pp. 244–5.
78 Smith, 'Scotland and Cromwell', pp. 106–21, 244; Dow, *Cromwellian Scotland*, p. 221.

with indifference.[79] Moreover, the regime never even got round to the formal abolition of feudal tenure in Scotland,[80] and even some regality and baron courts seem to have continued to meet on a feudal basis (rather than in the guise of the new 'courts baron' introduced in 1654 to replace them).[81] In religion few Scots had a real chance to exercise their new liberties, for the intolerant Kirk remained dominant in most parishes. It is doubtful if the vast majority of Scots noticed that they had new liberties, civil or religious, and as the regime moved towards reconciliation with landlords and with the Resolutioner majority of ministers the possibility of such liberties meaning anything in the future declined.

By the time of Cromwell's death in September 1658 there was in Scotland a growing feeling of returning normalcy – or acceptance of a new normalcy for the time being as there seemed no immediate prospect of anything better. At least the regime was now trying to make itself attractive to powerful interests such as landowners and ministers. It still had to be based on an army of occupation, but its numbers were declining – from about 18,000 in 1654 to an establishment of about 10,500 in 1657.[82] Increasingly English civilians were taking over from soldiers in civil offices, though their numbers remained small. The numbers of Scots prepared to hold office or sit in parliament grew – though again progress was slow.[83] Relations with English officers and officials were often good. Broghill in particular won a good reputation through both personality and policies, and General Monck was respected.[84] Yet the repeated themes of Robert Baillie's summaries of the state of the country from 1654 to 1659 are negative – military occupation, deep poverty ('the English hes all the moneyes'), high taxes, nobility broken, commons oppressed.[85] Monck's reports were little more optimistic: things were 'well' in that Scotland was quiet, but at heart the Scots were still malignant.[86] Cromwell himself, just months before his death, described Scotland as 'a very ruined nation'.[87] The mood seems one of desolation. If Cromwell had not quite made a desert, he

---

79   Trevor-Roper, 'Scotland and the Puritan Revolution', p. 418, cites enthusiastic Scots in 1651 crying 'Free the poor commoners and make as little use as can be either of the great men or clergy'. But though the cry did come from Scotland the context makes it clear that it was in fact the cry of the English conquerors. See C. H. Firth, *Scotland and the Commonwealth* (Scottish History Society, Edinburgh, 1895), p. 339.

80   See *C.J.* VII, pp. 407, 427 for attempts to do so.

81   Smith, 'Scotland and Cromwell', pp. 205–7.

82   C. H. Firth, *The Last Years of the Protectorate* (2 vols, Oxford, 1900), II, pp. 87–8.

83   Dow, *Cromwellian Scotland*, pp. 149–50, 177, 179–81, 185–8, 221–2; P. J. Pinckney, 'The Scottish representation in the Cromwellian parliament of 1656', *Scottish Historical Review*, XLVI (1967), pp. 95–114.

84   Nicoll, *Diary*, p. 183; Baillie, *Letters*, III, pp. 315, 321.

85   Baillie, *Letters*, III, pp. 249–50, 252, 287, 289, 317, 357, 387.

86   Dow, *Cromwellian Scotland*, p. 228.

87   Abbott, IV, p. 718.

had created something that Scots found hard to think of positively as peace.

That the great and idealistic ambitions of Oliver Cromwell for Scotland and Ireland were thwarted, that he remained conqueror rather than a liberator, is of course no surprise: the same is true in England, where his regime was endured rather than loved. Next to lack of positive support from the populations concerned, the most basic of all problems was money. Visions for reform often failed because they were expensive in themselves, or because they entailed alienating powerful interests – which in turn meant that increased military expenditure was necessary. Even after radical policies were abandoned Ireland and Scotland showed no prospect of becoming self-supporting. In 1659 Scotland's regime needed a subsidy from England of £164,000 – 53 per cent of total public expenditure.[88] Ireland at least covered 75 per cent of her own costs of government, but even here the expected deficit for 1658 to be met by England was anticipated as £96,000.[89] There was no realistic possibility of either nation being able to pay its own way until the armies of occupation were very greatly reduced in size – and there seemed little prospect in the near future of it being safe to do that.

Another major problem concerned the personnel of government. Who was to adjudicate and administer in Scotland and Ireland? There were three constraints that made this a problem. First was acceptability to the regime. In Ireland almost the whole population was disqualified from office, and the same was true of Scotland's ruling élites at first. In the early years civil government was very much subordinate to military, and leading officers held civil offices, later being joined by English civilians. Soon, particularly in Scotland, office was opened to those inhabitants regarded as suitable, the plan being for offices to be divided between natives and Englishmen. But here the second constraint appeared: many to whom the privilege of office was offered declined it, not being willing to serve the regime. And the final constraint was that the number of Englishmen of ability willing to accept office in the outlying countries of the commonwealth was very limited. The results were continuing involvement of army officers in civil affairs – since they were qualified and on the spot – and that the small numbers of English civilian administrators often held several positions at once, leading to inefficiency. And though the loyalty of English administrators might be certain, their experience of the countries they were helping to rule often limited their effectiveness.[90]

88   Dow, *Cromwellian Scotland*, p. 219.
89   Barnard, *Cromwellian Ireland*, pp. 26–7.
90   Ibid., pp. 12–13, 19–20, 25, 284, 287; Dow, *Cromwellian Scotland*, pp. 162–4; Smith, 'Scotland and Cromwell', pp. 102, 134.

Another problem lay in uncertainty as to where power in making decisions and appointments lay – in Dublin and Edinburgh, or in London? Frequently those unable to get their way in the sub-capitals of the Commonwealth by-passed them and got favourable decisions from Cromwell or parliament, thus undermining the authority of those struggling to rule in Edinburgh and Dublin.[91] Further, decisions based on ignorance of circumstances were often made in London which were difficult or impossible to implement in the peripheral nations of the commonwealth. Before the troubles Scotland and Ireland had suffered from being governed by a system of absentee monarchy. The 1650s experiments proved that absentee republican government could be just as blundering, ignorant and insensitive, with just as little time or priority for their concerns. That an act of union for Ireland was never passed; that Ireland was left without a civil government for two months in 1657 through delays in commissioning a new Lord Deputy, that Scotland was ordered to set up new courts baron based on 'manors' (which did not exist in Scottish land law) were all examples of the 'haphazard processes of the Cromwellian regime'.[92] In both countries news of Cromwell's death was greeted with apprehension, for it opened up worrying questions of what would follow, but in neither country was there much sorrow except among the members of the English armies and administrations of occupation. With the restoration of monarchy in 1660 the parliamentary unions with Scotland and Ireland were dissolved: not until 1801 were the three legislatures again to be united.

One final observation on Cromwell's attitude to the outlying kingdoms within the British Isles is called for. He conquered them and incorporated them into a single State. But it retained a tripartite name: the Commonwealth of England, Scotland and Ireland. Cromwell might rule the entire archipelago, but its periphery had only been conquered to protect England, and for 'God's Englishman' the name of England was sacrosanct, the concept of 'Britain' an unwelcome intrusion associated with the ambitions of the Stuarts and the covenanters which had threatened England's identity. He had dreams of just and godly futures for Ireland and Scotland – through making them little Englands: but England would remain England.

91   Barnard, *Cromwellian Ireland*, p. 25; Smith, 'Scotland and Cromwell', pp. 99, 101.
92   Barnard, *Cromwellian Ireland*, pp. 21–2, 98, 294; Smith, 'Scotland and Cromwell', p. 102; *Acts and Ordinances*, II, p. 883.

Timeline

1649	30 January	Execution of Charles I
	6 February	Rump votes to abolish House of Lords
	7 February	Rump votes to abolish monarchy
	13 February	Rump appoints executive Council of State
	17 March	Act abolishing monarchy
	19 March	Act abolishing House of Lords
	April	first Digger community established on St George's Hill, Surrey (driven away in August)
	14–15 May	Cromwell and Fairfax suppress Leveller mutineers at Burford
	19 May	England declared a Commonwealth
	15 August	Cromwell lands near Dublin
	11 September	massacre at Drogheda
	11 October	massacre at Wexford
1650	2 January	Engagement Act: all adult males to declare loyalty to the Commonwealth
	10 May	Adultery Act: death penalty imposed for adultery
	26 May	Cromwell leaves Ireland
	June	Charles agrees to sign both Covenants; arrives in Scotland
	17 July	Treason Act
	22 July	Cromwell invades Scotland

	9 August	Blasphemy Act
	3 September	Cromwell defeats Royalist forces at Dunbar
	27 September	Toleration Act: compulsory attendance at parish churches abolished
1651	1 January	Charles's Scottish supporters have him crowned at Scone
	July–August	Charles leads Scottish army into England
	3 September	Battle of Worcester: Cromwell defeats Charles, who escapes to the continent
	9 October	Navigation Act: introduces measures aimed against Dutch carrying trade
	28 October	Rump's declaration for incorporation of Scotland into a single Commonwealth with England
1652	January	Dalkeith Convention: cosmetic opportunity for Scottish representatives to consent to incorporative union
	24 February	Act of Pardon and Oblivion
	19 May	First Anglo-Dutch War begins
	12 August	Act for the Settlement of Ireland
1653	January	Beginning of Glencairn's Rising in Scotland
	20 April	Cromwell dissolves the Rump Parliament
	4 July	Barebone's Parliament convenes
	31 July	Battle of the Texel: Monck defeats Dutch
	12 December	Barebone's Parliament surrenders power back to Cromwell
	15 December	Council of Army Officers adopts Instrument of Government
	16 December	Cromwell installed as Lord Protector
1654	20 March	'Triers' established: a national body to vet all new clergy
	5 April	Treaty of Westminster ends Anglo-Dutch War
	12 April	ordinance for union of England and Scotland
	27 June	ordinances for elections in Scotland and Ireland
	June	Monck begins to quell Glencairn's Rising in Scotland (complete by May 1655)
	28 August	'Ejectors' established: county commissioners to expel inadequate ministers and schoolmasters
	3 September–22 January 1655	First Protectorate Parliament
	November–	George Cony, a London merchant, fined and

	December	then imprisoned for refusing to pay customs duties that had not been approved by Parliament
	13 December	Commons votes to imprison John Biddle, a Socinian
	December	Western Design launched
1655	12–16 March	Penruddock's Rising: abortive Royalist uprising in Wiltshire
	April–May	failure of Western Design: unsuccessful attempt to capture Hispaniola, although Jamaica is taken
	9 July	Henry Cromwell arrives as Major-General of the army in Ireland, and soon emerges as driving force in Irish Council
	9 August	rule of Major-Generals established in England and Wales
	22 August	first instructions issued to the Major-Generals
	21 September	Decimation Tax on former Royalists established
	11 October	further instructions issued to Major-Generals
	24 October	Anglo-French treaty
1656	12 May	publication of Sir Henry Vane, *A Healing Question Propounded*: critical of Cromwell
	17 September–26 June 1657	first sitting of second Protectorate Parliament
	October	James Nayler, a Quaker, re-enacts Christ's entry into Jerusalem
	6–17 December	Parliament debates Nayler's case: it convicts him of 'horrid blasphemy' and sentences him to savage mutilation
1657	28 January	Cromwell abandons the Major-Generals experiment and the Decimation Tax
	23 February	*The Humble Petition and Advice*: Cromwell offered the kingship
	13 March	Anglo-French treaty: offensive alliance against Spain
	8 May	Cromwell formally declines the kingship
	9–16 May	English troops begin campaign in Flanders
	25 May	Cromwell accepts revised version of *The Humble Petition and Advice*: he is to remain Lord Protector
	26 June	Cromwell's second installation as Lord Protector

	17 November	Henry Cromwell appointed Lord Deputy of Ireland
1658	20 January– 4 February	second sitting of second Protectorate Parliament
	28 March	Anglo-French alliance renewed
	14 June	Battle of the Dunes: Anglo-French force defeats Spanish; English troops occupy Dunkirk
	3 September	death of Oliver Cromwell

Index